A PROFESSION WITHOUT REASON

A PROFESSION WITHOUT REASON

The Crisis of Contemporary Psychiatry—
Untangled and Solved by Spinoza,
Freethinking, and Radical Enlightenment

Bruce E. Levine

A Profession Without Reason: The Crisis of Contemporary Psychiatry—Untangled and Solved by Spinoza, Freethinking, and Radical Enlightenment

© 2022 Bruce E. Levine

This edition © 2022, AK Press (Chico and Edinburgh)

ISBN: 978-1-84935-460-8
E-ISBN: 978-1-84935-461-5
Library of Congress Control Number: 2021944648

AK Press
370 Ryan Ave. #100
Chico, CA 95973
www.akpress.org
akpress@akpress.org

AK Press
33 Tower St.
Edinburgh EH6 7BN
Scotland
www.akuk.com
akuk@akpress.org

The above addresses would be delighted to provide you with the latest AK Press distribution catalog, which features books, pamphlets, zines, and stylish apparel published and/or distributed by AK Press. Alternatively, visit our websites for the complete catalog, latest news, and secure ordering.

Cover design by John Yates (stealworks.com)
Printed in the United States

CONTENTS

1. Introduction 1

2. Freethinking 15

3. Fear 29

4. *Ultimi Barbarorum* 41

5. Science 51

6. Unethical 63

7. Two Bibles 73

8. Three Noble Lies? 85

9. Tolerance and Stigma 95

10. Brain Disease 107

11. Genetics 117

12. Coercion 125

13. Madness and *Scientia Intuitiva* 137

14. Icarus and Recovery 151

15. Pals and Peers 163

16. Freedom from Bondage 175

17. *Tractatus Psychiatrico-Politicus* 187

18. Bento's Conclusions 199

Notes 215

Index 249

CHAPTER 1

INTRODUCTION

The guiding force of this book is the spirit of Baruch de Spinoza (1632–1677), who was banished from his community and risked death for the causes of free-thinking and tolerance.

Spinoza was a philosopher who used reason to understand everything. He was also a psychologist who provided antidotes to emotional suffering. His self-help ideas along with his courageous life were what first interested me, but Spinoza offers far more.

He was also a radical political thinker who championed democracy. He recognized the damage to individuals and society caused by authoritarianism, and he rejected unquestioning obedience to both monarchs and religious authorities.

A handful of mental health professionals are aware of Spinoza's wisdom about how our emotions can tyrannize us, but it would be a rare psychiatrist or psychologist who is aware of Spinoza's radical critique of theological dogma and his embrace of scientific rationality—and the relevance of this to modern ideas about mental illness.

In Spinoza's *Theological-Political Treatise* (1670), he put his life on the line disputing the sacredness of the Bible. He did not challenge the Bible's divinity to mock religion; rather, he did so because he knew that a divine Bible—the belief that it was the word of God—provided authorities with the power to co-erce obedience, suppress freethinking, and institutionalize intolerance.

Beyond Spinoza's liberating philosophical, political, and psychological insights, his life is a model of how we can refuse to be controlled by fear, and instead commit our lives to reason, truth, justice, and reducing suffering. Spinoza's experiences with others and a lifetime of thought informed him that fear undermines our capacity to understand nature, including human nature, and he sought to understand all of nature, including fear.

One thesis of this book is that societal ideas about *mental illness*, including the term itself, are the products of fear. Fear triggers intolerance, attachment to dogma, and irrational decision making. The idea that fear within an individual can fuel emotional difficulties is not a new one, however, this is not the only problematic effect of fear. The emotional suffering and behavior disturbances of others—especially when extreme—can be painful to observe and can trigger fear for family members, society, and mental health professionals. For all of us, fear can fuel irrationality, resulting in what Spinoza called *inadequate ideas*—confused and vague conceptualizations that are partially or completely false. A major goal of this book is to help readers transcend this fear, liberate themselves from fear-fueled dogma, and enjoy the pleasures of freethinking and reason.

Spinoza accepted nothing simply because an authority proclaimed it, and today he would most assuredly have applied his razor-sharp logic to modern beliefs about mental illness. Spinoza was unafraid to question the thinking of his day, and it is likely that today he would be asking the following questions about conceptualizations of mental illness: Are these reasoned ideas that truly help us understand human nature? Or are these beliefs unreasoned ideas that are products of our passions and which distort reality? And do these ideas improve the lives of individuals and society, or create intolerance, oppression, and resentment?

Asking such questions should not be considered radical. Unknown to most of the general public, there are psychiatrists at the highest institutional levels who today acknowledge their profession's lack of success. The National Institute of Mental Health (NIMH) is the lead U.S. government institution that funds research on mental illness, and psychiatrist Thomas Insel was the NIMH director—unofficially, "America's psychiatrist in chief"—from 2002 to 2015. In a 2011 interview, Insel candidly stated, "Whatever we've been doing for five decades, it ain't working. And when I look at the numbers—the number of suicides, number of disabilities, mortality data—it's abysmal, and it's not getting any better." Insel concluded his appraisal of psychiatry's performance with this: "All of the ways in which we've approached these illnesses, and with a lot of people working very hard, the outcomes we've got to point to are pretty bleak."

To discover why psychiatry, in Insel's words, "ain't working," a new type of magnifying tool is necessary. In *Spinoza: A Life* (1999), Spinoza scholar Steven Nadler reports, "As early as fall 1661, he was known for making not just lenses but also telescopes and microscopes." Spinoza provided himself and his lens customers with this then cutting-edge technology to better understand the natural world. Spinoza saw value in science and technology, but when it came to understanding fundamental truths about human nature, he trusted reason. A magnifying tool used in this book to more clearly see the essence of psychiatry and to understand its crisis is the rational mind of Baruch de Spinoza.

Spinoza's most well-known work is the *Ethics* (1677). With its Euclidean geometric format of definitions, axioms, propositions, and proofs, the *Ethics* is intimidating for most general readers. Unlike the *Ethics*, this book is not organized in such a manner, but paying homage to Spinoza, I will begin with a proposition: *What psychiatry calls mental illness is what psychiatry calls mental illness.*

This proposition, at first glance, appears to be a useless restatement (a tautology) or perhaps simply preposterous. However, consider these facts. Homosexuality was called a mental illness by psychiatry until 1973. Homosexuality was called a mental illness because homosexuality was classified by the American Psychiatric Association (APA), the guild of American psychiatrists, as a mental illness. The cure for the mental illness of homosexuality was the abolition of this classification. Psychiatry no longer calls homosexuality a mental illness because psychiatry no longer calls homosexuality a mental illness.

From this piece of history, there are two obvious questions: How relevant is the cause and cure of the mental illness of homosexuality to the cause and cure of all mental illnesses? If one concludes that the abolition of homosexuality as a mental illness has reduced unnecessary suffering, does that have any relevance to other mental illnesses?

Not that long ago, except on the fringes of society, homosexuality was extremely tension-producing. For most people, the image of a man deriving and delivering pleasure by inserting his penis into an orifice of another man created enormous tension. For the majority of society, the tension experienced by the very idea of homosexuality fueled fear and anger, and frightened and angry people readily accepted proclamations that homosexuality was an abomination, a sin, and a crime to be punished. Among people who viewed themselves as enlightened progressives, societal punishment seemed cruel; they believed that homosexuals were already self-punished by their homosexual compulsions and actions, and that homosexuality should be categorized as a mental illness to be psychiatrically treated.

Among advocates of homosexuality as a mental illness, many made the assumption that viewing homosexuality as a mental illness rather than as sinful or criminal would create greater tolerance for homosexuals. Advocates of homosexuality as a mental illness prided themselves on their altruism, and they believed that progress demanded providing psychiatric treatment for the condition of homosexuality. They embraced pseudoscientific notions about the cause of homosexuality which included defects in parenting and biology.

Among people self-certain of their essential altruism, it is often the case that far more energy is spent on self-celebrating their moral superiority than on struggling to acquire truths. History tells us that self-professed altruists have often been wrong and damaging with their classifications of tension-producing behaviors. Fortunately, there are individuals whose knowledge of history is an antidote to arrogance.

The treatment of homosexuality is not the only example of a society, piloted by self-celebrators of moral superiority, whose efforts at eradicating tension-producing behaviors resulted in catastrophes for certain groups of people. Consider how European American society dealt with their fear of and anger toward Native Americans and their culture—a tension that European American society termed as the "Indian Problem."

The earliest attempt by European Americans at eliminating their tension resulting from contact with Native Americans was extermination through a variety of means, including massacres, disease, and starvation. A more altruistic solution to this Indian Problem, concluded European American society, was to force Native Americans on to reservations. The most enlightened way to deal with the Indian Problem, European Americans next concluded, was the use of boarding schools, called residential schools, to forcibly assimilate Indians.

European Americans sanctimoniously believed Native Americans would have better lives if they were stripped of their Indian nature so they could behave like white people. "Kill the Indian in him, and save the man," was the infamous motto asserted in 1892 by the Carlisle residential school founder, Captain Richard Pratt. In such residential schools, authorities believed it to be highly altruistic to break Native children from their tribal values. There were brutal punishments for speaking Native languages and for refusals by young men to cut their hair. Such forced assimilation for Native Americans continued into the 1970s.

While perhaps there were some residential school authorities who derived sadistic pleasure out of inflicting pain on Native youngsters, most such authorities achieved self-satisfaction via their sense of moral superiority; they believed that they were doing the difficult work necessary to ensure these young Indians had better lives. The intergenerational trauma that resulted from these residential schools continues today to cause suffering for Native Americans.

For those who value truth, reason, justice, and reducing unnecessary suffering, the question is: How relevant is the atrocity of this forced assimilation of Native American young people to the current forced psychiatric treatments of American youngsters?

Consider the current mental illness of oppositional defiant disorder (ODD). In 1980, an APA task force of leading psychiatrists revised their diagnostic manual, the *Diagnostic and Statistical Manual of Mental Disorders* (the 1980 version known as *DSM-III*), to include ODD: "a pattern of negativistic, hostile, and defiant behavior lasting at least 6 months." For an ODD diagnosis, all that is required is four of the following eight symptoms for six months: often actively defies or refuses to comply with requests from authority figures or with rules; often argues with authority figures; often loses temper; often touchy or easily annoyed; often angry and resentful; often deliberately annoys others; often blames others for his or her mistakes or misbehavior; and spitefulness or vindictiveness at least twice within the past six months. ODD remains a *DSM* mental illness.

Are the above behaviors actually symptoms of a mental disorder? Or do many such young people who disobey all authorities, with maturity, learn to discriminate legitimate from illegitimate authority; and then as they mature, given their natural temperaments, are they best suited among us to resist illegitimate authority for the good of the entire society? And even if these young people continue as adults to resist all authority, is that because they are mentally ill, or because they have embraced a political ideology, for example, anarchism?

Baruch de Spinoza was a freethinker who, beginning at an early age, challenged the consensus reality of his community. In the eyes of exasperated Jewish authorities, Bento, as he was known in his Amsterdam community, likely had the required number of symptoms for ODD.

We don't know a great deal about Bento's childhood. According to Spinoza's friend and earliest biographer, Jean-Maximilian Lucas, "He was not yet fifteen years old when he raised difficulties which the most learned among the Jews found it hard to solve."

In Spinoza's early twenties, he was banished from his Jewish community for his refusal to comply with requests from authorities and their rules. In response to the threat of his excommunication, according to Lucas, Bento was annoyed, annoying, and spiteful, deliberately attempting to push the Rabbi over the edge. Lucas reported that Bento told the Rabbi: "That he knew the gravity of his threats, and that, in return for the trouble which he had taken to teach him the Hebrew language, he was quite willing to show him how to excommunicate." To which, Lucas reports that "At these words the Rabbi in a passion vented all his spleen against him . . . left the Synagogue, and vowed not to come there again except with the thunderbolt in his hand."

Spinoza's rejection of religious dogma enraged Jewish authorities. It also terrified them, as they worried that his ideas and actions would cause them grief with their Christian neighbors. And so these Jewish authorities pressured young Bento to repent, threatening him with excommunication. Spinoza did not repent, accepted the excommunication, and never returned to the Jewish community.

Neuroscientist Antonio Damasio, in his book *Looking for Spinoza* (2003), surmises the following about young Bento: "In my story he begins as the impossible child, inquisitive, opinionated, a mind aged beyond its years. As an adolescent he is insufferably quick-witted and arrogant."

My best clinical guess is that what made Bento an "impossible child" was more along the same lines of how a young Albert Einstein—who came to greatly admire Spinoza—enraged his teachers, which was by a more subtle insolence. In any case, if they were alive today, both may well have gotten an ODD diagnosis slapped on them.

While throughout his life, Spinoza's bold thinking did not diminish, he evidenced no such interpersonal obnoxiousness later on, as he was famously restrained in his relationships. The philosopher Bertrand Russell, in his *History of Western Philosophy* (1945), admired Spinoza's emotional self-control, "In controversy he was courteous and reasonable, never denouncing, but doing his utmost to persuade." Russell described Spinoza as "the noblest and most lovable of the great philosophers."

Spinoza was greatly admired and loved by a loyal inner circle of friends, and he was an intriguing figure for significant thinkers of his era, including the philosopher and mathematician Gottfried Leibniz who sought him out.

Biographer Matthew Stewart, in *The Courtier and the Heretic* (2006), a book about Leibniz, Spinoza, and their encounter, sums up the complexity of Spinoza's personality: "The peculiar combination of humility and pride, of prudence and valor, of icy rationalism and zealous passion; the guilelessness that opened doors to his adversaries; and the indifference bordering on insouciance that could drive them to extreme rage—all of these startling juxtapositions of character were present on the day of Spinoza's excommunication, and all would remain with him throughout his life."

Spinoza would not let himself be boxed in, and his uniqueness captivated those who knew him in his lifetime and has continued to captivate contemporary thinkers. Philosopher Rebecca Goldstein, in *Betraying Spinoza* (2006), recounts how as a teenager in her orthodox Jewish schooling, she was taught by Mrs. Schoenfield that Spinoza was a "monster of arrogance." However, she concluded that her teacher was completely mistaken and that Spinoza must have been a lovable man when she discovered that Bento had waited until his father died before he publicly questioned his father's religious beliefs. Goldstein recalled, "I sat in Mrs. Schoenfield's class and I felt that I loved him."

According to Lucas, Spinoza "had a wit so well seasoned that the most gentle and the most severe found very peculiar charms in it," and in the *Ethics*, Spinoza spells out how laughter and merriment are pleasurable and good. So it is likely Spinoza would be amused by the idea that his own defiance would be viewed as a mental illness. Since Spinoza also believed that public derision was not good, he would likely laugh privately at the psychiatrists who created the *DSM*, often referred to as psychiatry's bible.

In the *Ethics*, Spinoza pokes fun at the hypocrisy behind what society calls *madness*, stating: "But in reality avarice, ambition, lust etc. are kinds of madness, although they are not accounted as diseases." Though it is likely that he would have gotten a chuckle out of ODD, he would have been disturbed to discover that young people diagnosed with it are administered psychiatric treatments that include medication to treat their defiance.

Philosophers such as Spinoza and genuine scientists recognize that *consensus reality* is not synonymous with *reality*, and that *conventional wisdom* is not the same as *wisdom*, and that pursuing truth and reducing unnecessary suffering means a willingness to challenge the consensus and the convention. Consensus reality is the agreed upon reality by a society or community, and if a person rejects consensus reality, then such a person is routinely labeled as ignorant, wicked, delusional, or in some other way defective. Conventional wisdom refers to generally accepted beliefs about how best to navigate consensus reality. In U.S. history, the consensus reality of racial superiority of white people was used to justify slavery of African Americans, and there was conventional wisdom among slave holders about the wisest way to treat slaves so as to keep them from attempting to escape.

In any society, consensus reality is not viewed as consensus reality but as *reality*. In contemporary society, the concept of mental illness is consensus reality, and so those who view mental illness as an explanatory model or a paradigm—not reality—are accused of denying reality.

Today, consensus reality is that there are serious mental illnesses in which people behave in disturbing and frightening ways, and that these serious mental illnesses are brain disorders. The consensus reality is that schizophrenia, the most dreaded of all serious mental illnesses, is a chronic and incurable disease of the brain. Consensus reality is that brain disorders such as schizophrenia and bipolar disorder can be triggered by social and psychological stressors, and that while these serious mental illnesses cannot currently be cured, they can be effectively treated with medication.

Conventional wisdom for the seriously mentally ill is that they need medication for their own good and for the safety of society. Conventional wisdom is that although psychiatric medications are sometimes overprescribed and have adverse effects, they are essential tools. Conventional wisdom is that compassion for the mentally ill and their families means providing greater access to psychiatric treatment, including involuntary interventions to stop the downward spiral that results in the mentally ill becoming a danger to themselves and others. Conventional wisdom is that if society believed that mental illness is "an illness like any other," this would reduce the stigma of mental illness. Conventional wisdom tells us to keep in mind that psychiatry is a young science, and while it has much to discover about the workings of the brain, it has made great progress in understanding the causes and treatments of mental illness.

History—including recent history—tells us that consensus reality changes and that conventional wisdom may or may not be correct. This is why, for genuine scientists, neither consensus reality nor conventional wisdom are sacred. Genuine scientists are not attached to the consensus or the conventional. They are attached to facts and reason, and they are attached to creating explanatory models and paradigms that best fit facts and reason.

Spinoza, called by some "the apostle of reason," is a hero to many modern scientists because he modeled fearlessly challenging consensus reality. Albert Einstein, who himself challenged consensus reality, so admired Spinoza that he wrote a poem about him that begins: "How much do I love that noble man." Einstein shared a great deal with Spinoza, including a similar view of God, a contempt for religious superstitions and authoritarianism, a belief in determinism, and a devotion to tolerance and democracy.

A young Albert today, similar to Spinoza, would likely receive an ODD diagnosis, and Albert might also be "dual diagnosed" with attention deficit hyperactivity disorder (ADHD) or autism spectrum disorder (ASD). In *Einstein: His Life and the Universe* (2007), Walter Isaacson tells us that Albert's teacher, on one occasion, even though agreeing with him that he had not misbehaved, stated, "But you sit there in the back row and smile, and your mere presence here spoils the respect of the class for me." Albert was so slow to talk that his worried parents consulted a doctor; and as a young child, he was prone to temper tantrums. Isaacson notes, "His slow development was combined with a cheeky rebelliousness toward authority, which led one schoolmaster to send him packing and another to amuse history by declaring that he would never amount to much." These traits, Isaacson concludes, "made Albert Einstein the patron saint of distracted kids everywhere."

"I believe in Spinoza's God," Einstein said, "who reveals himself in the lawful harmony of all that exists, but not in a God who concerns himself with the fate and the doings of mankind." Spinoza's conclusions about God were radical ones, profound for some and misunderstood by many. He was called an atheist, a pantheist, and a God-intoxicated man.

The God of Spinoza is a very different God than the humanlike God depicted in the Bible. For Spinoza, self-centered humans confuse God's nature with human nature, as they anthropomorphize God with human characteristics and a human personality; for example being angry and punitive with the disobedient, and pleased and rewarding with the obedient. In one of Spinoza's correspondences, he pokes fun at anthropomorphic self-centered assumptions about God: "I believe that a triangle, if it could speak, would likewise say that God is eminently triangular, and a circle that God's nature is eminently circular. In this way each would ascribe to God its own attributes, assuming itself to be like God and regarding all else as ill-formed."

For Spinoza, triangles, circles, and humans are all only aspects of God—explicated by some Spinozists as "all of reality." In the words of Steven Nadler,

"God is Nature, and Nature is all there is. This is why Spinoza prefers the phrase *Deus sive Natura* ('God or Nature')."

When Spinoza equates God with Nature, Spinoza scholar Beth Lord clarifies, he doesn't only include "the trees and the forests and the animals." Spinoza's Nature, she explains, includes "all of being . . . the objects we engage with, the ideas we think, the concepts we come up with . . . the whole of being which goes beyond the world to include the entirety of the cosmos." For Spinoza, faith is not the way to relate to God. "Instead," Lord tells us, "we understand Spinoza's God through science or philosophy, through rational knowledge. Rational knowledge, for Spinoza, means true knowledge of the laws of Nature."

Spinoza took his version of God seriously, and he was adamant that he was neither an atheist nor anti-religion, but clergy and ecclesiastic authorities—who were either appalled by his version of God or could not understand it—didn't buy this. Similarly, the most well-known U.S. psychiatry critic in the twentieth century, psychiatrist Thomas Szasz, was adamant that he was neither anti-psychiatry nor anti-medication, but psychiatry authorities haven't bought that either. Spinoza and Szasz made it clear that what they opposed was coercion, as both believed in consensual pursuits. However, their challenging of the fundamental tenets that provide institutions with their authority compelled institutional defenders to attack them.

While Szasz is today discounted, ridiculed, and even scorned by psychiatry advocates—some of whom blame him for the current neglect of those diagnosed with mental illness—there are psychiatrists at the highest levels of institutional authority who are critical of psychiatry's most important paradigms, including the *DSM* diagnostic manual (discussed in Chapter 7: "Two Bibles").

Today, the very word *psychiatry* evokes boredom for many freethinkers for whom the topic of mental illness and its treatments have become tired ones. In virtually every dispute, apologists and critics can each point to empirical studies to back opposite positions, and a sea of data—absent an unbiased dedication to reason and truth—has left us lost in a fog. The field desperately needs a completely fresh look, but who has fresh eyes? Who is interested in this topic but has not been biased by their own experiences or by those of their family and friends?

If only we could bring back one of the most brilliant thinkers in history—a freethinking psychologist, philosopher, scientist, and theology critic who was a keen observer of politics. We need a realist but not a cynic, and we need someone who is unintimidated by authorities. If only we could have Baruch de Spinoza to cut through the fog, using his rational mind to get to truths that explain psychiatry's crisis.

The conventional picture of Spinoza has long been an incomplete one. "One of the cultural images of Spinoza that has come down to us is of an unworldly philosopher who shunned society and devoted his life to the articulation of a highly abstract metaphysical system," observes Spinoza scholar Susan James in *Spinoza on Philosophy, Religion, and Politics* (2012). This image of Spinoza, she concludes, "is not altogether wrong; but it is a partial representation, or what he would call an inadequate idea," and she explains that "we need to supplement it with a more sociable image of a man who was neither solitary nor isolated, but was deeply concerned about the condition of the society in which he lived." This more sociable Spinoza, James points out, "had many friends who shared his intellectual interests, and was connected to a number of outstandingly original scientists and philosophers. He was a close follower of Dutch theological and political debates, and his interventions in them made him a famous, and in some quarters a notorious, figure."

Spinoza was not only interested in the experiments of other scientists, he conducted his own, and so embracing Spinoza's rationalism does not mean a rejection of empiricism and the scientific method. Rather, it means restoring reason in its fullest sense to the scientific process of acquiring truths; this is necessary to counter psychiatry's poorly reasoned declarations of illness—homosexuality being the most well-known but not the only example—which have triggered leaps into research on causes and treatments that have not simply been a waste of time and money but have caused a great deal of suffering. Spinoza, who likely would have logically deduced the inadequacy of psychiatry's ideas, would be unsurprised that the failure of psychiatry would eventually become obvious even to those who trust only empirical observations.

In 2021, after covering psychiatry for twenty years, *New York Times* reporter Benedict Carey concluded that psychiatry had done "little to improve the lives of the millions of people living with persistent mental distress. Almost every measure of our collective mental health—rates of suicide, anxiety, depression, addiction deaths, psychiatric prescription use—went the wrong direction, even as access to services expanded greatly." This claim, Carey assures readers, is no radical one, as he quotes former NIMH director Thomas Insel from his forthcoming book: "While we studied the risk factors for suicide, the death rate had climbed 33 percent. While we identified the neuroanatomy of addiction, overdose deaths had increased by threefold. While we mapped the genes for schizophrenia, people with this disease were still chronically unemployed and dying 20 years early."

With the mainstream media now reporting psychiatry's failures with respect to treatment outcomes, and high-ranking psychiatrists now acknowledging the scientific failures of psychiatry's *DSM* and its "chemical-imbalance theory of mental illness" (discussed in Chapter 8: "Three Noble Lies?"), reform of psychiatry is not a radical idea. The question is whether moderate reforms are sufficient or is a "radical enlightenment" required?

In his classic essay "An Answer to the Question: What is Enlightenment?" (1784), philosopher Immanuel Kant explains, "Enlightenment is man's emergence from his self-incurred immaturity." By *immaturity* he is referring to "the inability to use one's own understanding without the guidance of another." Thus, Kant's "motto of enlightenment" is: "Have courage to use your own understanding!"

In *Radical Enlightenment: Philosophy and the Making of Modernity 1650–1750* (2001), historian Jonathan Israel explains that in addition to the moderate mainstream Enlightenment, there was a rival radical Enlightenment—an underground movement in which Spinoza had a major role. All Enlightenment thinkers embraced reason, science, toleration, and strove for greater freedom and an improved society; however, moderate Enlightenment thinkers aimed to accomplish this, Israel observes, "in such a way as to preserve and safeguard what were judged essential elements of the older structures." In contrast, radical Enlightenment thinkers such as Spinoza, Israel tell us, "rejected all compromises with the past," denying the Judeo-Christian view of God, miracles, afterlife rewards or punishments; and they scorned theologians' God-ordained hierarchies that sanctioned monarchies. Spinoza and other radical thinkers argued for democracy and the right to unfettered free thought and free speech, while moderate thinkers rejected democracy and placed limitations on which beliefs should be tolerated. Thus moderate thinkers did not threaten ecclesiastic and state authorities in the manner that Spinoza and other radical thinkers did.

Spinoza did not write for readers attached to Judaism, Christianity, or any dogma, but he also did not write for people attached to mocking religion and theism. In Spinoza's unfinished last work, the *Political Treatise* (1677), he makes clear: "I have taken great care not to deride, bewail, or execrate human actions, but to understand them."

This book is not written for people attached to the sacredness of psychiatry, nor is it written for those attached to mocking individuals who embrace their psychiatric diagnoses and medications.

A taboo is something proscribed by society as improper or unacceptable. It was taboo for Spinoza to challenge the dogma of organized religion and its notions of God. For his actions, Spinoza was viciously attacked, his books banned, and he may well have been assassinated if his respiratory illness had not killed him at age forty-four.

Today, in many circles, it is taboo to criticize psychiatry and its conceptualizations. Critics are ridiculed as "mental illness deniers," a purposeful ugly association to heartless Holocaust deniers; and they are paired with Scientologists in the manner that anti-war activists have been red-baited by falsely accusing them of being Communists.

Freethinkers, however, don't stop thinking about something because it has been declared taboo. For them, thinking freely is prioritized over pleasing authorities and political expediency.

Freethinkers take pleasure in not only questioning conventional wisdom and consensus reality but questioning themselves. Experiences—especially those that emotionally affect us—create bias. Like everyone, I carry biases based on my experiences. However, the more captivated I became by Spinoza's thought and life, the more I found it dissatisfying to merely validate my biases. For Spinoza, the more we discover about reality, the more empowerment and pleasure we experience; it is simply rational to re-evaluate our judgments and correct them so as to experience the pleasure of connecting with reality.

Original in Spinoza, Rebecca Goldstein concludes, is his "ecstatic rationalism," which she describes as "the exhilarating sense of expanding one's ideas to take in more of the world, and thus the exhilarating sense of one's own outward expansiveness into the world." Walking with Spinoza results in an exhilarating type of bliss that occurs with each new understanding of the essence of reality. Spinoza's ecstatic rationalism results in an addiction to the intoxication that accompanies each new understanding. To take a walk with Spinoza is to take an astonishing journey in which freethinking, reason, and understanding become exhilarating intellectual and emotional experiences.

This book is for freethinkers who recognize that suffering is part of life but believe that reason and tolerance can reduce unnecessary suffering. This book is for the beneficiaries of the wealth of wisdom bequeathed by Baruch de

Spinoza—for readers who believe that even when freethinking does not immediately result in greater truths, it can provide us with great pleasure in a world
that so often provides us with great pain.

CHAPTER 2

FREETHINKING

Merriam-Webster defines *freethinker* as "a person who thinks freely or independently; one who forms opinions on the basis of reason independently of authority."

Spinoza has been called a rationalist, but as much as anything, he can be seen as a freethinker. His *Theological-Political Treatise* (1670) is an argument for freedom of thought and expression. In this treatise, he explains that the *freedom to philosophize* means "everyone being allowed to think what he will and to say what he thinks." He declares, "Therefore the most tyrannical government will be one where the individual is denied the freedom to express and to communicate to others what he thinks."

In *A Short History of Freethought* (1915), historian and journalist John Robertson points out: "The words 'freethinking' and 'freethinker' first appear in English literature about the end of the seventeenth century." In the latter part of the 1600s, Robertson notes, we find Spinoza devoting his *Theological-Political Treatise* to advocating for *libertas philosophandi* (freedom to philosophize). "Such a work," Robertson concludes, "was bound to have a general European influence. It was probably, then, a result of such express assertion of the need and value of freedom in the mental life that the name 'freethinker' came into English use in the last quarter of the century."

Bertrand Russell, in his essay "The Value of Free Thought" (1944), states: "What makes a free thinker is not his beliefs, but the way in which he holds them. If he holds them because his elders told him they were true when he was young, or if he holds them because if he did not he would be unhappy, his thought is not free; but if he holds them because, after careful thought, he finds a balance of evidence in their favor, then his thought is free, however odd his conclusions may seem."

Freethought is exhilarating for some individuals; but for others, it is torturous, as for them the tension of uncertainty is so painful that they need the immediate relief provided by authority, tradition, and dogma. There is a tension in freethinking, as there is in skydiving, sex, gambling, democracy, and conversation; some of us relish the tension and its release in some of these activities but not in others. Then there are those people who attempt to control their lives so as to avoid *all* tension, and when they by chance encounter any tension, they attempt to immediately flee from it; and if they cannot immediately flee, they are enraged with whoever has placed them in a state of unavoidable tension. For Spinoza and his friends, freethought was exhilarating, but the tension that his freethinking created pained most of his society.

Spinoza did not relish putting people in pain with his freethinking. He made it clear that he wanted only freethinkers to read his books. In the Preface of his *Theological-Political Treatise*, Spinoza tells us he knows "that the masses can no more be freed from their superstition than from their fears . . . they are not guided by reason. . . . Therefore I do not invite the common people to read this work, nor all those who are victims of the same emotional attitudes."

As a teenager, during his Jewish schooling, it is likely that Spinoza felt oppressed by dogmas, articles of faith, and rituals that he viewed as superstitions. In addition to the oppressiveness of organized religion, a young Bento had also gotten a taste of the oppressiveness of business dealings.

His older brother Isaac died when Bento was seventeen, and his merchant father Miguel needed Bento in the family business, which included importing goods such as dried fruit. Miguel died in 1654 when Bento was twenty-one, and Bento found himself, along with his younger brother Gabriel, running a business that had financial problems. There are records from 1655 showing that Bento had to take legal proceedings against debtors, and it may well be that business dealings—not his heretical religious views—led to a knife attack on him.

For the freethinking Bento, religious indoctrination and financial dealings were oppressive. He is likely referring to this era when recalling the redirection of his life in his earliest work, the *Treatise on the Emendation of the Intellect*: "After experience had taught me the hollowness and futility of everything that is ordinarily encountered in daily life . . . I resolved at length to enquire whether there existed a true good . . . whether, in fact, there was something whose discovery and acquisition would afford me a continuous and supreme joy to all eternity." Spinoza recounts that he could see the "advantages that derive from honor and wealth" but that he wanted to devote himself to the search for something different and new so that he would have an opportunity for true happiness.

As a young man, Spinoza began to encounter other freethinkers. The curious Bento would have likely frequented the many bookshops of Amsterdam—there were perhaps as many as four hundred of them—and he would have been frustrated that he could not comprehend important books written in Latin. He decided to pursue a more secular education that included the study of Latin but that would include much more, especially when he connected with Franciscus van den Enden.

Spinoza biographer Matthew Stewart describes Van den Enden as "the bad boy of the early Dutch Enlightenment." Van den Enden, born in 1600 and thus thirty-two years older than Bento, had owned a bookshop in Amsterdam, been an actor, an author of banned plays, and was a fierce advocate of democracy. Van den Enden set up a school in his own house in Amsterdam, specializing in teaching classical languages as well as the most enlightened thinking of the time. His parenting was radical for his era, raising his eldest daughter Clara Maria to be involved in theater, painting, music, and to master Latin. Bento enrolled in Van den Enden's school, and some Spinoza biographers believe that Clara Maria helped tutor him in Latin. Bento moved into the Van den Enden household around 1655 or 1656, either immediately before or soon after his excommunication, and stayed there for a short time.

According to Spinoza's other early biographer, Johan Colerus—who, unlike Lucas, was unsympathetic to Spinoza's radical views—young Bento was smitten by Clara Maria. Though she was not considered all that physically attractive, Colerus claims that Spinoza was attracted to her "sharp mind and excellent learning," and he wanted to marry her; however, he lost out to a fellow student who was more skilled in the art of seduction, as his rival used an expensive pearl necklace to win her over.

The problem with this story is that, in 1656, Clara Maria would have only been twelve years old while Bento would have been twenty-four, and it is likely that Colerus just ran wild with his imagination. Spinoza scholars calculate Clara Maria's age from records showing her to be twenty-seven when she married in 1671, but those who fantasize that Bento had a thing for her speculate that she may have actually been somewhat older than what she stated at the time of her marriage. While a romantic today might contend that Elvis Presley was twenty-four when he became infatuated with a fourteen-year-old Priscilla, most Spinoza scholars would counter that Bento was in no way Elvis.

In the remainder of his life, as far as biographers know, Spinoza had no romantic partners, and he never married or had children. He was described by others as being of average height and having a "well-formed body" and a "beautiful face." Stewart summarizes Spinoza's looks: "He had an olive complexion; frizzy black hair, cut to shoulder length according to the fashion of the times; a thin mustache; long, thick, arched eyebrows, and dark, languid eyes." However, Stewart also points out that "his choice of a low-income lifestyle, his chronic illness, and his unenviable social status as an apostate Jew would hardly have made him an appealing prospect for the girls of Holland."

Spinoza's innate curiosity, fueled by the freethinking Van den Enden, resulted in Bento becoming immersed in the newest and coolest scientific, philosophical, and political thinking of his era, which included Galileo, Descartes, Machiavelli, and Hobbes. Bento developed a circle of freethinking friends and acquaintances (more on them in Chapter 15: "Pals and Peers").

Thus, when Spinoza was excommunicated before he turned twenty-four in 1656, it may well have felt much less a punishment than a relief. When he heard that he had been excommunicated, he is purported to have said: "All the better; they do not force me to do anything that I would not have done of my own accord if I did not dread scandal; but, since they want it that way, I enter gladly on the path that is opened to me, with the consolation that my departure will be more innocent than was the exodus of the early Hebrews from Egypt."

With both his parents dead—his mother, Hanna, had died shortly before Bento turned six years old—he would have no guilt about putting his parents in pain by his heresy; and with his banishment from the Jewish community, he would have no guilt about his freethinking causing them any trouble with Christian authorities. Moreover, he had no fear of entering a lonely wilderness, as he had already developed a freethinking community who dug this courageous, brilliant, likable heretic.

With no wife or children, the highly conscientious Bento was also freed up from guilt that his freethinking would be a selfish luxury that would make it financially difficult to support a family. In this, he was very much like the freethinker Henry David Thoreau. Both had no family to support, each had a community of close friends, and both were clever enough to scratch out a living. Thoreau famously lived simply and so did Spinoza. For Spinoza's final residence in The Hague, he rented a large single room that contained an inherited bed, a few tables, a chessboard, his lens-grinding equipment, and a bookcase that held, by the time of his death, approximately 160 books.

"As a Jew severed from his community," notes Spinoza scholar Stuart Hampshire, "equally at ease in several languages, absorbed in no national community, he was free, unattached and alone; and in this freedom and solitude, which he deliberately reinforced and protected, he set himself to construct by pure reason, and without appeal to any authority, a philosophy that he believed would be demonstrably complete and final."

"In a sense, Spinoza was always an outsider," observes philosopher Clare Carlisle, "and this independence is precisely what enabled him to see through the confusions, prejudices and superstitions that prevailed in the 17th century, and to gain a fresh and radical perspective on various philosophical and religious issues." Unlike many other thinkers in his and other eras, Carlisle notes, Spinoza was not a professional scholar constrained by an institution and thus, "He was free to be faithful to the pursuit of truth. This gives his philosophy a remarkable originality and intellectual purity—and it also led to controversy and charges of heresy."

Spinoza greatly cared about freedom, including freedom from oppressive institutions and freedom to philosophize. "The freedom that the freethinker seeks," notes Bertrand Russell, "is freedom within the intellectual law. He will not bow to the authority of others, and he will not bow to his own desires, but he will submit to evidence. Prove to him that he is mistaken, and he will change his opinion; supply him with a new fact, and he will if necessary abandon even his most cherished theories."

Freethinkers are oppressed by dogma, doctrine, rituals, and articles of faith, and they are compelled to question and challenge consensus reality and conventional wisdom. However, institutions are ruled by dogma, doctrine, rituals, and articles of faith, and are attached to beliefs about reality and wisdom. Thus, freethinkers will routinely feel oppressed by institutions, and such institutions will feel threatened by freethinkers.

When the beliefs and ideas that are tied to an institution's survival are threatened, the institution becomes fearful of those who have challenged it. Thus, it follows that institutions will in some way attempt to marginalize those challenging its ideas and beliefs. Marginalization ranges from burning a heretic at the stake, such as was the case with Giordano Bruno in Rome in 1600 for his denial of Catholic doctrines; to banishment from a community, such as in Spinoza's case; to a variety of legal, financial, and other intimidations and punishments. Spinoza understood the logic by which the Jewish community of Amsterdam had to excommunicate him, as he threatened their survival.

Psychiatry and its institutions also aim to persevere. As previously noted, the American Psychiatric Association (APA) is the guild of American psychiatrists, and the National Institute of Mental Health (NIMH) is the U.S. government's leading mental illness research-funding institution. The National Alliance on Mental Illness (NAMI) is an advocacy organization for the mentally ill and their families. The survival of all these institutions is tied to the idea that serious mental illness is a brain disease that requires medical treatment.

Self-preservation for an institution means discrediting and marginalizing critics who call into question ideas and beliefs that are tied to an institution's survival. The influence of powerful psychiatry institutions can be intimidating for public figures, even for artists—who fear being denounced as irresponsible in their depiction of the mentally ill.

Consider the Oscar-winning 2001 film *A Beautiful Mind*, about the life of the 1994 Nobel Prize–winning mathematician John Nash who, in the late 1950s, descended into irrationality and bizarre delusions, and was diagnosed with paranoid schizophrenia. How did he recover? In director Ron Howard's film, Nash states, "I take the newer medications." However, journalist Sylvia Nasar's 1998 book (with the same title) states that Nash stopped taking medication in 1970. Nasar reports that "Nash's refusal to take the antipsychotic drugs after 1970, and indeed during most of the periods when he wasn't in the hospital during the 1960s, may have been fortuitous. Taken regularly, such drugs, in a high percentage of cases, produce horrible, persistent symptoms like tardive dyskinesia . . . and a mental fog, all of which would have made his gentle reentry into the world of mathematics a near impossibility."

Nash, in a 2009 interview, confirmed that he had long ago stopped taking medication, "The movie is not quite accurate because it suggests that after many years of mental illness, in recovering I still depended on some medicine, whereas in . . . recovering from insanity and irrationality, I do not depend on medicine."

Why were the facts changed in the film *A Beautiful Mind*? Shortly after Nash's death in a car accident in 2015, *The Guardian* reported, "The change was apparently made because the screenwriter, Akiva Goldsman, whose mother was a prominent psychologist, was worried that the film might persuade people to stop taking their medication." *The Guardian* also reported that there were rumors that NAMI had "put pressure on the filmmakers to include the line about medication."

This would have greatly troubled Spinoza, who railed against the power of ecclesiastic authorities to shut down inquiry, and this was a major reason for his writing the *Theological-Political Treatise*. Experience told him, according to Steven Nadler, "Ecclesiastic meddling represents a threat not only to progress in philosophy and science but to the well-being of the state as well."

The conclusions that John Nash came to about his condition and his recovery are very different than the ideas and beliefs of prominent psychiatry institutions, and are of great value to some individuals attempting to understand frightening altered states and trying to uncover truths about recovery. Nash's reflections on the causes for his descent into irrationality and his beliefs about his recovery will be discussed later (in Chapter 13: "Madness and *Scientia Intuitiva*" and Chapter 14: "Icarus and Recovery").

There have been heretical psychiatrists, most famously Thomas Szasz, whose *The Myth of Mental Illness* (1961) brought the wrath of the psychiatric establishment against him. Szasz continues to be widely misunderstood.

"Szasz does not deny the existence of suffering," recounts psychiatrist Ron Leifer, a student of Szasz. "Szasz acknowledges the existence of mental illness. . . . The critical point is that mental illness is not a disease which exists in people, as pneumonia exists in lung tissue. Mental illness is, rather, a name, a label, a socially useful fiction, which is ascribed to certain people who suffer or whose behavior is disturbing to themselves or others."

Szasz's challenging of psychiatry's ideas about mental illness threatened psychiatry as an institution, and it retaliated. Psychiatrist Paul Hoch, New York state commissioner of mental hygiene, attempted to ban Szasz from Syracuse Psychiatric Hospital. Some of Szasz's colleagues protested, a local newspaper decried this breach of academic freedom, and Szasz, in order to retain his position, hired a lawyer and appealed to the American Association of University Professors and to the American Civil Liberties Union.

Just as Spinoza resented being called an atheist and anti-religion, Szasz resented being labeled as an anti-psychiatrist and anti-medication. In 2009, three years prior to Szasz's death at age ninety-two, journalist Natasha Mitchell asked him, "Would you describe yourself as an anti-psychiatrist?"

"Of course not," Szasz responded. "Anti-psychiatrist sounds like anti-Semite, or anti-Christian or even anti-religion. I'm not anti-religion, I just don't believe in it. Anybody who wants to have their religion is fine. Anybody who wants to go to a psychiatrist is fine. Anyone who wants to take psychiatric drugs is fine with me. That's why 'anti-psychiatrist' is completely inaccurate. I'm no more anti-psychiatry than pro-psychiatry. I am for freedom and responsibility."

While Szasz was adamant that he was not "anti-psychiatry," he was equally adamant in his opposition to coercive psychiatry. He was a fierce opponent of involuntary psychiatric treatment, believing the choice of psychiatry and psychotherapy should be a completely voluntary one.

For psychiatry defenders such as author and TV commentator Ron Powers—whose son was diagnosed with schizophrenia but rejected treatment and died by suicide—Szasz remains a villain. Powers, in his book *No One Cares about Crazy People: My Family and the Heartbreak of Mental Illness* (2017), concludes that Szasz exerted a "bombastic influence" that created a "post-Szaszian atrocity" in which the mentally ill are free to destroy their own lives and shatter the lives of their families.

A 1992 profile about Szasz in the *Syracuse Post-Standard* includes the opinions of two former APA presidents about him. Alan Stone (APA president, 1979–1980) declared that Szasz "gave patients the opportunity to deny they were sick, and he gave legislators the opportunity to deny they were responsible." The APA president at that time of this profile was Lawrence Hartmann (APA president, 1991–1992), and the *Post-Standard* reported: "The APA's Hartmann and some other psychiatrists also take issue with Szasz because they see him as the catalyst for laws that made it harder for families to treat or commit seriously ill relatives who won't admit they need help." Ironically, Hartmann was the first openly gay president of the APA and played a role in the 1973 abolition of homosexuality as a mental illness—an APA policy reversal that conservative psychiatrists at that time believed gave homosexuals the opportunity to deny they were sick. Szasz's sin, according to Powers and leading psychiatrists, was enabling the mentally ill to deny that they are mentally ill.

More recently, another former APA president declared a journalist to be a "menace to society." Medical and science reporter Robert Whitaker—whose co-written series for the *Boston Globe* on the abuse of mental patients in research settings was named as a finalist for the Pulitzer Prize in 1998—is the most well-known twenty-first century critic of psychiatry. In his 2010 book

Anatomy of an Epidemic, Whitaker concludes that increases in serious mental illness are in large part due to the adverse effects of psychiatric drugs, which can transform episodic conditions into chronic ones. In 2015, Whitaker was called a "menace to society" by Jeffrey Lieberman, a former president of the APA (2013–2014).

Attacks on critics on the grounds that they are responsible for unstable people rejecting institutional creeds to their detriment would strike a familiar chord to Spinoza. His *Theological-Political Treatise* was banned in 1674 in the Dutch Republic. In the ban, it was stated that Spinoza's depiction of God's attributes, the trinity, the divinity of Jesus Christ, the dogmas of the Christian religion, and the authority of the Holy Scripture "introduce doubt into weak, unstable minds."

Spinoza and Szasz had something else in common. As is the case with many freethinkers throughout history, political astuteness was not their strong suit.

In 1969, Szasz and the Church of Scientology co-founded the Citizens Commission on Human Rights (CCHR) to oppose involuntary psychiatric treatments, and Szasz served on CCHR's Board of Advisors as Founding Commissioner. Szasz made clear that "I don't believe in Scientology. . . . I no more believe in their religion or their beliefs than I believe in the beliefs of any other religion." Szasz's political judgment for his involvement with CCHR was that it was the only organization that had money and access to lawyers and that was, he recounted, "trying to free mental patients who were incarcerated in mental hospitals with whom there was nothing wrong, who had committed no crimes, who wanted to get out of the hospital. And that to me was a very worthwhile cause."

Szasz's political thinking neglected how his association with Scientology—a pseudoscientific and secretive institution with a reputation for financially exploiting members and retaliating against former members who speak out against the organization—would discredit not only himself, because he was the most well-known critic of psychiatry, but would also discredit other criticism of psychiatry. A more politically astute thinker would have recognized that, while Scientology had financially backed a few winning anti-coercion skirmishes, its presence as the most visible opponent of psychiatry was a great political benefit to psychiatry as an institution. "Thanks to Scientology," Robert Whitaker concluded, "the powers that be in psychiatry had the perfect storytelling foil, for they could now publicly dismiss criticism of the medical model and psychiatric drugs with a wave of the hand, deriding it as nonsense that arose from people who were members of a deeply unpopular cult, rather than criticism that arose from their own research."

Spinoza, despite his knowledge of politics, was also guilty of personal political judgments that were not astute. Spinoza had hoped that his *Theological-Political Treatise*, with its defense of the freedom of philosophizing, would "pave the way for publication (and welcome reception) of the *Ethics*," notes Steven Nadler. However, Nadler concludes, "It was a serious miscalculation." This treatise was condemned not simply by religious and political authorities, which Spinoza had expected, but it was attacked by even some of the more liberal members of Dutch society who felt Spinoza had simply gone too far. Spinoza's lack of political judgment about the reception of this treatise resulted in it not only failing to pave the way for the *Ethics*, but setting up a roadblock for the *Ethics* that could only be removed by his death.

Spinoza also showed little political acumen following the French invasion of the Netherlands in 1672, when he accepted an invitation in 1673 to meet with the leader of the French forces who was interested in him and his work. The French leader was called away before Spinoza could meet with him at his headquarters in Utrecht, but upon Spinoza's return to his home in The Hague, an angry mob, who had learned of what they believed to be Spinoza's traitorous trip, gathered outside his home, and only with some luck was he not torn to pieces.

In U.S. history, Spinoza's most famous radical Enlightenment successor, with respect to criticism of organized religion and monarchy, is Thomas Paine. While not an original philosopher such as Spinoza, Paine was a freethinker, and in the 1790s, in even bolder language than Spinoza, Paine promoted democracy in his *Rights of Man* (1791) and criticized organized religion in *The Age of Reason* (1795). Paine wrote that "all national institutions of churches, whether Jewish, Christian or Turkish, appear to me no other than human inventions, set up to terrify and enslave mankind, and monopolize power and profit." Paine dubbed Christianity as a "species of atheism" for it "professes to believe in a man rather than in God." Paine pulled no punches in his condemnation of Christianity: "Of all the systems of religions that ever were invented, there is none more derogatory to the Almighty, more unedifying to man, more repugnant to reason, and more contradictory in itself, than this thing called Christianity. Too absurd for belief, too impossible to convince, and too inconsistent for practice, it renders the heart torpid, or produces only atheists and fanatics."

"Paine emerges in most academic accounts," concludes historian Jill Lepore, "as a kind of idiot savant; savvy about adjectives but idiotic about politics." Despite the fact that Paine's *Common Sense* (1776) played a pivotal role in igniting the American Revolution, and his *American Crisis* (1776) was vital to keeping George Washington's troops from quitting on him, after Paine died in 1809, even the peace-loving Quakers refused Paine's request for burial in their cemetery. Six mourners attended Paine's funeral (compared to 20,000 mourners at Benjamin Franklin's funeral), with almost no mention of his death in the American press.

Freethinkers who can laugh at their own lack of political astuteness enjoy the following allegory retold by Fred Edwords, a former executive of the *American Humanist Association*. During the Reign of Terror in the French Revolution, the morning's executions began with three men: a rabbi, a priest, and a freethinker. First facing the guillotine, the rabbi cried out his last words, "I believe in the one and only true God, and He will save me"; the executioner then positioned the rabbi below the blade, pulled the cord, but the blade stopped inches above the rabbi's neck, and the crowd gasped and shouted out, "It's a miracle!"; and the rabbi was freed. Next the priest was given the chance to state his last words, which were, "I believe in Jesus Christ, the Father, Son, and Holy Ghost who will rescue me in my hour of need"; again the blade stopped inches from his neck and the crowd shouted, "Hallelujah"; and the priest was let free. Next it was the freethinker's turn, and before his head was positioned, he too was asked if he had any last words and initially he did not respond; but when prodded to speak, the freethinker cried out, "You gullible, superstitious fools. Those weren't miracles! You've got a blockage in the gear assembly, right here." Edwords concludes, "That might explain why there are so few freethinkers today."

Both Spinoza and Paine were pariah figures for many years after their death, as it was taboo in polite society to disclose any respect or affection for them. However, freethinker admirers of Spinoza and Paine kept their legacies alive. One of the most well-known U.S. freethinkers in the nineteenth century was Robert Ingersoll, who attempted to revive Paine's reputation. Ingersoll described Paine as having "more courage than politeness; more strength than polish." What would also be true for Spinoza, Ingersoll stated about Paine: "He loved the truth for truth's sake, and for man's sake."

The freethinker Bertrand Russell was an admirer of both Spinoza and Paine. In Russell's 1934 essay "The Fate of Thomas Paine," he said, "He had faults, like other men; but it was for his virtues that he was hated and success-fully calumniated." Though Spinoza had fewer personal faults than Paine, he was still hated by those who were not freethinkers. Spinoza recognized early in life that animosity for freethinkers such as himself came with the territory, and he appeared to have had no bitterness about this. Russell was a toughminded freethinker and not easy to impress, but he deeply admired the nobility of Spinoza who fit perfectly Russell's definition of a freethinker: "To be worthy of the name, he must be free of two things: the force of tradition, and the tyranny of his own passions."

During Spinoza's seventeenth century, there were three camps with respect to freethinking. The majority of society—including virtually all ecclesiastic au-thorities, most civil authorities, and much of the public—sought to maintain the status quo of faith in traditional authorities, and they rejected freethink-ing, religious tolerance, and democracy. A second camp consisted of moder-ately enlightened thinkers who saw value in science and tolerance, but they sought to limit the Enlightenment so as not to pose a threat to ecclesiastic and state institutions. The third camp consisted of an underground movement of radical thinkers that included Spinoza and his friends, who threatened institu-tions holding power by rejecting limitations on freethinking and by promoting democracy.

While the term *radical* can be used in many ways, in this book, as in histo-rian Jonathan Israel's *Radical Enlightenment*, it means a complete break with past tradition, including the dissolution of control by powerful societal in-stitutions. *Moderate* enlightenment, for Israel and in this book, refers to crit-icism and reform but no complete break from past traditions or dissolution of institutions.

By the time he left his position as NIMH director in 2015, Thomas Insel can be seen as a moderately enlightened thinker. He had rejected the validity of psychiatry's *DSM* diagnostic manual, and he had challenged the idea that all individuals diagnosed with serious mental illness, such as schizophrenia, need to remain on medications long-term (more in Chapter 12: "Coercion"); and, as previously noted, had acknowledged psychiatry's abysmal treatment outcomes. In his 2009 review of the research, he concluded: "For all classes of mental illness, rates of treatment increased from 20% to 33% during this 10-year period [between 1992 and 2002]"; however, he adds that "the results demonstrate no change in the prevalence of mental illness between 1992 and 2002." With respect to the lack of progress made on treating individuals diagnosed with serious mental illness, Insel pointed out: "Despite five decades of antipsychotic medication and deinstitutionalization, there is little evidence that the prospects for recovery have changed substantially in the past century. . . . In contrast to the steadily decreasing mortality rates of cardiovascular disease, stroke, and cancer, there is no evidence for reduced morbidity or mortality from any mental illness."

A further look at the data on suicide, mental illness disability, and mortality reveals more of the same—poor outcomes despite increased treatment. Between 1988 and 2008, the rate of antidepressant use in the United States increased nearly 400 percent, yet outcomes only have worsened. (1) Suicide: the Centers for Disease Control (CDC) reported in 2020: "From 1999 through 2018, the suicide rate increased 35%. . . . The rate increased on average approximately 1% per year from 1999 to 2006 and by 2% per year from 2006 through 2018." (2) Mental illness disability: in 1987, the U.S. mental illness disability rate was 1 in every 184 Americans, but by 2007 the rate had more than doubled to 1 in every 76 Americans. (3) Mortality among those diagnosed with serious mental illness: the World Health Organization (WHO) in 2020 ("Premature Death among People with Severe Mental Disorders") reported, "There is a 10–25 year life expectancy reduction in patients with severe mental disorders. . . . Mortality rates among people with schizophrenia is 2 to 2.5 times higher than the general population."

Correlation is not causation, and so this data on suicide, disability, and mortality rates coinciding with increased psychiatric medication use does not prove that such treatment is the cause of increased suffering. However, while psychiatric medication has many advocates who report that these drugs help them stabilize and lead normal lives, for society overall, the data shows that increased psychiatric treatment has not had a positive impact—and Spinoza and freethinking rationalists would apply reason as to why this might be the case.

CHAPTER 3

FEAR

Virtually every behavior and condition that has ever been termed an abomination, a sin, a crime, or a mental illness has been tension producing for others. Such tension routinely results in fear and perhaps anger—two of what Spinoza called "passions" that can tyrannize us, undermining our capacity to act with wisdom, justice, and kindness.

Susan James tells us that Spinoza "thinks of fear as a kind of depressing and disempowering emotion." We experience empowerment, liberation, and joy, Spinoza believed, to the extent that our mind is in union with the whole of nature. However, as James explains, "To varying degrees, fear undermines our capacity to engage with the world . . . fear encourages and preserves superstition." Superstition "is a form of obsession that disempowers the self by shutting down its capacity to modify its own beliefs." For Spinoza, fear-fueled superstitions block us from connecting with the truth of nature, including our own nature, and thus undermine our experience of empowerment.

A religion or any system of thought fueled by fear is not one that Spinoza respects. For him, a life controlled by fear, rather than informed by reason, is a life of bondage. He urges his freethinking readers to not be controlled by their fears, even the fear of death, stating, "A free man, that is, he who lives solely according to the dictates of reason, is not guided by fear of death. . . . A free man thinks of death least of all things, and his wisdom is a meditation of life, not of death." For Spinoza, a fear of death gives power to ecclesiastic authorities, as it makes people vulnerable to clerical interpretations of what will happen to them following their death. For him, obsessing about death deprives us of freedom to focus on living life.

Spinoza cared deeply about freedom—freedom from oppressive religious and political authorities, and freedom from one's own psychological bondage. With such freedom, there could be what he most loved—the freedom for free-thinking and philosophy. The less fear, the more freedom. The more fear, the more intolerance.

"On and off, then, from 1661 to 1674, Spinoza worked on the *Ethics*, his magnum opus," states Michael Morgan, philosopher and editor of *Spinoza: Complete Works* (2002). However, by the mid-1660s, Spinoza was becoming increasingly troubled by the assault on freethinking. With the barring by some Dutch provinces of the sale of his freethinking friend Lodewijk Meyer's anonymously published *Philosophia S. Scripturae Interpres* in 1666, followed by the arrest, imprisonment, and death of his outspoken friend Adriaan Koerbagh in 1669 (along with the arrest of Adriaan's freethinking brother), one senses that Spinoza was fed up with ecclesiastic authorities and those civil authorities afraid to buck them. So exasperated, he was compelled to take a break from the *Ethics* in order to fire off a defense of free speech.

That defense became the *Theological-Political Treatise* (1670), and here, unlike in his mostly dispassionate *Ethics*, Spinoza exhibited visceral disdain for fear-based irrational behavior. In his late thirties, upset by the plight of his freethinking pals, Spinoza cannot disguise his contempt for those who "implore God's help with prayers. . . . To such madness are men driven by fears . . . only while fear persists do men fall prey to superstition."

In the beginning of the *Treatise*, Spinoza spells out how fear results in irrational superstitions: "For if, while possessed by fear, they see something happen that calls to mind something good or bad in the past, they believe that this portends a happy or unhappy issue, and this they therefore call a lucky or unlucky omen, even though it may fail them a hundred times." Spinoza cannot disguise his lack of respect for people who give in to their fears and succumb to superstitious beliefs.

A group of people unified by fear, Spinoza knew, will develop a perverse bond, the kind of harmony that is absent of reason, as he concluded: "Harmony is also commonly produced by fear, but then it is untrustworthy. Furthermore, fear arises from weakness of spirit, and therefore does not belong to the use of reason."

For some philosophers and psychologists, there is a difference between *fear* and *anxiety*, with the distinction between the two most famously made by Søren Kierkegaard. For him, both fear and anxiety are responses to threats, but fear is triggered by a known external threat, while anxiety is the feeling of being threatened by an unknown cause that may not be external at all—such as a consciousness of freedom and becoming overwhelmed by possibilities. While this distinction is useful to understanding madness, or what today is called psychosis—more later on this—for now, I will use the word *fear* to convey the emotion we experience when threatened.

The emotional state of those psychiatrically diagnosed with generalized anxiety disorder, social anxiety, panic disorder, various phobias, obsessive compulsive disorder (OCD), and post-traumatic stress disorder (PTSD) is one of fear. Moreover, fear is routinely reported by people diagnosed with depression and many other mental illnesses including psychoses. Much of what we call mental illness is connected with fear—the fear within those being diagnosed, and the fear of those who are doing the diagnosing.

Oppositionally defiant young people create tension, fear, and anger for authorities, and they are today diagnosed with oppositional defiant disorder (ODD). There is no such disorder as "submissive compliant disorder," despite the reality that submissive compliance can cause a great deal of unnecessary suffering. Submissive compliance by one parent can enable emotional and physical child abuse by the other parent; and in societies and nations, submissive compliance can enable demagogic authorities. However, submissive compliance creates no tension for authorities, and thus, there is no mental illness called "submissive compliance disorder."

Fear, in the extreme, becomes terror. Parents often feel terrified when their child starts speaking incoherently or completely stops speaking; or refuses to leave their room; or chooses to sleep on the street; or claims to be Jesus Christ or his executioner; or hears or sees phenomenon that no one else does; or makes a serious suicide attempt; or threatens to physically attack someone; or reminds them of others they've known who have had multiple psychiatric hospitalizations and tragic lives.

An *axiom* is a self-evident truth. Axiomatic is that the greater the tension, fear, and anger that an individual who is considered to be mentally ill creates, the more serious their mental illness is considered to be.

Thus, the young person who refuses to comply with authority or pay attention to authority—behaviors that create some tension but not overwhelming tension—is diagnosed with ODD or attention deficit hyperactivity disorder

(ADHD), which are not considered serious mental illnesses. A person creates more tension by being immobilized or threatening suicide, and such a person is diagnosed with depression, which is seen as a more significant illness. And a person creates even more tension if, after repeated psychiatric treatment for their depression, they make a suicide attempt; and that person receives an even more serious mental illness diagnosis of treatment-resistant depression. Even more tension is created by the person who reports hearing voices that are unheard by others, and such a person is considered even more seriously mentally ill, especially so if such voices are instructing self-destructive or destructive behaviors.

What is a constant is: the greater the tension, fear, and anger that is created for others, the more serious a mental illness is considered to be.

Tension, fear, and anger create a vicious cycle of escalating tension, fear, and anger. Individuals, already frightened by their own thoughts, emotions, and behaviors, then experience the fear and anger of others. Anger—sometimes congruent and sometimes not—creates even more fear, escalating this vicious cycle.

Not only family members, but psychiatrists, psychologists, and other mental health professionals can become fearful and angry with individuals who create tension for them. Professionals are charged by society with evaluating whether or not a person is mentally ill, the severity of the illness, and whether that person poses a threat to themselves or others. There are multiple fears attached to this role.

At one level, professionals fear incompetence, the fear of making an incorrect assessment, diagnosing a person as not mentally ill or not a threat to themselves or others who then acts self-destructively or is violent with others. At another level, professionals fear how they will be judged by peers. And even if a professional is capable of transcending those fears, there are legal fears of being sued over their actions, and there are career fears that their actions can jeopardize their professional licenses. It is unprofessional to publicly blame one's fears on a patient, but professionals are human, and so professionals can become privately angry with patients for creating a condition that results in fear for them. When professionals have anger and don't admit that they do, they are vulnerable to taking retaliations.

Probably the most controversial and divisive issue in modern psychiatry is the use of coercive treatment for those individuals who have sufficiently frightened family and professionals and who are noncompliant with psychiatric treatment and refuse to take their medications. Advocates and critics of involuntary treatment agree that it is fear that triggers coercive court orders, and they also agree that it is societal fears that have resulted in coercion laws (more later on this in Chapter 12: "Coercion").

When I was twenty-four, in my training to become a clinical psychologist, I recall being overwhelmed by fear when I first began an internship at the psychiatry services in a hospital emergency room. Here, some patients entered the hospital voluntarily; a few of them were simply looking to get out of the rain and for a free baloney sandwich, but most were frightened by what they were thinking and feeling. Many other patients came there involuntarily; and while some of them were compliant with family wishes, many others were uncooperatively dragged there by emergency medical technicians or police.

In the psychiatry ER, a major part of the job was to evaluate whether a person was mentally ill and whether that person was a threat to self or others. If a patient is diagnosed as mentally ill and judged to be a threat to self or others, professionals are compelled to control them in some manner, including physical restraint and involuntary hospitalization.

Thus, there is professional fear of making a poor decision that results in releasing a person who then dies by suicide or is violent with others. There is also a fear of an over-reaction resulting in coercions that cause great resentment and distrust, leading to the patient forever rejecting professional care. And there is the fear that hospitalizing a patient who has no private health insurance will result in one fewer bed of the limited beds available for those without private insurance, an over-reaction that greatly annoys colleagues in the ER.

For the first month of that internship, my stomach would start tightening with fear on my drive to the hospital. I had been taught in classrooms and textbooks the symptoms of various mental illnesses and how to make a suicide evaluation, but all this academic instruction was of little value. For example, to evaluate suicide risk, we had been taught to ask patients if they had thoughts of suicide, if they had a suicide plan, and if so, exactly what it was. What was not in the textbooks was immediately obvious on the job. If you really wanted to kill yourself, would you be honest with your answers to those questions? And if you were mostly trying to get out of the rain and cold or get taken seriously or to simply torture a family member but had no real suicide intention, why not provide a chilling suicide plan?

When it comes to assessing self-destructive and violent behaviors, mental health professionals are aware that males are more likely than females to act self-destructively and violently; and professionals routinely look to an individual's history of self-destructive or violent behaviors, their access to a gun, and their alcohol/drug use. But this history may not be known about a stranger entering the ER, and even if known, could be irrelevant in any particular situation.

"After Decades of Research, Science Is No Better Able to Predict Suicidal Behaviors" was a 2016 report by the American Psychological Association. The report quoted researcher Joseph Franklin, lead author of a 2016 meta-analysis of 365 studies examining the use of risk factors (such as previous suicide attempts, depression, stressful life events, and substance abuse) to predict suicidal behaviors. Franklin concluded, "Our analyses showed that science could only predict future suicidal thoughts and behaviors about as well as random guessing. In other words, a suicide expert who conducted an in-depth assessment of risk factors would predict a patient's future suicidal thoughts and behaviors with the same degree of accuracy as someone with no knowledge of the patient who predicted based on a coin flip."

In my first couple of weeks as an intern, I recall being so overwhelmed by fear that I found it difficult to listen to what a patient was communicating. A month into my internship, I had a fortuitous encounter with a psychiatrist who worked there and whose position in the hierarchy gave him freedom to enjoy eccentricity. On an overnight shift at around 3:00 a.m., with only the two of us present, he turned to me after assessing a patient who was completely noncommunicative and thus difficult to evaluate. He said, "Sometimes, you just have to flip a coin," and he proceeded to do so. As a naïve trainee, it was shocking to see how his decision to hospitalize had been made (which now with knowledge of the research such as Franklin's, his coin flipping is not shocking at all); but at another level, what the eccentric psychiatrist said and did considerably reduced my level of fear over my own adequacy, which paradoxically enabled me to better listen to patients.

I was hired to work an additional year at the psychiatry ER after my one-year internship ended. I am glad that I was there for two years but not longer. It was long enough to understand why mental health professionals develop such strong biases about people who are diagnosed with serious mental illnesses such as schizophrenia, but it was not so long that reason could not rehabilitate these biases.

Mental health professionals who work in hospitals routinely see individuals who stop taking their medication and become psychotic. These professionals don't see individuals who have had a psychotic episode, took medications for a brief time, recovered, and no longer use medications or have any contact with mental health professionals. The bias developed by many mental health professionals is what Patricia Cohen and Jacob Cohen called "The Clinician's Illusion," in which clinicians' sense of long-term prognosis is biased by the skewed population that they see.

Spinoza wrote about the phenomenon of bias in his second work, the *Short Treatise on God, Man, and His Well-Being* (probably completed by 1662). He discusses how one can form an incorrect general opinion based on a specific sample, "like one who, having never seen any sheep except with short tails, is surprised at the sheep from Morocco which have long ones." Spinoza might tell mental health professionals who have based their opinions on a select sample to consider the sheep from Morocco.

When it comes to mental illness, fear is everywhere. Fear is the internal experience of many people diagnosed with mental illness. Family members, friends, and strangers are often terrified by people diagnosed with mental illness. And while professionals vary in their degree of fear, they have professional reasons to fear the consequences of their actions. Thus, there is often a situation in which already frightened patients interact with frightened people. And when one is already frightened, another's fear, especially an authority's fear, can push one to points beyond fear—to terror and severe breakdowns.

A psychotic breakdown—when people enter into a condition in which they appear to have disconnected from reality—can be extremely frightening. It can be frightening for the person in that condition, for their friends and family, and for a community. And it can be frightening for professionals.

For Spinoza, "It is fear, then, that engenders, preserves, and fosters superstition" and "spurious religious reverence." When we are overwhelmed by fear and terror, our capacity to reason evaporates and we are vulnerable to superstitions, which include unscientific explanations of causes and fixes.

For nearly three thousand years, individuals diagnosed as mad or insane were given the treatment of bloodletting. Some of these individuals did then improve, but today all agree that they got better despite that treatment and not because of it. When fueled by fear and terror, even those who pride themselves on their critical thinking can become irrational, and all of us are vulnerable to scientific-sounding language about pseudoscientific conceptualizations.

While possessed by fear, we will return to anything that we associate with relief from that fear, even though, as Spinoza said, "it may fail them a hundred times." Thus, Spinoza would fully understand why barbaric treatments don't disappear. When patients improved after bloodletting, doctors attributed it to the treatment, even though they may have seen bloodletting fail a hundred times. When the bloodletting failed, doctors could attribute it to a failure to administer bloodletting early enough in the disease process or to not removing enough blood. Fear maintains superstition. For Spinoza, only reason and science can deactivate superstition.

"Man's emotional nature masters, more often than not, man's rational nature and leads him astray," notes Spinoza scholar Joseph Ratner in *The Philosophy of Spinoza* (1927). Our anger and fear—especially when we deny our anger and fear or are ashamed of these passions—can fuel irrational explanations; and as Ratner points out, "Their stark immediacy vitiates man's judgement."

Our judgments about others, especially when fear-based, tell us more about ourselves than who we are judging. For Spinoza, Ratner tells us, "Paul's idea of Peter tells us more about Paul than about Peter . . . the prophets' ideas about God tell us more about the prophets than about God."

Taking Spinoza to heart, when a psychiatrist or psychologist tells me that a patient has a borderline personality disorder, this tells me more about the professional than the patient. It tells me that the professional is likely extremely frightened by this patient. The professional might report having assessed the symptoms of a borderline personality disorder (extreme emotional swings and explosive anger, unstable relationships, impulsivity, self-destructive behaviors, and boundary violations); but what the professional is mostly communicating by a borderline diagnosis is that the patient scares the hell out of the professional. The professional is likely afraid that the patient will assume a relationship that is problematic for the professional. Individuals diagnosed with borderline personality disorder are routinely unaware that patients do not get that diagnosis without a professional, consciously or unconsciously, being frightened of them.

There is another important fear-driven phenomenon for individuals who are emotionally suffering and behaving in disturbing ways: the fear of blame and ostracism for creating tension, which makes them vulnerable to fear-fueled remedies. Western society prioritizes efficiency and productivity; and so those individuals who are insufficiently paying attention, immobilized by their anxiety and depression, or acting in some other way deemed inefficient and nonproductive and seen as disrupting their family, school, or workplace can create tension, anger, and resentment. These individuals fear of blame and ostracism for their tension-producing behaviors, and this fear, like all fear, renders them vulnerable to inadequate ideas about remedies.

One such fear-driven inadequate idea is that a mental illness diagnosis with biochemical causality is an antidote to ostracism and stigmatization. While the research does show that individuals are less likely to be blamed for their behavior if they are seen as suffering from a biochemical mental illness, this biochemical mental illness attribution also causes others to have greater fear of such individuals, resulting in stigmatization. Specifically, the research shows that the idea that emotional and behavioral disturbances are caused by a biochemical illness communicates to others that such disturbances are beyond control, which creates fear of unpredictable and violent behaviors, which of course leads to avoidance (more in Chapter 9: "Tolerance and Stigma").

From my experience, the following are axioms about fear:

1. The source of much of what is termed mental illness is some type of fear, of which there are several types, including: the fear of isolation, the fear of relationships, the fear of abandonment, the fear of engulfment by others, the fear of death, the fear of life, the fear of being out of touch with reality, and the fear of reality.

2. Virtually all of what is termed as mental illness is tension-producing for other people.

3. Tension-producing conditions routinely result in fear and sometimes anger. If loved ones say with conviction that they are considering suicide, this is going to create tension, which is going to result in fear and sometimes anger. When loved ones, or sometimes even strangers, claim to hear or see things that others don't, believe things that seem to be clearly untrue, or act in ways that are socially unacceptable, this is going to create tension, which is going to result in fear and sometimes anger.

4. There is a vicious cycle of fear in which an individual, already fearful, creates tension for others, which results in fear and anger for others, which creates even more fear for that individual.

5. Fear and anger undermine reason and critical thinking, resulting in what Spinoza called inadequate ideas that are partially or completely false. Such inadequate ideas result in irrational decision making.

6. Significant tension leads to the desire for simple answers that are easy to grasp and promise a quick tension reduction, but such answers may be superstitions or other such inadequate ideas.

7. When we feel so threatened that we have moved into a flight-or-fight state, we are vulnerable to handing over decision making to authorities whose credentials may well give them the appearance of being legitimate but who often, by virtue of their role, are not in the best position to de-escalate the fear cycle.

8. After we have handed over power to authorities, it creates tension to continue evaluating whether such authorities are legitimate ones. We are vulnerable to being attached to our decision, as a re-evaluation of such a decision creates more tension.

9. Fear and anger over tension-producing conditions truncate dialogue. Conversations that do not immediately result in eliminating tension can create more tension, and so lengthy discussions that ensue in dialogue can be unwelcome.

10. Reason dictates not fleeing from the tension but attempting to transcend it, which includes maintaining dialogue and reassessment.

11. We become less fearful of ourselves to the extent that we can accept the unusual in ourselves, and to the extent that we are less fearful of the unusualness in ourselves, we are less fearful of the unusualness in others.

12. While some mental health professionals are skilled at de-escalating fear, often the best ways to break the cycle of fear is peer-to-peer support (more later in Chapter 15: "Pals and Peers"). Individuals who themselves have experienced the unusual—including extreme emotional states and atypical behaviors—are less likely to be as terrified of

these conditions compared to those who have never experienced them. In contrast to family members or to mental health professionals with liability concerns, peers can more easily listen with curiosity, compassion, and playfulness, which is more likely to de-escalate fear.

Spinoza recognized how tension-producing conditions and resulting fear undermine our capacity for reason and ability to understand human nature. He knew that the more we understand, the greater pleasure we experience, which energizes us to want to understand more. He knew that if we can understand the source of tension, we can better tolerate it, and that this can prevent barbaric attempts to immediately eradicate the source of tension.

Spinoza's philosophy is an antidote to arrogance. For Spinoza, the more we understand reality, including our own emotional reality, the more we are empowered and the greater our joy. And so the rational individual is incentivized to be open to correcting false notions of reality so as to gain the pleasure of connecting with what is truly real. As Rebecca Goldstein explicates: "Since the very process of correcting erroneous judgments is expansive—to understand is to expand ourselves into the world, reproducing the world in our own minds, appropriating it into our very selves—to understand one's emotions, even the most painful of them, is necessarily pleasurable." However, she adds, this "requires one's getting out of oneself, seeing oneself clearheadedly as just another thing in the world, treating one's own emotions as dispassionately as a problem in geometry."

CHAPTER 4

ULTIMI BARBARORUM

Throughout history, including recent U.S. history, human behaviors that are unfamiliar, foreign, bizarre, and inexplicable create tension and fear resulting in barbarism. Psychiatry advocates and critics agree that many individuals diagnosed with mental illnesses such as schizophrenia have been victims of intolerance and barbarism.

It was obvious to Spinoza that the fear of uncommon beliefs can trigger anger, intolerance, and barbaric violence. Throughout his life, he repeatedly saw this occur. His Jewish ancestors were the victims of intolerance and violence in Portugal, as they fled from an inquisition that was similar to the Spanish Inquisition. And Spinoza himself became personally acquainted at an early age with the ugly effects of fear of the unconventional, and he would repeatedly encounter anger, intolerance, and violence throughout his life. This greatly informed all his works.

Even though the Dutch Republic was extraordinarily tolerant compared to the rest of Europe, when Spinoza's *Theological-Political Treatise* was published in 1670, the ideas in his book threatened many people. Spinoza knew it could provoke violent retribution, so he published it anonymously, falsifying the actual publisher and the city of publication. However, word got out that Spinoza was the author, and prison or even assassination became possibilities. By 1675, when he wanted to publish the *Ethics*, it was simply too dangerous to do so, and it could only be published after his death in 1677. Both books were banned, and individuals caught selling them faced the possibility of prison.

As a young man, before publishing a word, Spinoza provoked tension and fear that resulted in anger and intolerance. Spinoza's views on religion had so angered and terrified his Jewish community that, in 1656, he received the harshest writ of *herem* (banishment) that had ever been pronounced upon a member of the Portuguese-Jewish community in Amsterdam. Spinoza was accused of unspecified "evil opinions and acts," "monstrous deeds," and "abominable heresies." And because he refused to "mend his wicked ways," he was punished with a *herem* that proclaimed: "By decree of the angels and by the command of the holy men, we excommunicate, expel, curse and damn Baruch de Espinoza, with the consent of God." Spinoza was cursed, literally and repeatedly: "Cursed be he by day and cursed be he by night; cursed be he when he lies down and cursed be he when he rises up. Cursed be he when he goes out and cursed be he when he comes in."

The writ concludes with the specifics of his shunning: "no one should communicate with him, not even in writing, nor accord him any favor nor stay with him under the same roof nor come within four cubits [approximately six to seven feet] in his vicinity." Spinoza might be amused to learn that during the coronavirus epidemic, people were instructed to keep that same distance away from one another to prevent the spread of the virus.

Spinoza was well aware of the likely reaction by Jewish authorities to his noncompliance. He knew the tragic story of Uriel da Costa, a member of the Amsterdam Jewish community, whose emotional instability would today likely garner him a serious mental illness diagnosis. In 1640, da Costa killed himself after being humiliated by Jewish authorities. After da Costa's rejection of dogma and various Jewish rituals, a *herem* was issued against him. Da Costa was offered an opportunity to repent and retract his words, which he rejected for seven years, but loneliness and perhaps poverty forced him to surrender. The ritual for lifting the *herem* included not simply his retraction and penance but a public lashing followed by da Costa being forced to lie down at the synagogue exit while the members of the congregation stepped over his body. Overwhelmed by the humiliation, a few days later, after writing a denunciation of Jewish authorities, he shot himself.

Bento was eight years old at the time of da Costa's suicide, a major event in his community and one that certainly would have made a major impression on him. Bento was determined not to suffer Uriel's fate. In response to his own banishment, Spinoza would practice what he ultimately preached, maintaining his cool, perhaps even welcoming the expulsion. While in the instance of his own banishment, Spinoza was a model of composure, on another occasion of mob violence, Spinoza's anger overcame his reason.

Though famously levelheaded, in 1672, Spinoza became so incensed by barbarism that he had to be restrained so as not to act rashly and jeopardize his life. In Dutch history, 1672 has been called "the disaster year." It was then that Johan de Witt, the Grand Pensionary of Holland, essentially the leader of the Dutch Republic, along with his brother were brutally killed by a mob. The mob was terrified and angered by a French invasion that they blamed on Johan de Witt. Though de Witt was not, as was Spinoza, an advocate of democracy, de Witt did adhere to republican ideals, opposed monarchy, and was a proponent of religious tolerance.

Spinoza was greatly upset by the murder of the de Witt brothers. Spinoza was especially enraged by the brutality of it. After the de Witt brothers were killed, their bodies were stripped naked, hung up by the feet, torn to pieces, and, according to one report, their flesh roasted and served up to the mob, with some body pieces sold as souvenirs.

This barbarism resulted in one of the few instances in Spinoza's life in which he lost control over his emotions, according to the philosopher Leibniz, who visited Spinoza a few months before Spinoza's death. Spinoza told Leibniz that, after discovering the atrocity, he "wanted to go out at night and post a placard near the site of the massacre, reading *ultimi barbarorum* [you are the greatest of barbarians]. But his host [his sympathetic landlord] locked the house to keep him from going out, for he would be exposed to being torn to pieces."

Throughout history, tension, fear, intolerance, and anger has resulted in barbarism. Tension and fear are created by the unfamiliar, the strange, and the unknown. And so those, throughout history, diagnosed as insane and mentally ill have been victims of barbarism.

Commonly referred to as "Bedlam," Bethlem was founded in London in 1247 and is history's most infamous madhouse. Jailers would shackle naked, starving people and taunt and beat them. Standard medical treatments included bleeding, freezing baths, scarification, and bruising. The public paid to gawk, mock, poke with sticks, and sexually abuse patients. Such barbarism occurred there well into the eighteenth century.

In the late-eighteenth and early-nineteenth century, the most well-known American physician who treated the mad was Benjamin Rush, a signer of the Declaration of Independence. Rush today is called "the father of American psychiatry," his image adorning the seal of the American Psychiatric Association

(APA). Rush proclaimed himself a slave abolitionist though he had owned a slave; and his views on race included the idea that blackness in skin color was caused by leprosy, and so he advocated "curing" skin color. Rush also invented treatments for the mentally ill. Based on an earlier imbalance theory that improper flow of blood caused madness, Rush used bloodletting, and he also devised two mechanical devices to treat madness: a "tranquilizing chair" and a "gyrator" in which patients were strapped down, immobilized, and violently spun.

In the early part of the twentieth century, the United States led the world in forced sterilizations of the mentally ill. The eugenics movement—aimed at improving the genetic composition of a society—received strong political and financial support in the United States. By 1928, twenty-one states had compulsory sterilization laws. Between 1907 and 1939, more than 30,000 people in twenty-nine U.S. states were sterilized (nearly half of them in California). In the twentieth century, over 70,000 psychiatric patients in the United States were sterilized.

In 1941, at the annual meeting of the APA, neurologist Foster Kennedy presented a paper entitled: "The Problem of Social Control of the Congenital Defective: Education, Sterilization, Euthanasia." He argued that "It was a merciful and kindly thing to relieve that defective—often tortured and convulsed, grotesque and absurd, useless and foolish, and entirely undesirable— of the agony of living." In 1942, the *American Journal of Psychiatry* published that paper.

Fear can make any society, including U.S. society, barbaric. When people in a society become convinced that their survival is jeopardized by those who are unproductive burdens, barbarism emerges. In the midst of the Great Depression in 1934, ten years after Virginia passed its 1924 sterilization act, Joseph DeJarnette, superintendent of Virginia's Western State Hospital, noted Nazi Germany's increasing rates of sterilizations and lamented in the *Richmond Times-Dispatch*: "The Germans are beating us at our own game." And that year, Leon Whitney, executive secretary of the American Eugenics Society, said about the Nazis, "While we were pussy-footing around . . . the Germans were calling a spade a spade."

While the United States and Great Britain were most responsible for igniting the eugenics movement, it was Nazi Germany that acted most decisively, with both massive sterilization and murder, to accomplish eugenics goals of ridding society of individuals considered burdensome. Prior to the

Nazi regime, Germany had been reluctant to force sterilizations, but when Hitler—an admirer of U.S. eugenic policies—came into power, he sought to first catch up with and then surpass the United States in eliminating those individuals that the Nazi's infamously labeled as having a "life unworthy of living."

In Hitler's Germany, there would be an estimated 300,000 to 400,000 forced sterilizations, followed by murder (euphemistically called "involuntary euthanasia"). Approximately 200,000 to 300,000 psychiatric patients were murdered in Nazi Germany in what was later referred to as its T4 program. Grotesquely, in 1941, the staff of Hadamer Psychiatric Institution in Hessen, Germany had a ceremony in which each member of the staff was given a bottle of beer to celebrate the murder and cremation of their 10,000th patient.

During the Nazi regime, the German public had little to be proud of, but when word got out about the organized murder of psychiatric patients, there were public protests led by prominent religious figures; and in 1941, Hitler actually ordered the suspension of T4. However, the murdering secretly continued, orchestrated by enthusiastic doctors, including psychiatrists. A 2012 *Public Health Reviews* article, "How Ethics Failed—The Role of Psychiatrists and Physicians in Nazi Programs from Exclusion to Extermination, 1933–1945," notes: "Psychiatrists deceived their patients and patients' families. Physicians were complicit in forcing their patients to be sterilized, arranged their deaths, used them as test subjects for research, performed 'involuntary euthanasia' and participated in the Final Solution."

The tension created by psychiatric patients has continued to bring out the worst in U.S. society in both its treatment and research methods, which if practiced on other populations—including animal populations—would be considered sadistic and criminal.

Consider U.S. physician Walter Freeman, whose mental illness treatment specialty was transorbital lobotomy. Freeman had no surgical training, yet over four decades beginning in the 1930s through the 1960s, he performed approximately 3,500 to 4,000 lobotomies. Approximately 2,500 of these lobotomies were his own invention, which he called a transorbital lobotomy: a metal pick was inserted into the corner of each eye-socket and hammered through the thin bone with a mallet, moved back and forth, severing the connections between the prefrontal cortex and frontal lobes. Freeman performed his final surgery in 1967 on a woman he had already performed two previous lobotomies; she died of a cerebral hemorrhage, as did at least a hundred of his other patients, and many more simply lost all interest in life. He lobotomized 19 minors, most famously twelve-year old defiant Howard Dully, who told his story with the help of a co-author in the 2007 best seller *My Lobotomy*.

Today, Freeman appears to us as a sadistic egomaniac, but he performed this procedure throughout the United States at many of its most respected institutions. Lobotomy is not the only example of the sad reality that virtually any idea that is confidently proclaimed by a physician to be capable of reducing the tension created by psychiatric patients is an idea welcomed by U.S. society. The hope for such tension reduction trumps rational thought about adverse effects.

Other recent psychiatric treatments that much of society now considers barbaric include aversion therapy to treat homosexuality and insulin coma therapy for those diagnosed with serious mental illness. Homosexuality, as noted, was a *DSM* mental illness until 1973, and aversion therapies for it included electric shock to the genitals and nausea-inducing drugs administered simultaneously with the presentation of homoerotic stimuli. In insulin coma therapy, used extensively through the 1950s and into the 1960s, patients were repeatedly injected with large doses of insulin in order to produce daily comas over several weeks.

Barbarity extends beyond treatment to research on psychiatric patients. The Nuremberg Code, established after the horrific human experiments by doctors in Nazi Germany, states that medical experiments on human subjects "should be so conducted as to avoid all unnecessary physical and mental suffering and injury." Thus, it shocked many Americans to discover that following World War II and through the 1990s, several of the most renowned U.S. psychiatrists conducted research that attempted to provoke and exacerbate psychotic symptoms in psychiatric patients.

Paul Hoch (prior to becoming New York state commissioner of mental hygiene and attempting to ban Thomas Szasz from Syracuse Psychiatric Hospital) was the director of the Department of Experimental Psychiatry at the New York State Psychiatric Institute between 1948 and 1955. Here, Hoch administered LSD and mescaline to nonpsychotic psychiatric patients to see if this would trigger psychotic symptoms. After his death in 1964, a bust of Hoch was placed in the lobby of the New York State Psychiatric Institute.

By the 1970s, the most prominent theory for the cause of schizophrenia was an excessive amount of the neurotransmitter dopamine, and so researchers went about testing this "dopamine hypothesis of schizophrenia." Psychotic symptom exacerbation and provocation (psychotogenic) experiments were pioneered in the 1970s by physician David Janowsky. He discovered that giving the dopamine-enhancing psychostimulant drug methylphenidate (Ritalin) to patients diagnosed with schizophrenia caused a significant intensification of psychotic symptoms; and that other psychostimulants also exacerbated psychosis.

These psychotogenic experiments continued in the United States through the 1980s and 1990s. In 1998, the *Boston Globe* series of reports, "Doing Harm: Research on the Mentally Ill," authored by Robert Whitaker and Dolores Kong, uncovered how several renowned psychiatrists conducted experiments on more than two thousand patients in which certain drugs were administered and other drugs withheld in the expectation of worsening symptoms.

One of those psychiatrists who conducted such psychotogenic research aimed at inducing symptoms of psychosis was Jeffrey Lieberman. In 1987, in his investigation "Prediction of Relapse in Schizophrenia," Lieberman administered Ritalin to thirty-four stable outpatients previously diagnosed with schizophrenia. They were not only administered Ritalin but taken off standard antipsychotic drugs until psychotic symptoms reappeared. In a 1990 study co-authored by Lieberman, "Behavioral Response to Methylphenidate [Ritalin] and Treatment Outcome in First Episode Schizophrenia," the article abstract states: "In order to examine the relationship of behavioral response to psychostimulants and acute treatment response, we administered methylphenidate [Ritalin]. . . to 38 patients who met Research Diagnostic Criteria (RDC) for definite or probable schizophrenia or schizoaffective disorder, [who] were experiencing their first acute episode of psychosis."

These psychotogenic researchers were self-certain of their essential altruism. For them, these studies were done to gain greater knowledge about schizophrenia that would lead to improved treatments. Because they deemed their mission so important, and because the general public prefers not to think about psychiatric patients, ignored was the reality that human subjects received interventions—such as drug injections designed to create or exacerbate psychotic symptoms—that caused suffering.

Important here to keep in mind is that this psychotogenic research was not done by a rogue psychiatrist in a distant era but by several of the most renowned psychiatrists as late as the 1990s; and that one such psychotogenic researcher, Jeffrey Lieberman, remained so respected within psychiatry that he was later elected president of the APA.

Standard twenty-first century psychiatric treatment in the United States appeared barbaric to *60 Minutes* reporter Katie Couric in her September 30, 2007 story "What Killed Rebecca Riley?" about the 2006 death of four-year-old Rebecca Riley. When Rebecca was twenty-eight months old, following complaints by her mother that she was "hyper" and had difficulty sleeping, psychiatrist Kayoko Kifuji, at the Tufts-New England Medical Center in Boston, Massachusetts, diagnosed Rebecca with attention deficit hyperactivity disorder (ADHD). Kifuji prescribed clonidine, a hypertensive medication with significant sedating properties, a drug Kifuji also had prescribed to Rebecca's older sister and brother. When Rebecca was three years old, Kifuji added the diagnosis of bipolar disorder and prescribed two additional drugs, the antipsychotic Seroquel and the anticonvulsant Depakote. At age four, Rebecca died. The medical examiner concluded that the cause of death was intoxication of clonidine, Depakote, and two over-the-counter cold and cough medicines that led to heart failure, lungs filled with bloody fluid, coma, and then death.

Rebecca's parents sedated their children to make them easier to manage, and they attained psychiatric diagnoses for their children so as to garner disability payments; and they were charged with murder and convicted. A juror, who voted for the second-degree murder conviction of Rebecca's mother, spoke for her fellow jurors: "Every one of us was very angry. Dr. Kifuji should be sitting in the defendant's chair, too." However, Kifuji returned to practicing child psychiatry without any restrictions, penalties, or supervision. She was not considered by Tufts-New England Medical Center a "bad apple."

While lobotomist Walter Freeman is now seen as a bad apple, he wasn't in his day; in 1941, Freeman was so well-regarded that he was chosen by Kennedy family patriarch Joseph Kennedy to perform a lobotomy on his twenty-three-year-old daughter Rosemary Kennedy. Today, psychotogenic researcher Jeffrey Lieberman is certainly not considered a bad apple, as he served as the APA president between 2013 and 2014. And Kayoko Kifuji's treatment of Rebecca Riley was defended by Tufts-New England Medical Center, whose spokesperson told *60 Minutes* the following: "The care we provided was appropriate and within responsible professional standards."

Would Spinoza, if alive today, have considered posting a placard at Tufts-New England Medical Center stating *ultimi barbarorum*? I can't say. But as a freethinker in the early part of what we now call the Enlightenment, Spinoza would be deeply saddened to discover that in the twenty-first century, a girl aged twenty-eight months could end up being the victim of such barbarism.

He would have hoped that what we now call the Enlightenment would have been more successful.

Today, many Americans are surprised to discover that electroconvulsant therapy (ECT), commonly called electroshock, continues to be used as a psychiatric treatment. Despite being controversial, owing to adverse effects such as memory loss, there has been little recent effort in establishing ECT's effectiveness; and so whether or not one considers ECT to be barbaric, the lack of scientific effort in justifying it is, if not barbaric, at best cavalier. A 2019 review of the research on ECT effectiveness for depression, published in *Ethical Human Psychology and Psychiatry*, reported that there have been no randomized placebo-controlled studies (ECT versus simulated/sham ECT) since 1985. In assessing the five meta-analyses (based on eleven studies) prior to 1985, the quality of the studies was found to be so poor that conclusions about efficacy are not possible. The authors concluded that given ECT's adverse effect of permanent memory loss (and its smaller risk of mortality) that the "long-standing failure to determine whether or not ECT works means that its use should be immediately suspended until a series of well designed, randomized, placebo-controlled studies have investigated whether there really are any significant benefits against which the proven significant risks can be weighed."

While, as noted, there is agreement between psychiatry advocates and critics that many individuals diagnosed with mental illness are victims of intolerance and barbarism, advocates and critics sharply disagree about how to reduce this intolerance and barbarism. While mental illness advocacy groups such as the National Alliance on Mental Illness (NAMI) work to destigmatize people diagnosed with mental illness, self-identified "psychiatric survivors" believe that the very concept of *mental illness* is a source of intolerance and barbarism (more later on this in Chapter 9: "Tolerance and Stigma").

For Spinoza, freedom and tolerance are what a society should strive for. He would understand why many individuals who have been diagnosed with serious mental illness have anger that the population diagnosed as mentally ill has such high mortality rates, and he would empathize with their anger about their friends from this population who have died prematurely. It might make Spinoza think about his high-spirited friend Adriaan Koerbagh.

Spinoza, so as to remind himself of the dangers of freethinking, wore a signet ring engraved with the word *caute* (caution); however, his friend Adriaan threw caution to the wind, as his actions got him in major trouble with ecclesiastic and civil authorities. Koerbagh was a radical democrat who opposed church authorities having any civil authority. In Koerbagh's books, he mocked the irrationality of organized religion, making fun of superstitions, dogma, and ceremonies. He was so rash—some might say "crazy"—that, unlike Spinoza, he published his views in Dutch with his name on his books; thus, the general public could read his views, and authorities were certain who wrote it and sought his arrest. As a fugitive living under an assumed name, Jonathan Israel tells us, "Apparently in a manic mood, he was reportedly engaging all kinds of people in conversation and 'disseminating his obscenities.'" After his arrest, under interrogation, Koerbagh denied the divinity of Jesus and the virginity of Mary, and in 1668, he was sentenced to ten years of prison, banished from Amsterdam for another ten years, and received a steep fine. A year later, in 1669, Koerbagh died in prison.

"Spinoza was deeply touched by Koerbagh's death," notes Steven Nadler. He reports, "By the mid-1660s, Spinoza and Koerbagh seem to have developed an intimate, mutually influential intellectual relationship." They were, Nadler believes, "kindred spirits," and so with his death, "Spinoza lost a good companion, a philosophical and political fellow traveler, and an intrepid ally in his campaign against sectarianism and superstition." Nadler concludes that Spinoza's 1670 *Theological-Political Treatise* is a personal book, "a response to the loss of a dear friend, and his reply to what he perceived to be the calumnies increasingly being leveled at him."

CHAPTER 5

SCIENCE

Spinoza was very much interested in science and technology. He followed the latest developments in optics, and he studied insects and other phenomena with the lenses that he made, using microscopes that he constructed. He was curious about the results of scientific experiments and discussed them with other scientists, including the renowned Dutch astronomer and physicist Christiaan Huygens.

Valuing science was a major part of the Enlightenment, the goal of which was to make life better for humankind. Given Spinoza's chronic respiratory problems, he cared very much about medical advances, as he valued all technological advances that could make living easier and free one up to philosophize. "The depth of his devotion to science," reports historian and journalist Anthony Gottlieb in *The Dream of Enlightenment* (2016), "may be gauged from the fact that at the time of his death about one-third of the books in his personal library were scientific or mathematical works."

In standard philosophy courses, Spinoza is routinely classified as a "Continental Rationalist" (along with Descartes and Leibniz) as contrasted with the "British Empiricists" (Locke, Hume, and Berkeley), but it is a mistake to conclude that Spinoza did not value the experimental method. However, he believed that the experimental method had its limitations. For Spinoza, notes Jonathan Israel, "Observed data are only the raw material of scientific discourse and tell us little in themselves . . . experiments can only prove or disprove propositions once a coherent theoretical framework has been set up."

Spinoza knew that the best of experiments, based on inadequate ideas and invalid conceptualizations, would yield worthless results. Also, he believed that scientific experiments were sometimes unnecessary for someone capable of reason. Furthermore, the experimental method would have little value for Spinoza in discovering truths that he believed were of supreme importance, such as the essence of reality and happiness. So, while Spinoza valued experimentation and conducted experiments—including ones on hydrodynamics that he details in one of his letters—he recognized that without adequate ideas, we will have misconceptions that will undermine the discovery of essential truths.

Spinoza cared deeply about understanding the essential nature of things. He grappled with this issue his entire life. In his twenties, he began working on the *Treatise on the Emendation of the Intellect*. He never finished it, perhaps concluding it best to finish his more comprehensive *Ethics*, in which he included some of the material from this earlier treatise (which, like the *Ethics*, was not published until after his death).

It was critical for him to learn how, as Steven Nadler explains, "to distinguish 'true ideas'—ideas that reveal the essences of things—from fictions, 'clear and distinct' perceptions from confused ones." Understanding the essential nature of things is no easy matter. "This," as Nadler puts it, "is not a project to be undertaken haphazardly."

Absent strenuous reason, we are likely to have ideas that are not true. This, for Spinoza, should compel us to be more self-critical about the basis of our knowledge. Stuart Hampshire notes, "In studying logic or the theory of knowledge . . . we explicitly recognize that most of our so-called knowledge does not reflect the true order of causes in the Universe, but is only a logically confused association of ideas, reflecting our individual reaction to our limited environment."

In our attempts at understanding, we can rely on methods that are inadequate or limited. In Spinoza's *Treatise on the Emendation of the Intellect*, he describes four methods that we use to acquire knowledge, the first two being inadequate ones. In the first method, we can acquire information through hearsay (others' report); but this method is not a reliable method for gaining essential truths about the nature of reality. In the second method, we can acquire knowledge by casual, random, or anecdotal experience, but this mode too has limited value. For Spinoza these first two methods provide us with inadequate ideas, as adequate knowledge can only be obtained by the third and fourth methods. In the third method, we acquire truths through reasoning and deduction; in a Spinoza example, once we understand "the nature of vision and realize that it has the property of making us see [something] as smaller at a distance than if we were to see it near at hand, we can infer that the sun is bigger than it appears"; this third mode can provide us with, as he says, "the idea of a thing," however, it cannot provide us with the essence of a thing, which includes the properties that make it distinct—this requires a fourth method. Spinoza tells us that "only the fourth mode comprehends the adequate essence of the thing," and this is the mode of perceiving a thing so that we can immediately intuit it; examples of this fourth mode, he tells us, are the "kind of knowledge we know that two and three are five, and that if two lines are parallel to a third line, they are parallel to one another."

In his later *Ethics*, Spinoza distinguishes three categories of knowledge. Knowledge of the first kind combines his previous two categories of inadequate methods and includes opinion, imagination, hearsay, and random experience. Knowledge of the second kind is reason, deduction, logic, and scientific understanding. Knowledge of the third kind is what he calls *scientia intuitiva* or intuitive knowledge. He tells us, "Knowledge of the first kind is the only cause of falsity; knowledge of the second and third kind is necessarily true." This is clearly important for Spinoza, as to make sure we get it, he immediately adds an additional proposition, "Knowledge of the second and third kind, and not knowledge of the first kind, teaches us to distinguish true from false."

Spinoza's three types of knowledge, according to philosopher Alasdair MacIntyre, connect to three psychological stages. Specifically, the first type of knowledge (opinion, hearsay imagination, and random experience) results in inadequate and confused ideas causing the psychological condition of human bondage. The second type of knowledge (reason and scientific understanding) corresponds to human freedom and liberation by providing understanding of how things are caused and determined. The third type of knowledge (intuitive knowledge) corresponds to the "intellectual love of God," which for Spinoza is "blessedness"—as good as it gets.

Spinoza's concept of intuitive knowledge is not an easy one, and I will discuss it later (in Chapter 13: "Madness and *Scientia Intuitiva*" and Chapter 16: "Freedom from Bondage"). For now, what's important to understand is that Spinoza recognized that acquiring knowledge in the first way—opinion, hearsay, imagination, and random experience—will result in ideas that are inadequate and confused.

Questioning the truthfulness of attributions that are made about phenomena is a major activity of philosophers and scientists who recognize that humans are prone to confused and false understandings—what Spinoza called inadequate ideas. Some people who consider themselves to be scientists are in fact dogmatists attached to canon and doctrine. Unlike philosophers or scientists, dogmatists react angrily to anyone who creates tension for them by questioning the truthfulness of their ideas.

Similar to Spinoza's concept of adequate ideas, and crucial in contemporary science, is the concept of *validity*. In the most general sense, validity means truthfulness and calling things by their proper name.

In *The Analects*, Confucius (551–479 BC) tells us: "When names are not correct, what is said will not sound reasonable." This proverb is better known through its paraphrased form: "The beginning of wisdom is to call things by their proper name." Calling things by their proper name is one way of describing validity.

In the history of medicine, there are many examples of something not being called by its proper name. Invalidity that is obvious can help us understanding validity. In 1851, physician Samuel Cartwright, in the *New Orleans Medical and Surgical Journal*, reported his discovery of *drapetomania*, the disease that caused slaves to flee captivity. Cartwright believed that absent of this illness, they were "like children . . . constrained by unalterable physiological laws to love those in authority over them." At that time, slavery was legal in Louisiana and the rest of the U.S. South, and racial superiority of white people was consensus reality; and so when a slave attempted to flee captivity, this was a violation of not simply law but consensus reality, creating a great deal of tension.

Today it is obvious that Cartwright attempted to enable slavery and the consensus reality of racism by labeling a slave who fled captivity as ill. Among slavery abolitionists in Cartwright's time, the concept of drapetomania was ridiculous, as absurd as it is for most of us today. Calling people diseased because they flee captivity for freedom is obviously not calling a phenomenon by its proper name, and it is obviously invalid. A crucial lesson taught in the history of science is that what a society proclaims as *reality* is often merely something that is a consensus reality that has been politically, economically, and culturally determined.

For those who recognize how critical establishing validity is to reducing unnecessary suffering, there are questions: Given the history of mental illness proclamations, should we question the validity of all such proclamations of mental illness? Given history, is it not possible that the consensus reality of any society will later be discovered to be untrue or to have excluded aspects of reality?

Today, challenging the validity of mental illnesses, especially so-called serious mental illnesses such as schizophrenia, can meet with harsh consequences for the challenger. Psychiatry institutions such as the National Alliance on Mental Illness and the American Psychiatric Association allow challenges to the causes and treatments of all mental illnesses, including schizophrenia, however, NAMI and APA do not question the validity of schizophrenia as a mental illness. While the National Institute of Mental Health has questioned whether the construct of schizophrenia is a scientifically valid one, it does not question whether this phenomenon is primarily a brain disease.

In a genuine scientific community, the validity of everything can be challenged. Albert Einstein questioned the validity of his hero Isaac Newton's theory of gravity because it didn't appear to Einstein to completely explain the phenomenon. Challenging the revered Newton caused tension, and certainly some scientists wanted Einstein to be proven wrong. But genuine scientists know that anger is not a professional reaction to a proposed theory; rather a professional reaction is a demand for proof.

A genuine scientist would not become angry by the questioning of the validity of any mental illness or even by the questioning of the concept of mental illness. And so when an institution does lash out angrily at those who pose such questions, that institution gives away its essence as being much closer to a theological one than a scientific one.

For scientists, the validity of what we label a phenomenon is vital. There is another important kind of validity, the validity of a phenomenon's measurement. Regardless of a consensus of a condition being a valid illness, how it is being measured may be invalid and thus provide invalid conclusions about its cause and treatment.

Consider the measurement of depression. One of the most commonly used depression measurements in research is the Hamilton Rating Scale for Depression (HAM-D), originally created by Max Hamilton in 1960. Researchers using the HAM-D rate subjects on items that are considered to be symptomatic of depression; the higher the point total, the more one is deemed to be suffering from depression. The HAM-D version used in much of the research on the effectiveness of antidepressants has three separate two-point items about insomnia (early, middle, and late), and so one could receive up to six points for sleep difficulties; and there is an "agitation" item in which one receives four points for "hand wringing, nail biting, hair-pulling, biting of lips." However, there is only one suicide item, in which one is awarded either two points for wishing to be dead, or four points for a serious suicide attempt. The validity issue for scientists is obviously this: In assessing depression, is it valid to place three times more emphasis on insomnia than on suicidal thoughts, and is it valid to view a serious suicide attempt as being equal to hand wringing, nail biting, hair-pulling, and biting of lips? If depression is measured by this HAM-D, then antidepressant medications—which may have a positive effect on sleep difficulties and agitation but no such positive effect on suicidality—will be more likely to be quantified as an effective treatment for depression.

In addition to the validity of a measurement, in order to empirically study a phenomena, science requires reliability of measurement. There are many kinds of reliability, but in a general sense, reliability means agreement and consistency. For example, if a measurement of mental illness is reliable, researchers using the same measurement on an individual will consistently agree on results.

Spinoza would have immediately grasped, without any empirical study, why mental illness diagnoses are unreliable. With respect to depression, as noted, one symptom indicating it is suicidal thoughts, but such thoughts are only discovered through a patient's self-report. However, patients may feel highly suicidal but be too afraid to report it because previously that self-report resulted in an unpleasant hospitalization, or they may not actually have suicidal thoughts but report them because they want to be taken seriously. Among individuals I've known who have been patients in psychiatric hospitals and were able to convince professionals to discharge them, none needed Spinoza's signet ring engraved with the word *caute* to remind them to be very careful as to what they said.

Beginning with *DSM-III* (1980) and its use of publicly observable behaviors to diagnose mental illnesses, psychiatry proclaimed that *DSM* diagnoses were reliable, but this turned out to be untrue. Spinoza would immediately recognize that psychiatric diagnoses are acquired through "hearsay" and "opinions," which result in confused, false, inadequate ideas. He would not need to see the APA field trials revealing *DSM-5*'s lack of reliability (detailed in Chapter 7: "Two Bibles"). For Spinoza, a scientific experiment such as *DSM-5*'s expensive field trials that revealed *DSM-5* unreliability would have been a waste of time and money—and unnecessary for someone capable of reason.

Behaviors are not necessarily consistent and reliable over time and place. For example, a young child may not pay attention and may be restless in one teacher's classroom, and that teacher may fill out a questionnaire that results in that child being diagnosed with attention deficit hyperactivity disorder (ADHD)—such teacher questionnaires are routinely used in the diagnosis of ADHD. But that same child may pay perfect attention to a teacher whom that child likes and finds interesting, and that child may not be restless in that teacher's classroom; and so that other teacher will fill out the same questionnaire differently. Individuals' behaviors change in different environments and around different people. This would have been obvious to Spinoza, as he would recall himself paying far less attention to dogmatic teachers and peers than freethinking ones.

Even if something can be reliably measured, that doesn't make it a valid illness. Drapetomania could be reliably measured, since exiting a plantation without permission and not returning is a publicly observable, objective phenomenon. However, saying a person who flees from a plantation is suffering from a mental illness is obviously invalid. For scientists, this is an example of "garbage in, garbage out." If one takes seriously invalidity or "garbage," even if it can be reliably measured, conclusions about it will be garbage.

While drapetomania, determined by a publicly observable objective measure, can be reliably diagnosed, this is not the case for virtually all the mental illnesses listed in the *DSM*, for which the variables used in diagnosis are nowhere near as objective. Despite what the public may hear about mental illnesses being associated with brain abnormalities, psychiatrists and psychologists don't use brain-scanning technologies, lab tests, or any other such objective physiological measure to diagnose mental illnesses. Instead, professionals rely on behavior observations and patient self-reports of their emotions and thoughts, which can often be difficult for patients to put into words and are easily misinterpreted and misunderstood, and thus are routinely unreliable.

In addition to validity and reliability, the issue of superstition is also a source of concern for scientists, as it was for Spinoza who wrote at length about it. Superstitions are attachments to unscientific causes, supernatural or otherwise. The following are two examples of superstitious behaviors: (1) a gambler, playing a game of craps, kisses the dice to influence them; (2) a farmer prays to God for rain. The gambler and the farmer may in fact get what they are looking for but, clearly for Spinoza and modern scientists, dice kissing and prayer had no influence on the outcome.

Spinoza was, as modern scientists are today, surrounded by people who engaged in superstitious behaviors followed by their desired outcome. But that is not, for Spinoza or scientists, evidence of causality. In science this is called "anecdotal evidence," which is not considered scientific proof. For Spinoza, this falls in the realm of that first kind of knowledge, which includes random experience, and which results in false and inadequate ideas.

A major goal of science is to discover true causality as opposed to superstitions and false beliefs about causality. In any area in which there is great fear, we are more susceptible to superstitions. That which causes us tension and resulting fear is routinely termed a mental illness, and so it is no surprise that, in the history of explanations for the causes and cures of mental illnesses, we will find many superstitions.

Genuine scientists fully expect that any society's consensus reality is replete with superstitions. Genuine scientists take seriously the scientific methods necessary to distinguish superstitions from truthful explanations.

It was clear to Spinoza that organized religion is replete with superstitious rituals that were promoted by clergy so as to create obedient congregants. All explanations for the causes and cures of mental illness increase the power of some and decrease the power of others. So, if the cause of our suffering is a supernatural one, this gives power to clergy. If the cause is associated with psychological variables, this gives power to psychologists. If the cause is associated more with variables such as housing and living environment, this gives power to social workers. If the cause is associated more with biological variables, this gives power to psychiatrists and other physicians. If the cause is associated specifically with biochemistry, this gives power to drug prescribers and pharmaceutical companies.

What scientists call the "placebo effect" is in some ways similar but in other ways different from superstitions. Placebos are substances or procedures that in themselves have no intrinsic therapeutic value but can be associated with patient improvement for a variety of reasons. A common placebo is a sugar pill that is prescribed as a medication; less common would be a sham surgery in which a person is put to sleep but no surgery is done.

Placebos may appear to be effective in the same way that a superstition can appear to be effective. A patient recovers after taking the placebo but would have done so without it, yet the doctor or patient attribute the recovery to the placebo. This is true for superstitions. As previously noted, sometimes patients got better after bloodletting, and patients and doctors attributed recovery to it when, in fact, the patient got better in spite of the bloodletting and not because of it.

Sometimes a placebo is no different than a superstition, but not always. Belief or faith in the power of a substance or intervention can actually alter chemical processes and promote recovery in a scientific sense. Thus, an important aspect of scientific evaluation of any treatment is to control for what is called the "placebo effect." This necessitates the use of the so-called "gold standard" of randomized control trials (RCT), in which patients and researchers are blind as to whether or not the patient is receiving a placebo or a hypothesized therapeutic substance or intervention. Unfortunately, unless scientists are truly seeking truth with no other agenda, it is easy to self-deceive and deceive others that they are truly implementing RCT when they are not (more on this with respect to psychiatric drug trials in Chapter 8: "Three Noble Lies?").

In modernity, science is viewed as the authority best relied on to provide us with truths. Thus, there are obviously political and financial incentives for individuals who prize power and money over truth to corrupt the scientific method—for example, to give an inquiry the appearance of being scientific when it is not.

The issue of pseudoscience is one that philosophers of science consider and analyze. Validity, reliability, and controls are only some of the criteria and tools that scientists use to distinguish science from pseudoscience.

The criterion of falsifiability to distinguish science from pseudoscience was famously emphasized by scientific philosopher Karl Popper. Falsifiability (or refutability or testability) means that a theory is not a scientific theory unless it can be proven false. An example of pseudoscience, Popper tells us, is astrology because it is a theory that cannot be refuted by science. In contrast, Einstein's theory of general relativity could have been refuted, and so it is an example of science.

Is psychiatry's theory of serious mental illness as a brain disease falsifiable? Yes, and no. Specific biological theories of mental illness are falsifiable, and many such theories have in fact been refuted, including various chemical imbalance theories (detailed in Chapter 8: "Three Noble Lies?" and Chapter 10: "Brain Disease"). However, since there are likely an infinite number of biological theories, another brain-disease theory can always be proposed and claimed to be the true one. So even if the current biological theory is again disproved, the general theory of mental illness as a brain disease cannot be refuted.

Today, thinking freely about the validity of the general brain disease theory of mental illness is as taboo as when Spinoza thought freely about the validity of prayer to God as a way of getting our desires met. Spinoza knew that if we are attached to the general theory of prayer, even if our specific prayers fail, we can maintain a belief in prayer—concluding that perhaps we didn't use the correct words in our prayer, or perhaps we had sinned too many times that week for God to reward us. Spinoza did not need Popper to tell him that the general theory of prayer is not falsifiable and so is not a scientific theory.

Einstein's general theory of relativity could have been refuted, but it was not, as Eddington and other astronomers confirmed it by solar eclipse observations. In contrast, the *general* theory of brain disease as the cause of mental illness—as opposed to any *specific* brain disease theory such as serotonin imbalance—cannot be refuted by any observations or experiments, and so in Popper's sense is unscientific.

Brain activity is certainly connected to thoughts, emotions, and behaviors. However, it is only opinion—the first kind of knowledge that results in inadequate ideas and falsity—as to the normality or abnormality of these thoughts, emotions, and behaviors. Any brain disease theory assumes that psychiatry's declarations of illnesses are valid. Such declarations in the past have been retracted by psychiatry, and present declarations are in dispute even among psychiatrists who created previous *DSMs* (detailed in Chapter 7: "Two Bibles"). As in Spinoza's day, clergy continue today to declare, based purely on opinion, which thoughts, feelings, and actions are sins; and so too does contemporary psychiatry—also based purely on opinion—declare which thoughts, feelings, and actions are symptoms of mental illnesses. While our thoughts, feelings, and actions are associated with brain activities, this does not mean our opinion of them as sins or as illnesses are correct.

A major goal of science is to discover a model or paradigm that accounts for observations. Spinoza had a keen interest in paradigms, though he did not use that word but instead talked about imaginative knowledge and fictions, which he makes clear are not necessarily false but cannot be declared as true without applying reason and science to test them.

"Imaginative knowledge," Beth Lord explains, "is not wholly false or illusory. It's just partial and subject to error. Spinoza says that imaginative knowledge is confused knowledge. . . . Fictions are kind of organized systems of images . . . fictions can be coherent anticipations about the future. . . . They can also be scientific hypotheses, predictions, or beliefs upheld for the sake of

argument. . . . These fictions are strictly neither true nor false. They are organized sets of images which we hold up for scrutiny and critique until the truth
becomes clear to us."

In *The Structure of Scientific Revolutions* (1962), philosopher of science
Thomas Kuhn concluded that most scientists accept the current paradigm, and
they attempt to solve problems within that paradigm—a practice that Kuhn
termed as *normal science*. However, when a current model cannot account for
a large accumulation of observations, and when facts simply cannot be explained within the established paradigm, normal science becomes fruitless.

There are increasing observations and facts that challenge the value of
the current mental illness paradigm. These include the assessment of psychiatry's record of treatment outcomes as "abysmal" by the long-time director
of the National Institute of Mental Health (NIMH) and by others; the NIMH
declaring the *DSM* diagnostic system to be invalid and jettisoning it for future research (discussed in Chapter 7: "Two Bibles"); psychiatry jettisoning its
chemical-imbalance theory of mental illness (discussed in Chapter 8: "Three
Noble Lies?"); and no biological markers found that can be used in diagnosis
despite many decades of research. Despite this, it remains taboo to reconsider
the validity of the brain-disease paradigm, and Kuhn would know why.

The problem, Kuhn makes clear, is that no matter how poorly an established paradigm accounts for data, most scientists continue to engage in
normal science; in other words, they continue to attempt to solve problems
within the established paradigm. For Kuhn, it will only be a minority of scientists who judge that there are so many observations and facts not fitting into
an established paradigm that science requires reconsidering whether the paradigm itself is correct. This reconsideration results in what Kuhn called *revolutionary science*. Such revolutionary science means considering alternatives to
the established paradigm.

For Kuhn, it is axiomatic that most scientists who are practicing normal
science will oppose a paradigm shift, as they are working on problems within
the established paradigm. In psychiatry, also undermining a pursuit of a superior explanatory model is that the current paradigm is protected by financial
and political forces, ones that create conflicts of interest that compromise and
corrupt scientific inquiry. This is psychiatry's ethical crisis, detailed in the following chapter.

CHAPTER 6

UNETHICAL

In the *Ethics*, Spinoza observed how money will routinely "obsess the minds of the populace, because they can scarcely think of any kind of pleasure that is not accompanied by the idea of money as its cause. . . . But those who know the true use of money set the limit of their wealth solely according to their needs, and live content with little."

Spinoza practiced what he preached. "His wants were few and simple," notes Bertrand Russell, "and he showed throughout his life a rare indifference to money." Spinoza has been esteemed by many philosophers such as Russell and scientists such as Albert Einstein not simply for his insights but for how he conducted his life. Given how much Spinoza materially sacrificed to maintain his freedom of thought, he would today be saddened to see the blatant disregard by many doctors and medical researchers with respect to conflicts of interest that compromise and corrupt freethinking and science. Given his views on money and how he lived, he would view psychiatry as unethical.

Spinoza's friend and biographer Lucas notes, "Not only did riches not tempt him at all, but he also had no fear whatever of the consequences of poverty. . . . When he heard that somebody who owed him two hundred francs had gone bankrupt, he was so far from being upset thereby that he said laughingly, 'I must reduce my daily fare in order to make up for this small loss. It is at such a price,' he added, 'that one buys fortitude.'"

Among Spinoza's many friends, one of them, Simon de Vries, was financially well off. De Vries attempted to provide Bento with a stipend so he wasn't financially dependent on his lens crafting, but Spinoza rejected this idea.

When de Vries tried to make Spinoza his heir, Bento persuaded him not to do so, agreeing only to a small annuity of 500 guilders; but after de Vries died, Spinoza told de Vries's brother that he would only accept 300 guilders.

After the 1672 murder of the de Witt brothers, tolerance in the Dutch Republic diminished, making life for Spinoza and other freethinkers increasingly precarious. In 1673, Spinoza's fame overseas garnered him an offer for a prestigious job. Spinoza received a flattering letter from J. Ludwig Fabricus, a professor at the University of Heidelberg, inviting him to be a professor at that university. Fabricus made clear he was acting on behalf of Karl Ludwig, Elector of Palantine (one of the German imperial states), and he included this: "You will not find elsewhere a Prince more favorably disposed to men of exceptional genius, among whom he ranks you." After Spinoza considered this attractive offer for over a month, he politely declined. One reason that he rejected the offer was that he was troubled by a sentence in Fabricus's invitation that stated: "You will have the most extensive freedom in philosophizing, which he [Karl Ludwig] believes you will not misuse to disturb the publicly established religion." This stipulation clearly bothered Spinoza, as in his return letter he stated: "I do not know within what limits the freedom to philosophize must be confined if I am to avoid appearing to disturb the publicly established religion." Spinoza was not about to allow any financial dependency to dictate his thought and expression.

Spinoza knew that it is difficult enough without conflicts of interest to discover truths about nature; and so he would likely conclude that only the naïve would trust researchers and doctors who are financially dependent on giant pharmaceutical corporations. Yet, financial relationships between drug companies and psychiatry institutions have increasingly become normalized.

An early prominent critic of such financial conflicts of interest was Marcia Angell, physician and former editor-in-chief of *The New England Journal of Medicine*. In her book, *The Truth about the Drug Companies* (2004), she documents the widespread corruption of medicine by drug companies, with some of the most egregious examples being in psychiatry. For example, Angell details how the head of the psychiatry department at Brown University Medical School made over $500,000 in one year consulting for drug companies that make antidepressants; she remarked, "When *The New England Journal of Medicine*, under my editorship, published a study by him and his colleagues of an antidepressant agent, there wasn't enough room to print all the authors' conflict-of-interest disclosures. The full list had to be put on the website."

Investigative journalists at *ProPublica* published "Dollars for Docs: The Top Earners" in 2013, reporting: "When Dollars for Docs first launched in 2010, *ProPublica* spoke with several of the dozens of doctors who had earned more than $200,000 from their speaking and consulting work for drug companies. Now, with records from more companies and more years of data, we've identified 22 doctors who've earned at least $500,000 since 2009. . . . Half are psychiatrists, including three of the top four earners."

Unsurprisingly, receiving money from drug companies influences prescribing practices. The *New York Times* ("Psychiatrists Top List in Drug Maker Gifts") reported in 2007: "Psychiatrists who took the most money from makers of antipsychotic drugs tended to prescribe the drugs to children the most often." A 2007 analysis of Minnesota psychiatrists revealed that psychiatrists who received at least $5,000 from makers of the then-newer-generation antipsychotic drugs (such as Risperdal, Seroquel, Zyprexa, and Abilify) wrote, on average, three times as many prescriptions to children for these drugs as psychiatrists who received less money or none.

One of psychiatry's most influential "key opinion leaders" in the twenty-first century has been Harvard psychiatrist Joseph Biederman, Director of the Johnson & Johnson Center for Pediatric Psychopathology Research at Massachusetts General Hospital. Biederman is credited with creating pediatric bipolar disorder; and it was his research that psychiatrist Kayoko Kifuji said influenced her use of a bipolar disorder diagnosis for three-year old Rebecca Riley, whose drug treatment resulted in her death at age four. Due in great part to Biederman's influence, the number of American children and adolescents treated for bipolar disorder increased forty-fold from 1994 to 2003.

Biederman's financial relationships with drug companies was discovered by the general public in 2008, when Congressional investigations revealed that he had received $1.6 million in consulting fees from drug makers from 2000 to 2007. As part of legal proceedings, Biederman was forced to provide documents about his interactions with Johnson & Johnson, the giant pharmaceutical company. Biederman had told Johnson & Johnson that his proposed research studies on its antipsychotic drug Risperdal would turn out favorably for Johnson & Johnson—and such studies did in fact turn out favorably.

Those Congressional hearings revealed that Biederman was far from alone among influential psychiatrists having financial relationships with drug companies. The then-president-elect of the American Psychiatric Association, Alan Schatzberg, had $4.8 million stock holdings in a drug development company.

The APA itself, the guild organization of American psychiatrists, has also had a financial relationship with drug companies. In 2008, the *New York Times* reported the following about the APA: "In 2006, the latest year for which numbers are available, the drug industry accounted for about 30 percent of the association's $62.5 million in financing." The APA publishes the *DSM*, and according to the journal *PLOS Medicine* in 2012, "69% of the *DSM-5* task force members report having ties to the pharmaceutical industry."

Pharmaceutical companies seek every means possible to use their financial influence. The National Alliance on Mental Illness, as previously noted, is an advocacy organization for the mentally ill and their families. Psychiatry historian Anne Harrington in *Mind Fixers* (2019) reported, "By 2010, as much as 75 percent of NAMI's budget came from the pharmaceutical industry." NAMI strongly supports the use of psychiatric medication.

How did the psychiatry-pharmaceutical industrial complex come to be?

First, a few words about industrial complexes in general. An industrial complex means giant corporations with great financial resources and political clout become enmeshed with social and political institutions. Historically, at the advent of an industrial complex, there is concern and even protest. But in time, the industrial complex becomes normalized.

The first industrial complex that became well known to the general public was the *military-industrial complex*, a term used by Dwight Eisenhower in his January 1961 farewell speech. Eisenhower warned that "we must guard against the acquisition of unwarranted influence, whether sought or unsought, by the military-industrial complex." The military-industrial complex is a powerful partnership between defense contractors and the U.S. military that poses a major threat to democratic government. Sadly, despite this warning from Eisenhower—a former general and U.S. president for eight years—the military-industrial complex has grown dramatically and has increasingly become normalized.

The psychiatry-pharmaceutical industrial complex came into being because the institution of psychiatry was under threat in the 1970s. Psychiatry had become, for much of U.S. society, an object of derision. The film *One Flew Over the Cuckoo's Nest*, which confronts authoritarianism and dehumanization in a psychiatric hospital, won an Oscar for Best Picture of 1975. With increasing competition from other types of mental health professionals, psychiatry was at risk of disappearing, and this crisis made it vulnerable to financial support from pharmaceutical companies—a welcome idea for some but not all psychiatrists.

Psychiatry's crisis was one of the public's lack of faith as to whether it was in fact a science with valid illnesses, reliable diagnoses, and effective treatments. In 1973, as previously noted, gay activism had succeeded in forcing the APA to abolish homosexuality as a mental illness, an overturning that made the general public question whether mental illness declarations were more political than scientific in nature.

In addition to mental illness validity being mocked, so too was diagnostic reliability. Specifically, also in 1973, psychologist David Rosenhan, in *Science*, published the study "On Being Sane in Insane Places," which showed psychiatry could not distinguish between normal individuals and those so psychotic they needed to be hospitalized. In the study, eight pseudopatients were sent to twelve hospitals, all pretending to have this complaint: hearing empty and hollow voices with no clear content. All pseudopatients were able to fool staff and get hospitalized. Immediately after admission, the pseudopatients stated the voices had disappeared and they behaved as they normally would but none were immediately released. The length of their hospitalizations ranged from seven to fifty-two days. Though Rosenhan's veracity was challenged in 2019 by journalist Susannah Cahalan in her book *The Great Pretender*, in the 1970s, his findings greatly threatened psychiatry.

In the 1970s, being critical of psychiatry was not the risky career choice for mental health professionals, journalists, and film makers that it would later become. Psychiatry as an institution was seen by society as unscientific, and its treatments were seen as more authoritarian and no more effective than less expensive helping professions. Psychiatry desperately needed the public to perceive its special value.

To alter public perception, psychiatry found an influential natural ally. This ally is the pharmaceutical industry, which, while helping psychiatry gain credibility with the general public, has acquired a lucrative expanded market. In 1992 in the *New York Times*, the then-APA Medical Director, Melvin Sabshin, responding to criticism of psychiatry's relationship with the pharmaceutical industry, defended the APA's relationship with the industry, calling it "a responsible, ethical partnership that uses the no-strings resources of one partner and the expertise of the other to help the one person in five who needs help and hope in struggling with mental illnesses." The obvious conflict of interest inherent in a *partnership* between drug companies and the APA (and other major psychiatric institutions and individual psychiatrists) has become as normalized as the military-industrial complex.

The institutional corruption of psychiatry was the subject of the 2015 book *Psychiatry Under the Influence,* authored by investigative journalist Robert Whitaker and psychologist Lisa Cosgrove, both of whom undertook the research as fellows at Harvard's Edmond J. Safra Center for Ethics, which had launched a "Lab" to study institutional corruption. At the time, the Center was directed by Lawrence Lessig, who wrote: "I was drawn to this conception of corruption through my own reflections on the dysfunction of Congress . . . it seems clear enough that the institution has allowed the influence of campaign funding to weaken its effectiveness, and certainly weaken its public trust."

Whitaker and Cosgrove note that since the 1980s, "financial conflict of interest came to pervade every corner of the psychiatric enterprise. Editors of journals had such ties to industry; so too did writers of psychiatric textbooks; authors of clinical practice guidelines; developers of diagnostic criteria; and chairs of psychiatric departments at medical schools."

In 2021, utilizing the Open Payments database (which resulted from the 2013 federal legislation that requires pharmaceutical companies to disclose their direct payments to physicians), Whitaker reported: "From 2014 to 2020, pharmaceutical companies paid $340 million to U.S. psychiatrists to serve as their consultants, advisers, and speakers, or to provide free food, beverages and lodging to those attending promotional events." Open Payments lists 31,784 psychiatrists (roughly 75 percent of the psychiatrists in the United States) who, Whitaker noted, "received something of value from the drug companies from 2014 through 2020." During that time period, sixty-two psychiatrists received one million dollars or more; nineteen psychiatrists received over two million dollars; and the leading recipient, Stephen Stahl, received over eight million dollars.

There are doctors who do not receive money from drug companies but who are ignorant of scientific truths because professional journals that they rely on for information have been corrupted. For example, many doctors are unaware of truths about antidepressant effectiveness as compared to placebos (detailed in Chapter 8: "Three Noble Lies?") because their professional journals have not informed them of such. In 2008, researcher and physician Erick Turner, at the Department of Psychiatry and Center for Ethics in Health Care, Oregon Health and Science University, analyzed published and unpublished antidepressant studies registered with the Food and Drug Administration (FDA) between 1987 and 2004. Turner found that thirty-seven of thirty-eight studies having positive results were published; however, he reported, "Studies viewed by the FDA as having negative or questionable results were, with 3 exceptions, either not published (22 studies) or published in a way that, in our opinion, [falsely] conveyed a positive outcome (11 studies)."

How can doctors and researchers convince themselves they are unaffected by drug company financial rewards? Much of their denial has to do with self-certainty about their essential integrity, and a failure to recognize that conflicts of interest inherently compromise integrity. Spinoza scrupulously eschewed conflicts of interest because he recognized such conflicts compromise free thought. But those who accept such conflicts rationalize that they—because of how ethical they believe themselves to be—are uninfluenced by them. Whitaker and Cosgrove document several studies revealing that doctors and researchers recognize that such conflicts can create vulnerability to influence for others, but they believe that they themselves are so ethical that such conflicts will not influence them. In one University of California San Francisco study, 61 percent of physicians believed that their prescribing practices would not be influenced by free gifts, but they believed that among "other physicians," only 16 percent would be uninfluenced.

The APA guide for psychiatrists, "Commentary on Ethics in Practice" (2015), includes the topic: "Relations with the Pharmaceutical and Other Industries." It specifically states: "Psychiatrists may interact with industry in many ways, including presenting at industry sponsored lectures and appearing in industry sponsored publications and advertisements, accepting and distributing sample products, recommending patients for industry sponsored clinical trials, and accepting personal or office gifts or corporate donations from industry."

What's telling is that psychiatrists are only advised of the potential for compromised integrity but that it is not necessarily wrong to have such a conflict of interest. Specifically, the guide states: "Although the mere appearance or existence of a conflict of interest does not by itself imply wrongdoing, the failure to recognize and actively address such conflicts does compromise professional integrity and threatens the independence of the psychiatrist's judgment." The guide, however, does not prohibit conflicts of interest.

For Spinoza and many genuine scientists today, it is simply arrogant—and perhaps even delusional—to believe that one is so morally superior that one can have financial conflicts of interest and that simple awareness of the potential influence can inoculate one from being compromised and corrupted. In the APA's professional ethics, there is no requirement to forego financial conflicts of interest, just be honest about them.

Politicians also claim ethical behavior if they properly disclose their financial relationships with industries. This is exactly what troubled Lawrence Lessig at the Safra Center for Ethics, as it was clear to him that campaign funding by industry, even honestly revealed, is a form of institutional corruption that is damaging for the public.

In U.S. society, it has become increasingly normalized for societal authorities, including those in government and psychiatry, to have corrupting conflicts of interest. While it has been normalized, it still creates enormous tension for some individuals who are anxious that authorities who are financially influenced by large corporations cannot be trusted to care about the public good. This normalization of corruption creates such great tension that many people must simply ignore or deny it so as to function at all.

In Spinoza's lifetime, the major forces that could manipulate and enslave people were state and clergy authorities. Spinoza's political solution was to have a democratic state governed with the consent of the governed, one that is not controlled by ecclesiastic authorities.

Today, while the influence of clergy over politicians persists (especially the influence in the United States by evangelical Christian authorities), there exists an even more powerful force subverting democracy—giant transnational corporations.

The financial resources of these giant corporations—which include pharmaceutical companies—gives them political power to control government officials. Such corporations, for example, routinely reward friendly government officials with high-paying jobs after they leave government. In 2019, former FDA Commissioner Scott Gottlieb, two months after leaving the FDA, joined the Board of Directors at the giant drug company Pfizer (whose products include the antidepressant Zoloft and the benzodiazepine Xanax). Pfizer's board members were paid a minimum of $335,000 in stock and cash in 2018, and so by rewarding Gottlieb, Pfizer sent a clear message to high-level officials currently at the FDA.

Moreover, the enormous financial resources of these corporations provide them with the power to directly and indirectly popularize ideas that result in greater profits for them. It would be irrational for a drug company not to use their financial resources to persuade doctors to prescribe and promote their drugs; to persuade government officials to legalize direct advertising; and to then use every technological means to manipulate consumers.

While there are individuals within any corporation who are genuinely concerned about the public interest, the "ethics" of any corporation must prioritize profit. And so employees financially dependent on their salaries must either deny certain realities, recognize them and rationalize them, experience some manner of angst, or quit their job.

Today, while some people continue to feel tyrannized by ecclesiastic and civil authorities, increasingly, people feel tyrannized by giant corporations and by their financial dependencies on them. Spinoza lived his ethics. He boarded inexpensively, ate enough to survive, acquired an excellent reputation as a lens maker, and only agreed to a small annuity left to him by his deceased friend because it in no way compromised his freedom to philosophize.

While Spinoza today would continue to be concerned about the influence of clergy over civil society, given how much Spinoza cared about freedom from bondage, if alive today, he may have felt compelled to write a "Corporatist-Political Treatise."

CHAPTER 7

TWO BIBLES

In comparing the Bible to what is often referred to as the "bible of psychiatry," the *Diagnostic and Statistical Manual of Mental Disorders* (*DSM*), Spinoza would see differences but also commonalities.

For Spinoza, an advantage of the *DSM* would be that its publisher, the American Psychiatric Association (APA), acknowledges that it is authored by a committee of humans—specifically psychiatrists who, after debate among themselves, declare what are and what are not mental illnesses. Spinoza would see this admission as superior to the claim of ecclesiastic authorities that the Bible is the word of God.

The major advantage of the Bible over the *DSM*, for Spinoza, is the Bible's moral narrative. Spinoza saw Bible writers as gifted story tellers, and he saw the Bible as powerful literature, useful for those lacking philosophical understanding as to why acting morally is rational. The Bible, for Spinoza, is a good way of engendering the non-philosophical to practice justice and charity. No *DSM* advocate claims that the *DSM* provides a moral narrative that compels justice and charity; and some *DSM* critics claim that it provides a very different kind of moral narrative, one that declares individuals who do not comply with societal norms to be mentally disordered.

I will first discuss Spinoza's critique of the Bible. Then, given what this reveals about his thinking, I will follow with what I believe would be Spinoza's critique of the *DSM*.

Spinoza's *Theological-Political Treatise* was banned shortly after it was published anonymously in 1670. According to Steven Nadler, "More than any other work, it laid the foundation for modern critical and historical approaches to the Bible." In Spinoza's day, his treatise was shocking. Spinoza argues that the Bible is a work of human literature, not the literal word of God, and that the prophets were not rational philosophers but gifted only in their capacity to combine moral insights with superior imaginations so that they could inspire moral behaviors. Since, for Spinoza, God and Nature are one and the same, miracles—which are violations of nature—are impossible, and thus the belief in miracles is evidence of ignorance or delusions. The *Theological-Political Treatise* was soon denounced as the most dangerous book ever published, as one critic called it, "'a book forged in hell' written by the devil himself," notes Nadler in his book, *A Book Forged in Hell* (2011), about this treatise.

In this treatise, Spinoza also made what was, in his day, a radical political argument—that societal stability and security is enhanced by freedom to philosophize and by democracy. For Spinoza, it was clergy who most threatened the freedom of thought and expression by exploiting the fears of people. Fear made people vulnerable to superstitions, which were used to maintain power over them. Spinoza's radical solution was to strip clergy of political power over civil society. Spinoza believed that this would allow scientists and philosophers the freedom to do their work, which would make for a better society. Obviously, ecclesiastic authorities were none too pleased with the idea of relinquishing power. For Nadler, "Spinoza is, without question, one of history's most eloquent proponents of a secular, democratic society and the strongest advocate for freedom and toleration in the early modern period."

In order to delegitimize the authority of clergy, Spinoza demonstrated that the Bible was not sacred, not revealed by God; and that instead, it had numerous human authors over many years. Spinoza concluded that the Hebrew Bible was assembled in the Second Temple period, most likely under the editorship of Ezra the Scribe (480–440 BCE), who attempted to synthesize sources. For Spinoza, the Bible is simply a work of literature, a "faulty, mutilated, adulterated, and inconsistent" work.

Spinoza was not the first to see obvious inconsistencies in the Bible. Other critics had also recognized such discrepancies; for example, Moses, the reputed author of Pentateuch (the first five books of the Hebrew Bible), includes an account of his own death and burial. The Bible's authors, for Spinoza, were deficient in both a philosophical and a scientific sense. In Spinoza's day, learned people knew of the astronomical discoveries of Copernicus, and it was an insult to Spinoza and his pals' intelligence to expect them to believe the Bible story in which Joshua's prayers cause the sun to stand still.

For Spinoza, God/Nature includes all of reality, including all the laws that govern nature. Spinoza rejected the idea of supernatural occurrences. The God of Spinoza is in accordance with laws of nature; and so a belief that miracles can occur outside of the laws of nature is, given Spinoza's concept of God, a rejection of God. What appears to be supernatural miracle occurrences are simply natural phenomenon that are not yet understood by humans. For Spinoza, only the delusional believe that God acts toward some end; and it is only the conceited who believe that God can be manipulated by prayers to show favor on them. For Spinoza, the idea that God would reward or punish people in the hereafter is an ecclesiastic manipulation to frighten and control people.

Routinely accused of being atheist and anti-religion, Spinoza was always offended by these attributions. He only opposed those religions that, as Nadler points out, "were led by ambitious clergymen and that introduced divisive sectarian loyalties into society." Spinoza believed in what he called a "true religion," a basic rational morality of justice and charity.

Spinoza respected the Bible's moral message of justice and charity, but he had contempt for the ceremonies and rituals of organized religion that he viewed as superstitions used to control people. Viewing the Bible as the word of God resulted in power for one group, clergy, to rule over the general public, and it created intolerance and hindered free thought.

The goal of theology and religion, for Spinoza, is obedience, while the aim of reason and philosophy is understanding the essence of reality. By showing that the Bible was the work of men and not God, the political goal of the *Theological-Political Treatise* was to limit the authority of its clergy interpreters. Spinoza's goal was not to abolish religion or the Bible, but to curtail the political power of clergy and create greater tolerance.

Spinoza would likely recognize similarities between the Bible and the *DSM*. Similar to the Bible, he would see the *DSM* as replete with "inadequate ideas" and scientific invalidities. The *DSM* would have no philosophical value for Spinoza, but he would be interested in the *DSM* because of its political implications. He would see how the *DSM*, similar to the Bible, provides power for one group of people over others, and he would see how the *DSM*, similar to the Bible, narrows the range of acceptability and creates intolerance. Spinoza was troubled by how the false idea that the Bible was the word of God provided power for its professional interpreters, and he would likely be troubled by how the false idea that the *DSM* is scientific provides power for its professional interpreters.

The *DSM* is used not only by clinicians and researchers but by the legal system in civil society. The first *DSM* was published in 1952 and had 106 separate disorders (depending on how counted, *DSM* disorder totals vary); *DSM-II* was published in 1968 and had 182 disorders; *DSM-III* published in 1980 had 265 disorders; *DSM-IV* published in 1994 had 410 disorders. The *DSM-5* (foregoing Roman numerals), published in 2013, has roughly the same amount of disorders as *DSM-IV*, however, classification and criterion changes in *DSM-5* increased the number of people who could be diagnosed with mental illness.

In 1978, I began my graduate school training to become a clinical psychologist, and all such PhD programs, in order to meet accreditation standards, had compulsory psychopathology courses, including adult psychopathology and child psychopathology. At that time, psychiatrists and psychologists knew that the APA was in the process of revising the 1968 *DSM-II*, but nobody knew exactly when *DSM-III* would be published. Given that gay activism had successfully abolished homosexuality as a mental illness in 1973, it was known that homosexuality would be excluded in *DSM-III*, but mental health professionals did not know if any other conditions previously pathologized would also be excluded, or which conditions not previously pathologized would be added (oppositional defiant disorder was added to the 1980 *DSM-III* and remains today in the current *DSM-5*).

In my first year of graduate school, I recall stating in a psychopathology class that it felt as if we were in seminary school waiting for Exodus II, unsure whether in the revision, instead of the Red Sea parting, the Red Sea would be traversed by a miracle tunnel or a miracle bridge. At that time, I had minimal knowledge of Spinoza. I had no idea of the nature of his critique of theological dogma, including his rejection of the possibility of miracles. So back then, I had no idea that if Spinoza would have been in my class and heard my smartass quip, he would have found it a lot funnier than did my psychopathology professor.

More than thirty years later, the mental illness expansionism of the *DSM* created smartass remarks about the *DSM* from even leading psychiatrists. The chair of the *DSM-IV* task force, Allen Frances, was so appalled by *DSM-5* that, in 2013, he published *Saving Normal: An Insider's Revolt against Out-of-Control Psychiatric Diagnosis, DSM-5, Big Pharma, and the Medicalization of Ordinary Life.*

Even prior to his harsh critique of *DSM-5*, in a 2010 *Wired* interview with Gary Greenberg ("Inside the Battle to Define Mental Illness"), Frances had criticized the concept of *mental disorder* employed in every *DSM* including his own *DSM-IV*, as he shocked the media and the general public by stating that "there is no definition of a mental disorder. It's bullshit. I mean, you just can't define it."

Greenberg went on to author *The Book of Woe: The DSM and the Unmaking of Psychiatry* (2013), which exposed the internal politics of psychiatrists involved in the creation of *DSM-5*. Spinoza would be unsurprised that the *DSM*, similar to the Bible, has created a large number of critics. In addition to the books by Frances and Greenberg, some of the more influential *DSM*-debunking books are Paula Caplan's *They Say You're Crazy: How the World's Most Powerful Psychiatrists Decide Who's Normal* (1995); Herb Kutchins and Stuart Kirk's *Making Us Crazy: DSM: The Psychiatric Bible and the Creation of Mental Disorders* (1997); Allan Horwitz and Jerome Wakefield's *The Loss of Sadness: How Psychiatry Transformed Normal Sorrow into Depressive Disorder* (2007); Christopher Lane's *Shyness: How Normal Behavior Became a Sickness* (2007), and Stuart Kirk, Tomi Gomory, and David Cohen's *Mad Science: Psychiatric Coercion, Diagnosis, and Drugs* (2013).

Frances and other critics challenged the validity of several mental illnesses in the *DSM-5*. One Frances criticism that garnered the most public attention was the removal of the "bereavement exclusion" for depression. Specifically, in *DSM-III*, if one had depression symptoms following the loss of a loved one, this was considered a normal reaction, and one received a so-called "bereavement exclusion" and was not diagnosed with the mental illness of depression. In *DSM-IV*, a time limit was imposed, as the griever could have symptoms of depression for two months before being considered mentally ill, but if depression symptoms persisted longer, then it was a mental illness. This time limit was derided by many mental health professionals, and the derision grew far louder with the *DSM-5* revision. In *DSM-5*, this bereavement exclusion was removed altogether, so that if one had the required depressive symptoms immediately after the loss of a significant other, one was seen to have the mental illness of depression. This upset even Frances, the chair of the 1994 *DSM-IV* task force.

Frances stated in 2012 that, while he did not agree completely with Thomas Szasz, he did agree with Szasz that no mental disorders are diseases, and Frances viewed all of them, including schizophrenia, as "constructs." Specifically, Frances stated, "Schizophrenia is certainly not a disease; but equally it is not a myth. As a construct, schizophrenia is useful for purposes of communication and helpful in prediction and decision making—even if . . . the term has only descriptive, and not explanatory power."

One of the most significant symptoms for schizophrenia is the presence of delusions. In *DSM-IV*, the presence alone of "bizarre delusions" was considered sufficient by itself for a diagnosis of schizophrenia. Given Spinoza's criticism of the Bible—which for him was replete with stories that had no basis in fact and were patently absurd—he would be curious as to exactly what psychiatry considers to be a "bizarre delusion."

Due to the importance of the concept of *bizarre* in diagnosing schizophrenia, *Schizophrenia Bulletin* in 2010 published the article "What is Bizarre in Bizarre Delusions? A Critical Review." It summarized recent various *DSM* definitions of a bizarre delusion: "(1) 'the content [is] patently absurd and has no possible basis in fact' (*DSM-III*); (2) 'involving a phenomenon that the person's culture would regard as totally implausible' (*DSM-III-R*); and (3) 'clearly implausible and not understandable and not derived from ordinary life experiences' (*DSM-IV*)."

According to psychiatry's definition of bizarre delusions, Spinoza would be curious as to how psychiatry would label people who believed that Moses wrote about his death and burial after he was dead or that he parted the Red Sea so that the Israelites could exit Egypt; or believed that Aaron's rod turned into a serpent; or believed that Joshua made the sun stand still; or believed that a virgin could give birth to a child. Spinoza saw many Biblical notions as patently absurd, clearly implausible, and certainly not derived from ordinary life experiences, which would make them bizarre delusions.

A 2017 Gallup poll of Americans reported that 24 percent believe that the Bible is the literal word of God. Thus, it is easy to understand the politics behind why psychiatry continues to maintain a "Biblical Belief Exclusion" for bizarre biblical delusions. If psychiatry attempted to classify 24 percent of Americans who believe in bizarre biblical delusions as schizophrenic, given that group's political power, psychiatry would face a far larger assault than it faced from gay activists in the early 1970s.

Even if one believes that the *DSM* list of mental illnesses are valid, the scientific question remains: Can they be reliably diagnosed? Specifically, do different doctors who see the same patient agree on that patient's diagnosis?

The APA claimed that this reliability problem had been solved by removing the more subjective psychological notions such as "neurosis" and replacing them with behavioral checklists that were first installed in the 1980 *DSM-III*. However, in *Making Us Crazy* (1997), Kutchins and Kirk reported there is not a single major study showing high reliability in any version of the *DSM*.

Kutchins and Kirk reported on a major 1992 study conducted at six sites. Mental health professionals were given extensive training in how to make accurate *DSM* diagnoses and then assessed six hundred prospective patients. Kutchins and Kirk summarize the results: "Mental health clinicians independently interviewing the same person in the community are as likely to agree as disagree that the person has a mental disorder and are as likely to agree as disagree on which of the . . . *DSM* disorders is present." This was true even though the standards for defining agreement were very generous; for example, Kutchins and Kirk reported that "if one of the two therapists . . . made a diagnosis of Schizoid Personality Disorder and the other therapist selected Avoidant Personality Disorder, the therapists were judged to be in complete agreement of the diagnosis because they both found a personality disorder—even though they disagreed completely on which one!"

To assess the reliability of the current *DSM-5*, the APA conducted field trials assessing the degree of agreement between clinicians diagnosing the same individuals. However, these field trials yielded embarrassing results for psychiatry. A standard statistic used to assess reliability is called *kappa*. A kappa value of 0 means zero agreement and no reliability; a kappa of 1.00 means perfect reliability; and a kappa of less than .59 considered weak reliability. *DSM-III* task force chair, Robert Spitzer, had proclaimed with respect to assessing the reliability of the *DSM* that a kappa of less than .40 indicated "poor" agreement and .70 was "only satisfactory."

For the *DSM-5* field trials, here is a sample of kappa results: .20 for generalized anxiety disorder; .32 for major depressive disorder; .41 for oppositional defiant disorder; and .46 for schizophrenia. When *DSM-5* task force vice-chair, psychiatrist Darrel Regier, announced these results at the 2011 APA annual convention, Greenberg observed the following: "Here he was, announcing a miserable failure, but if he grasped the extent of the debacle, nothing about his delivery showed it."

One reason why even schizophrenia has such poor diagnostic reliability is that clinicians routinely disagree on what constitutes a bizarre delusion. In a 1995 *American Journal of Psychiatry* study ("Interrater Reliability of Ratings of Delusions and Bizarre Delusions"), fifty senior psychiatrists were asked to distinguish between bizarre delusions versus non-bizarre delusions. Their inter-rater reliability kappa was between .38 and .43. The researchers concluded, "The symptom of bizarre delusions does not have adequate reliability."

In this sense of reliability, the *DSM* is less scientific than the 613 Torah Commandments (Mitzvot). For example, with regard to kosher laws and circumcision, there is going to be far higher rabbinical agreement about compliance than there is clinician agreement on *DSM* mental illnesses. Similar to the Bible, Spinoza would see the *DSM* as "faulty, mutilated, adulterated, and inconsistent." Given the aspirations of the *DSM* creators to be viewed as scientists, Spinoza might take pity on them.

Spinoza would have been amused by Greenberg's *Book of Woe*. Greenberg had gained access to the internal debate among psychiatrists who were creating *DSM-5*, along with exacting candidness from psychiatrists who had created *DSM-III* and *DSM-IV* but who were excluded from the *DSM-5* creation process. The *DSM* creation process would strike Spinoza as remarkably similar to how the Bible was put together in the Second Temple period under the editorship of Ezra the Scribe. Each *DSM* has had its own Ezra. The Ezra of *DSM-III* was psychiatrist Robert Spitzer, and the Ezra of *DSM-IV* was psychiatrist Allen Frances. What would have amused Spinoza was how those Ezras battled the Ezra of *DSM-5*, psychiatrist David Kupfer.

It would not surprise Spinoza that some psychiatrists are willing to question some aspects of the *DSM*. Nadler tells us, "Even the sages of the Talmud, committed as they are to the principle that all of the Torah was written by Moses, concede that the last eight verses were added by Joshua." The battle by psychiatrists over diagnoses might strike Spinoza as similar to the Amsterdam rabbinical battle in his time between Rabbi Morteira and Rabbi Aboab over beliefs about how God treated sinners in the hereafter (these rabbis did, however, join together on Spinoza's excommunication).

For their attack on *DSM-5*, Spitzer and Frances, two of the most influential psychiatrists in the history of U.S. psychiatry, were attacked by the then-current APA leaders. In response to Frances's rebuke of *DSM-5*, APA leaders attempted to discredit him by pointing out that once *DSM-5* was published, Frances would stand to lose his $10,000 annual royalties from *DSM-IV*. Spitzer had publicly criticized the APA for mandating that *DSM-5* task force members sign a confidential agreement (a gag order) enabling the APA to create *DSM-5* in secrecy. It was a major blow to psychiatry for Frances and Spitzer to cast aspersions on psychiatry's newest diagnostic bible, and Greenberg notes that both were placed on the "APA's enemies' list."

Psychiatrist Michael First was the text editor for *DSM-IV*, and Greenberg concludes his book with a quote from First about *DSM-5*: "The good news about the *DSM-5* is also the bad news . . . [*DSM-5*] relies on categories that facilitate clinician communication but have no firm basis in reality. So I think it's an improvement, but it's also an acknowledgment that psychiatry, especially in its understanding of mental illness, is still in its infancy."

Spinoza would come to a full stop to ponder First's acknowledgment that *DSM* categories "have no firm basis in reality." However, psychiatry apologists speed past that and applaud First's reprise of the conventional wisdom that psychiatry "is still in its infancy," a nod to conventional wisdom that psychiatry is a young science with much to discover but making great progress.

Spinoza viewed Bible authors as imaginative story tellers who were not philosophers or scientists. Spinoza would view *DSM* authors as having no aptitude as scientists, philosophers, or story tellers. Spinoza had a strong interest in human psychology and in discovering the sources of human misery, but the behavioral classification system of the *DSM* would likely provide no intellectual stimulation for him.

What would likely interest Spinoza about the *DSM* is that it provides authority for psychiatrists to declare mental illness. This would strike Spinoza as similar to the Bible, which viewed as the word of God provides authority to its interpreting clergy to declare who are sinners. If the Bible is God's word, and if ecclesiastic authorities are superior to others in the Bible's interpretation, then clergy can exercise control over others. Spinoza noted, "We see that nearly all men parade their own ideas as God's Word, their chief aim being to compel others to think as they do, while using religion as a pretext."

Spinoza was, Nadler tells us, "Troubled by the expansion of ecclesiastic power in the Dutch Republic, and especially the meddling of Calvinist preachers in public affairs and in the lives of private citizens." Spinoza recognized that clergy derived their moral, social, and political authority by claiming the Bible as the word of God. "Moreover," Nadler continues, "they set themselves up as the sole qualified interpreters of Scripture and read it to suit their purposes." Nadler concludes, "Spinoza hopes to undercut ecclesiastic influence in politics and other domains and weaken the sectarian dangers facing his beloved Republic."

For Spinoza, in order to delegitimize the intolerant ecclesiastic authorities, it was crucial to delegitimize the sacredness of the Bible. Just as he saw how clergy derive their authority by positioning themselves to be the interpreters of a pseudosacred Bible, he would see how psychiatrists derive their authority by positioning themselves to be the interpreters of a pseudoscientific DSM. And so, just as it was necessary for him to critique the sacredness of the Bible, Spinoza would see it necessary to criticize the pseudoscience of the DSM. Spinoza would recognize that DSM criticism is not simply scientifically important but politically necessary.

Those at the top of psychiatry institutions have long recognized that the public perception of a lack of science behind the DSM threatens the legitimacy of psychiatry, and so in the past, the APA has revised the DSM several times to respond to criticism. However, more recently, some leading figures in psychiatry have recognized that for psychiatry to have any scientific credibility, the DSM must be jettisoned. In 2013, Thomas Insel, then director of the National Institute of Mental Health (NIMH), stated that the DSM's diagnostic categories lack validity, and he announced that "NIMH will be re-orienting its research away from DSM categories."

Insel explained that the NIMH would be re-orienting to something called RDoC, which stands for Research Domain Criteria (announced by the NIMH in 2010). At present, most of the general public and many mental health professionals remain unaware of RDoC, and even among professionals who are aware of it, few can explain it, as its language is unfamiliar to most of them. The major RDoC research domains, Insel reported, are negative valence systems; positive valence systems; cognitive systems; systems for social processes; and arousal/modulatory systems. The NIMH has appropriated scientific-sounding language such as "negative valence" (a term in science used to mean a negatively charged ion); however, by "negative valence," the NIMH simply means unpleasant emotional states such as fear and anger. Insel proclaimed that the NIMH will now be supporting research that connects these research domains with "genetic, imaging, physiologic, and cognitive data to see how all the data—not just the symptoms—cluster and how these clusters relate to treatment response." For example, RDoC research will map the connection between emotions such as fear and anger with biological correlates. Unlike the DSM, RDoC would not organize its research domains with reference to disease categories.

The conflict between the DSM and RDoC was termed by psychiatrist Stuart L. Kaplan in a 2016 Psychology Today article to be "The Most Important Controversy in Current Psychiatry" (his article title). One of the major criticisms of RDoC by psychiatrists attached to the DSM, notes Kaplan, is that the so-called "dimensional approach" of RDoC "does not permit the discrimination between health and illness. . . . To have more or less of some biological quality does not distinguish between who is well and who is ill." If psychiatrists are unable to state whether an individual is healthy or ill, then it means psychiatrists are unable to proclaim who should be treated, which is obviously a major problem for the profession. In a political compromise, Kaplan notes, "The NIMH RDoC group and the American Psychiatric Association [APA] quickly managed to paper over their differences and present something of a united front on the brink of the launch of *DSM-5*."

This "united front" was a political compromise. Even though the then-NIMH director declared the *DSM* to be invalid and thus unscientific, the *DSM* continues to be used for patient diagnosis and treatment, while RDoC will be used for research. This compromise has not been widely publicized; once known, it will be difficult for psychiatry to evade the derision that will likely ensue over its continuing to use an invalid *DSM* for diagnosis and treatment to appease the APA—America's guild of psychiatrists that publishes the *DSM*.

The inconsistency here, for Spinoza, would be strikingly similar to Biblical inconsistencies that are irrationally reconciled by theologians.

CHAPTER 8

THREE NOBLE LIES?

Psychiatrist Allen Frances, chair of the *DSM-IV* task force, as previously noted, received a great deal of public attention for his 2010 statement that "there is no definition of a mental disorder. It's bullshit. I mean, you just can't define it." However, perhaps even more illuminating was Frances's 2011 warning to *DSM* critic Gary Greenberg not to "puncture that noble lie." Specifically, Frances told Greenberg that even if "the diagnostic label is just a description, and not really an explanation for what has gone wrong" that it is still crucial to treatment, and he cautioned Greenberg, "If you puncture that noble lie, you'll be doing a disservice to our patients. . . . A lot of false beliefs help people cope with life."

While Frances pointed out that a *DSM* diagnostic label is "not really an explanation for what has gone wrong," he recognized that many people embrace their diagnosis as just such an explanation. They become very much attached to their diagnosis, which explains to them why they are behaving self-destructively; and they hope that their diagnosis will provide an explanation to others that will result in greater compassion. This is what is behind Frances's declaration that "false beliefs help people cope with life," and this is why he cautions against puncturing the noble lie of psychiatric diagnoses.

Another leading psychiatrist, in 2011, revealed a second false belief, one about the cause of mental illness—a belief that continues to be widely accepted and also considered by some psychiatrists to be a noble lie. Before detailing this false belief about the cause of mental illness as well as discussing treatment fictions, some background from philosophy and political science about the *noble lie,* and why the elite embrace it.

The noble lie, a concept often associated with Plato, was originally seen as a myth or untruth propagated by the elite to achieve social harmony by convincing citizens to accept their status in a hierarchy. The noble lie has come to mean an altruistic use of deceptions and falsehoods to achieve ends that are beneficial.

Condemners of the noble lie include propaganda critics Edward Herman and Noam Chomsky. They do not trust either the motives or the wisdom of the elite, pointing to the damage created by these so-called noble lies. Herman and Chomsky's book *Manufacturing Consent* (1988) derives its title from presidential advisor and journalist Walter Lippman's phrase "the manufacture of consent"—a necessity for Lippmann, who believed that the general public is incompetent in discerning what's truly best for them, and so their opinion must be molded by a benevolent elite who does.

In contrast to Chomsky and Herman, political scientist John Mearsheimer views himself as a "realist," and his book *Why Leaders Lie* (2011) contends that lying by leaders is not essentially immoral. Mearsheimer provides us with a window into the thinking of those among the elite who view themselves as altruistic. He states, "I look at international lying from a strictly utilitarian perspective, mainly because there are compelling reasons that justify it and, not surprisingly, we find a considerable amount of it in the historical record." For him, lying itself is not essentially immoral; the moral issue is whether the lie results in a good or bad end.

From this pragmatic perspective, Mearsheimer evaluates the lies of U.S. presidential administrations. He details how the George W. Bush administration, in its attempt to sell the American people on the 2003 invasion of Iraq to accomplish regime change, told four major lies: (1) claiming with certainty that Iraq had weapons of mass destruction (WMDs); (2) asserting there was foolproof evidence that Saddam Hussein was allied with Osama bin Laden; (3) implying that Saddam Hussein was responsible for the September 11, 2001 attack; and (4) claiming that the Bush administration was open to a peaceful resolution when the decision had already been made to go to war. The lying by the Bush administration was bad for Mearsheimer only because it resulted in a war that had a disastrous outcome.

However, Mearsheimer evaluates positively a major lie of the John F. Kennedy administration. In order to peacefully conclude the Cuban Missile Crisis in 1962, Kennedy lied to the American people, denying he had cut a secret deal with the Soviet Union in which U.S. missiles were pulled out of Turkey.

Spinoza's regard for democracy—his belief that the best government is one that has the consent of the governed—was an extremely radical idea for his era. However, in another sense, he was an elitist. Spinoza believed that only a minority of people could reason their way to morality. For Spinoza, most people are incapable of the kind of philosophical reasoning that leads to rationally concluding that justice and charity are good ideas that reduce resentment in society and improve lives. Thus, the belief that the Bible is the word of God is useful for such non-philosophers, enabling their compliance with prophets' messages of justice and charity. For non-philosophers, it is useful to believe that justice and charity are commanded by an anthropomorphic supernatural God. For Spinoza, the falsehood of the divinity of the prophets and the Bible is, in this sense, a noble lie, resulting in greater social harmony. However, also for Spinoza, the falsehood of proclaiming the Bible as the word of God is politically dangerous. By transforming the Bible into dogma that ecclesiastic authorities use to establish control over civil society, intolerance is created, which diminishes justice and charity and increases suffering.

Back to psychiatry. For patients and even many doctors, there was something even more shocking than the 2010 psychiatric diagnosis invalidity admission by psychiatrist Allen Frances. This was the public rejection of the chemical imbalance theory of mental illness in 2011 by psychiatrist Ronald Pies, Editor-in-Chief Emeritus of the *Psychiatric Times*. Pies stated: "In truth, the 'chemical imbalance' notion was always a kind of urban legend—never a theory seriously propounded by well-informed psychiatrists."

That the chemical imbalance theory of depression is not true came as a great surprise to National Public Radio (NPR) correspondent Alix Spiegel, the granddaughter of psychiatrist John Spiegel, a former president (1974–1975) of the American Psychiatric Association. In a 2012 NPR story, Spiegel reported on researchers who confirmed that the chemical imbalance theory was not true. She began her story on a personal note:

When I was 17 years old, I got so depressed that what felt like an enormous black hole appeared in my chest. Everywhere I went, the black hole went, too.

So to address the black-hole issue, my parents took me to a psychiatrist at Johns Hopkins Hospital. She did an evaluation and then told me this story:

"The problem with you," she explained, "is that you have a chemical imbalance. It's biological, just like diabetes, but it's in your brain. This chemical in your brain called serotonin is too, too low. There's not enough of it, and that's what's causing the chemical imbalance. We need to give you medication to correct that."

Then she handed my mother a prescription for Prozac.

Was Alix Spiegel's psychiatrist at the prestigious Johns Hopkins Hospital, in Pies's terms, not "well-informed"? Or was this psychiatrist telling Alix a noble lie? We don't know. Spiegel did not interview her ex-psychiatrist, but she did interview other psychiatrists and researchers, including Alan Frazer and Pedro Delgado, who both believe that this lie was a noble one.

Alan Frazer, professor of pharmacology and psychiatry and chairman of the pharmacology department at the University of Texas Health Sciences Center, told Spiegel that by framing depression as a deficiency—something that needs to be returned to normal—patients feel more comfortable taking antidepressants. Frazer stated, "If there was this biological reason for them being depressed, some deficiency that the drug was correcting, then taking a drug was OK." For Frazer, the story that depressed people have a chemical imbalance and that the antidepressant is correcting that imbalance is a story that has enabled people to come out of the closet about being depressed and take their antidepressant medication.

Pedro Delgado, chairman of the psychiatry department at the University of Texas, had actually helped debunk the serotonin deficiency theory of depression, but he told Spiegel that the fiction of the chemical imbalance theory has benefits. Delgado pointed to research showing that uncertainty can be harmful; and so simple and clear explanations, regardless of how inaccurate, can be more helpful than complex truthful explanations. Delgado knows as well as anyone that it was an inaccurate belief that low levels of serotonin are associated with depression. In his 1999 review of the research, "Antidepressants and the Brain," he detailed how in serotonin depletion studies that "depletion in unmedicated patients with depression did not worsen the depressive symptoms, neither did it cause depression in healthy subjects with no history of mental illness."

Spinoza would be intrigued by Frazer and Delgado's admissions, as he is clear about the difference between science and religion. Beth Lord notes that for Spinoza, "The aim of science, philosophy, and reason is to get at the truth. . . . the aim of religion is rather different . . . its aim is not to tell the truth or even to discover the truth, its aim is to make people behave better, and to keep people obedient." For Spinoza, Lord continues, "The role of religion is really in controlling and . . . helping to manage people's feelings and images when they're in this irrational state." Religion is a fiction but can have considerable utility, as Lord explains that for Spinoza, "Useful fictions are those that promote tolerance and community." However, there are also malevolent fictions, which Lord describes as "ones which people are controlled, oppressed, and enslaved."

Since the 1990s, it has been clear to scientists that the chemical imbalance theory of depression was a disproved hypothesis. In *Blaming the Brain* (1998), Elliot Valenstein, professor emeritus of psychology and neuroscience at the University of Michigan, detailed research showing that it is just as likely for people with normal serotonin levels to feel depressed as it is for people with abnormal serotonin levels, and that it is just as likely for people with abnormally high serotonin levels to feel depressed as it is for people with abnormally low serotonin levels. Valenstein concluded, "Furthermore, there is no convincing evidence that depressed people have a serotonin or norepinephrine deficiency." But how many Americans heard about this?

Pies claims that the APA fulfilled its obligation to inform the general public of the truth with a 2000 public statement about depression that begins: "The exact causes of mental disorders are unknown, but an explosive growth of research has brought us closer to the answers." However, in 2014, Pies did admit psychiatry should have been clearer and louder, "Shouldn't psychiatrists in positions of influence have made greater efforts to knock down the chemical imbalance hypothesis, and to present a more sophisticated understanding of mental illness to the general public? Probably so."

A 2006 survey revealed that 80 percent of Americans believed that depression is caused by a chemical imbalance. When people constantly hear something, they continue to believe it unless they hear it retracted many times. That is also why many Americans continue to believe that WMDs were discovered in Iraq. A 2015 survey reported that 42 percent of all Americans (51 percent of Republicans) continued to believe that WMDs were found in Iraq.

The astronomer Carl Sagan, a fierce advocate of skeptical inquiry, observed: "One of the saddest lessons of history is this: If we've been bamboozled long enough, we tend to reject any evidence of the bamboozle. We're no longer interested in finding out the truth. The bamboozle has captured us. It's simply too painful to acknowledge, even to ourselves, that we've been taken. Once you give a charlatan power over you, you almost never get it back" (Carl

Sagan was a Spinozist according to his daughter Dorion Sagan who recalled, "My father believed in the God of Spinoza and Einstein").

Prior to the public's acceptance of the chemical imbalance cause of depression, many people were reluctant to take antidepressants—or to give them to their children. But the idea that depression is caused by a chemical imbalance that can be corrected with Prozac or some other selective serotonin reuptake inhibitor (SSRI) sounded similar to taking insulin for diabetes (the comparison that the Johns Hopkins psychiatrist made to a teenage Alix Spiegel and her parents). So the use of SSRI antidepressants skyrocketed (as previously noted, between 1988 and 2008, the rate of antidepressant use in the United States increased nearly 400 percent).

The case for the chemical imbalance theory of depression as a noble lie rests in large part on the answers to two questions: (1) What is the effect of the belief in the chemical imbalance theory on treatment expectations? (2) Given that the belief in the chemical imbalance theory is largely responsible for the increased use of antidepressant medications, exactly how effective are these drugs?

A study published in 2020 in the *Journal of Affective Disorders* ("Stressors and Chemical Imbalances: Beliefs about the Causes of Depression in an Acute Psychiatric Treatment Sample") examined the effects of causal beliefs about depression in 279 patients and reported the following results: "The chemical imbalance belief related to poorer treatment expectations . . . with more depressed individuals showing a stronger relationship between chemical imbalance beliefs and lower treatment expectations. Finally, the chemical imbalance belief predicted more depressive symptoms after the treatment program ended for a 2-week measure of depression."

The question about the scientific effectiveness of antidepressant medications requires a deeper inquiry. Ironically, the effectiveness of these drugs has much to do with a variation of the noble lie—the placebo effect: the power of expectations creating actual benefits. Psychiatrist Allen Frances notes, "Like most medical specialties, our field depends heavily on placebo effects."

The power of the placebo with respect to the effectiveness of antidepressants such as Prozac and other SSRI drugs is uncontroversial. What is controversial is just how powerful the placebo effect is.

A leading researcher of the placebo effect is psychologist Irving Kirsch, professor emeritus at the University of Hull in the United Kingdom and later at Harvard University. Kirsch's "expectancy theory" is simply that our experience depends in large part on what we expect to experience, and this is the basis of the placebo effect. Kirsch's major career interest has been the placebo effect, not in criticizing psychiatric treatment. His analysis of antidepressant effectiveness was spurred by his general interest in the placebo effect.

In 2002, Kirsch examined forty-seven drug company studies on SSRIs such as Prozac, Paxil, Zoloft, and other antidepressants. These studies included published and unpublished trials, but all had been submitted to the Food and Drug Administration (FDA), so Kirsch used the Freedom of Information Act to gain access to all data. He discovered that in the majority of the trials, antidepressants failed to outperform placebos, and he reported that "all antidepressants, including the well-known SSRIs (serotonin selective reuptake inhibitors), had no clinically significant benefit over a placebo." While in aggregate, antidepressants slightly edged out placebos, the difference is so unremarkable that Kirsch and others describe it as "clinically negligible."

Some antidepressant critics go even further than Kirsch in criticizing the value of antidepressants. They say that if the drug research had not been "dice loaded" by drug companies, there would be no difference at all in the effectiveness of antidepressants compared to a placebo. As previously noted, in antidepressant effectiveness studies, depression measurements such as the HAM-D scale provide antidepressants with an edge, but that's not the only way the drug company studies are biased in favor of making their drug appear more effective than it actually is.

A critical scientific standard in drug studies is the double-blind control, which means that neither subject nor experimenter knows who is getting the drug and who is getting the placebo; however, drug company antidepressant studies use blinds that are not all that blinding. Sugar pills used as placebos don't create side effects, and so subjects can more easily guess if they are getting the actual drug. In order to make it more difficult to penetrate the blind, what needs to be used is what scientists call an "active placebo"—that creates side effects—so that a subject cannot so easily guess whether they are being administered the drug or a placebo, but drug company research does not use active placebos. Drug company research also uses the dice-loading technique called "placebo washout," in which subjects who respond favorably to placebos in initial trials are weeded out from final trials.

Moreover, pharmaceutical companies are not required to do long-term outcome studies to acquire FDA drug approval. The FDA's "Major Depressive Disorder: Developing Drugs for Treatment Guidance for Industry" states the following: "Antidepressants in established classes (e.g., SSRIs, SNRIs) typically need studies of 6 to 8 weeks duration to demonstrate efficacy." Thus, the general public is unaware of studies that show antidepressants, over the long-term, may result in more, not less, depression.

In the 1990s, psychiatrist Giovanni Fava concluded that it appeared that antidepressants could increase the likelihood that an individual experiencing a single depressive episode could become chronically depressed.

In 2017, the journal *Psychotherapy and Psychosomatics* published "Poorer Long-Term Outcomes among Persons with Major Depressive Disorder Treated with Medication," in which researcher Jeffrey Vittengl, controlling for depression severity, examined outcomes of 3,294 subjects over a nine-year period. He reported that while antidepressants may have an immediate, short-term benefit for some individuals, subjects who took antidepressants had significantly more severe symptoms at the nine-year follow-up than those who did not take medication, and patients who received no medication did better than those who used medication.

In 2006, an NIMH-funded study "The Naturalistic Course of Major Depression in the Absence of Somatic Therapy" reported that 85 percent of the non-medicated patients recovered within a year, and the authors concluded: "If as many as 85% of depressed individuals who go without somatic treatments spontaneously recover within one year, it would be extremely difficult for any intervention to demonstrate a superior result to this."

Even proponents of antidepressants recognize that the primary variable in determining a patient's report of the effectiveness of these drugs is their expectation of effectiveness—in other words, the placebo effect. Antidepressant proponents and critics differ in that proponents believe the actual chemical effect of antidepressants greatly enhances effectiveness, while critics believe the effect is completely or almost completely the result of the placebo effect or simply the passage of time.

Spinoza would be very much interested in the placebo effect. Given how much Spinoza wrote about superstitious behaviors, it is a safe bet that he would be fascinated by the idea that a placebo could, in some cases, have scientific value.

Praying in order to manipulate God to get your needs met is a superstitious behavior that Spinoza derided as such. However, while praying to God for rain has no value, praying to God may improve psychophysiological (psychosomatic) conditions created in part by stress (such as hypertension and tension headaches). If you believe strongly enough that your prayers will be answered, it can reduce your stress, which may have a positive biological effect on physical conditions that are in part caused by stress.

Given Spinoza's rejection of the mind-body dualism asserted by René Descartes, and Spinoza's embrace of the oneness of mind and body, the placebo effect would fit well into his monism.

It is safe to say that Spinoza would be fine with the noble lie of prescribing harmless sugar pills to people suffering from depression, especially since science confirms how powerful the placebo effect is for any pill used for depression. A placebo works as well or almost as well as antidepressants in the short-term and eliminates the long-term detrimental effects of antidepressants.

However, even though the placebo is indisputably a safe and effective in reducing patient suffering, it is considered professionally unethical for psychiatrists to prescribe placebos. In contrast, psychiatry considers it ethical to use diagnostic labels deemed invalid and unreliable, which psychiatrist Alan Frances has termed "noble lies" that "help people cope with life." And psychiatry has deemed it ethical to promote a disproven chemical imbalance theory of depression because it provides a biological rationale for depression that results in greater medication compliance.

It would be clear to Spinoza that whether psychiatry uses or does not use lies has to do with whether the lie advances psychiatry's authority and power—and satisfies the interests of pharmaceutical companies which have grown to have great influence over psychiatry. Falsehoods about diagnostic labels and chemical imbalance theories about causality promote psychiatrists' authority and are helpful for pharmaceutical companies. Obviously, if sugar pills were routinely prescribed for depression rather than antidepressants, pharmaceutical companies would lose billions of dollars.

Jonathan Israel concludes, "No other element of Spinoza's philosophy provoked as much consternation and outrage in his own time as his sweeping denial of miracles and the supernatural."

Today, denying psychiatry's claims of medication effectiveness often result in consternation and outrage. While I'm unaware of any antidepressant critic who has denied the power of expectations and the placebo effect or has derided individuals for their use of antidepressants, Spinoza would not be surprised that such critics are denounced by some antidepressant advocates as "pill shamers."

CHAPTER 9

TOLERANCE AND STIGMA

Spinoza cared a great deal about tolerance. Happiness for him and his friends was predicated on freedom of thought and expression, and such freedoms are predicated on societal tolerance.

Spinoza's ancestors had immigrated to the Dutch Republic because it was the most tolerant nation in Europe. After the Dutch liberated themselves from Spain's Catholic rule, their Union of Utrecht (1579), which served as the provinces' constitution, stated: "Every individual should remain free in his religion, and no man should be molested or questioned on the subject of divine worship." This was a dream come true for the Spinoza family and other Jews who flocked to the Netherlands, especially to Amsterdam, the most liberal and tolerant city in the Dutch Republic.

This era, now called the "Dutch Golden Age," did not have unlimited tolerance, but relative to the rest of Europe, the degree of religious freedom was astonishing. The Dutch recognized the practical economic value of a tolerant society. Such a society attracts artists, philosophers, and individuals who will discover scientific truths that result in new technologies, which are good for business. In the 1600s, the Dutch Republic was a draw for the French philosopher René Descartes and, later, the British philosopher John Locke, and also for merchants from various cultures—such as Spinoza's ancestors—who had foreign business connections and created material wealth.

While Dutch Calvinist authorities attempted to keep control over the Jewish population, the type of stigma for being a Jew that existed in the rest of Europe did not exist in the Amsterdam that Bento was born into. However, there was great stigma to being an atheist, which despite Spinoza's protestations, he was often called because of his distinctly different understanding of God.

While Spinoza believed in tolerance for all beliefs and non-beliefs—including atheism—he fought his diagnostic label of *atheist*. He had a deep intellectual love of God, and he resented being labeled as an atheist by people he considered to be irrational Scripture worshipers who believed in a false notion of God—an anthropomorphic God who could be manipulated by selfish prayers. For Spinoza, believing in such a false notion of God made his accusers, not him, God deniers. Spinoza also knew that it was dangerous to be diagnosed as an atheist, as the term was associated with a libertine rejection of social conventions and mores, and Spinoza prided himself on being a good citizen of the Dutch Republic.

While another seventeenth-century philosopher, John Locke, is today often given the credit for promoting ideas about religious tolerance, which resulted in the right to "freedom of religion" being included in the U.S. Bill of Rights, Spinoza actually had a more expansive tolerance than Locke. In Jonathan Israel's comparison of *moderate* Enlightenment thinkers, which included Locke, to *radical* Enlightenment thinkers, which included Spinoza, he concludes that "the two Enlightenments forged powerfully contrasting notions of toleration."

The moderates, Israel notes, advocated "freedom of worship and peaceful coexistence of dissenting Churches." In contrast, the radicals demanded complete freedom of thought and expression, Israel explains, "including the expression of ideas incompatible with the core tenets of revealed religion." Locke advocated tolerance for freedom to worship, but not for those who eschewed worshiping. Locke was explicitly intolerant of atheists, proclaiming in his *A Letter Concerning Toleration* (1689), "Those are not at all to be tolerated who deny the being of a God." For Locke, atheism was tantamount to having no respect for morality, and so atheists were a threat to their fellow citizens.

This contrast between moderate and radical Enlightenment thinkers with respect to toleration has a parallel in psychiatry. Moderately enlightened thinkers such as former NIMH director Thomas Insel are tolerant of: those who are critical of psychiatry's performance; those who reject the *DSM*; and those who embrace the idea that not all individuals diagnosed with serious mental illness need lifelong medication (more in Chapter 12: "Coercion").

However, in contrast to moderates, only radical thinkers find it acceptable to reject: the medical model/construct of mental illness; the legitimacy of psychiatry as a scientific authority; and the idea that treatment requires professional credentials.

While Locke's views around religious tolerance were progressive for the 1600s, Spinoza's belief in the toleration of *all* thought and expression—including atheist and irreligious thought and expression—was radical for the 1600s and remain so today in many parts of the world. Spinoza had intimate knowledge of the violent history of the stigmatization of his Jewish ancestors as well the barbarism perpetuated on others who rejected the consensus reality of the nature of God and conventional religious practices. And so it is likely that today he would be very much sensitive to those who are being stigmatized.

Merriam-Webster defines *stigma* as "a mark of shame or discredit." Sociologist Erving Goffman described how an individual, owing to an attribute—for example, being a "mental patient"—is ostracized, scorned, shunned, and ignored. For those who accept their stigmatization, it can result in an internalized sense of defectiveness. In his books *Asylums* (1961) and *Stigma* (1963), Goffman described what he called "institutionalization"—a process by which a psychiatrically hospitalized patient is conditioned to be a "good patient" in the sense of being compliant, harmless, and inconspicuous. Goffman contended that such institutionalization causes the development of a "mental patient identity" that results in an individual becoming chronically dysfunctional.

Among both psychiatry advocates and critics, there is agreement that those who have been diagnosed with serious mental illness are stigmatized by society. Those identified as seriously mentally ill are viewed in a variety of unfavorable ways, including being unpredictable and dangerous, resulting in difficulties finding housing and gaining employment.

Today's conventional wisdom includes the idea that if mental illnesses such as schizophrenia had as little stigma as other illnesses such as diabetes, then those afflicted with schizophrenia would feel more comfortable seeking treatment and remaining in treatment; and this would result in not only less suffering for them but less suffering for their family and society. The conventional wisdom is that since people with medical diseases such as diabetes are not routinely stigmatized, then if there was parity for mental illness with physical illness, the stigmatization of the mentally ill would be reduced. Thus, an often used slogan of the conventional mental illness anti-stigma campaign is "an illness like any other."

Spinoza questioned everything, and he would question whether the anti-stigma strategy of "an illness like any other" is a well-reasoned, adequate idea.

According to contemporary conventional wisdom, it is absurd to believe that psychiatry and mental illness advocates themselves are stigmatizing the mentally ill. After all, nobody more loudly proclaims the need to abolish the stigma of mental illness. However, philosophically minded people such as Spinoza know that it is quite possible that those who proclaim and promote an ideal can actually create its opposite. Sometimes this happens because of corruption, disingenuousness, and hypocrisy; but this can also happen because people are so self-certain of their moral superiority that they forego rationality, empiricism, and scientific analysis.

As early as 1961, the U.S. Joint Commission on Mental Illness and Health had concluded: "The principle of sameness as applied to the mentally sick versus the physically sick has become a cardinal tenet of mental health education." The ensuing efforts to de-stigmatize mental illness has resulted in several questions: Does labeling people who are acting in extremely disturbing ways as mentally ill increase or decrease stigma and intolerance? Has viewing these tension-producing conditions as brain diseases created more or less intolerance and stigmatization? Or would such people be less stigmatized if their conditions were seen as having different causes? Does viewing people as "ill" and in need of "treatment" increase or decrease stigma compared to viewing them as "in crisis" or "experiencing extreme states" and in need of understanding and support?

Both empirical research and rational analysis point in the opposite direction of the conventional wisdom that is currently being employed in the anti-stigma "illness like any other" campaign. First some of the empirical research, and then why Spinoza would not have needed it.

There have been many studies examining the relationship between mental illness stigmatization and beliefs about mental illness. In 2006, *Acta Psychiatrica Scandinavica* published "Prejudice and Schizophrenia: A Review of the 'Mental Illness is an Illness Like Any Other' Approach." The lead author was psychologist John Read, and the review was an examination of the many studies investigating: (1) whether there has been an increase in the belief that mental illness is caused by biological factors such as biochemistry and genetics; (2) whether a biological (biogenetic) causal belief is associated with less or more negative attitudes; and (3) whether labeling people with mental illnesses such as schizophrenia rather than a non-illness label is associated with less or more negative attitudes.

In the United States between 1950 and 1996, Read reported that there was an increase in the public's willingness to apply the label "mental illness" to unusual or problematic behaviors; but he notes that "over the same period, perceptions that 'mentally ill' people are violent and frightening increased." Such perceptions obviously increase stigma.

Read examined several studies that attempt to answer the question whether labeling someone with "schizophrenia" rather than describing them as "in crisis" was associated with more or less negative attitudes. These studies conclude that labeling behaviors as "schizophrenia" increases the belief in biological causality and increases the perceived seriousness of the person's difficulties, which produces a more pessimistic view about recovery. If a person is seen as having the serious mental illness of schizophrenia, the public more desires to keep their distance from them rather than if the person is seen as "in crisis."

A critical question with regard to contemporary anti-stigma efforts is whether or not biological causal beliefs are associated with more or less negative attitudes. Read examined twenty-one studies, and he summarizes the findings: "From 1970, studies in several industrialized countries have found that biogenetic causal beliefs are related to negative attitudes. This has been demonstrated among patients and professionals as well as general populations. Biogenetic beliefs are related to perceptions of dangerousness and unpredictability, to fear, and to desire for social distance." The research clearly shows that the brain disease conceptualization and the "an illness like any other" anti-stigma campaign have resulted in greater stigmatization.

Psychologist Shelia Mehta examined how our beliefs about the cause of mental disturbances translate into behaviors. In Mehta's 1997 study, "Is Being 'Sick' Really Better? Effect of the Disease View of Mental Disorder on Stigma," subjects were told that a confederate—who was actually in league with the experimenter—had a history of either being (1) normal; (2) psychiatrically hospitalized for psychosocial reasons ("things that happened to me when I was a kid"); or (3) psychiatrically hospitalized because of a brain disease ("a disease just like any other, which affected my biochemistry"). In the experiment, subjects attempted to teach the confederates a task. When the confederate purposely responded incorrectly, subjects gave the confederate electric shocks. Mehta found that confederates self-identified as normal were shocked least harshly by subjects. Most importantly, confederates who gave a biochemical disease explanation for their history of psychiatric hospitalization were shocked significantly more severely than those who had reported a psychosocial explanation for their psychiatric hospitalization.

In "Myth: Reframing Mental Illness as a 'Brain Disease' Reduces Stigma," the Canadian Health Services Research Foundation (CHSRF) reported in 2012: "Despite good intentions, evidence actually shows that anti-stigma campaigns emphasizing the biological nature of mental illness have not been effective, and have often made the problem worse." The CHSRF concludes, "Biological explanations can also instill an 'us vs. them' attitude, defining individuals with mental illness as fundamentally different." Alternately, the CHSRF concludes, "Presenting mental illness in the context of . . . psychological and social stressors normalizes symptoms."

Spinoza was very much interested in science, and if alive today, would be interested in the above empirical research, but it is likely that he would conclude that a person who is capable of reason would not have needed these studies about stigma. It would have been obvious to him that viewing people who create tension and fear as having mental illness caused by a brain disease would set them more apart from others—and make them more vulnerable to stigma.

Mehta concludes, "Biochemical aberrations make them almost a different species." In contrast, psychosocial explanations—such as the trauma of physical or emotional abuse—as the reason for a psychiatric hospitalization results in a greater likelihood that a person who was not psychiatrically hospitalized could feel that it was only a matter of good luck that they were not traumatized. A psychosocial traumatization can be healed; however a biological disease whose symptoms can only be treated but not cured indicates permanence and greater potential for relapse. Most people, excepting the extraordinarily tolerant, would rather not befriend or date an individual with a brain disease who is likely to once again behave bizarrely.

Both psychiatry advocates and critics agree that people diagnosed with mental illness are stigmatized. However, both the empirical research and reason conclude that ascribing to the "mental illness is an illness like any other"-view results in increased stigma. And the empirical research and reason tell us that individuals who offer a biological reason for their psychiatric hospitalization will be more stigmatized and treated more harshly than those who offer a psychosocial reason. So, why has the "illness like any other" campaign persisted despite both reason and the empirical evidence revealing the failed nature of this campaign? Again, the answer would be obvious to Spinoza, who would not need the following empirical research to see who benefits from this failed anti-stigma campaign.

A 2012 review ("Evolution of Public Attitudes about Mental Illness: A Systematic Review and Meta-Analysis") published in *Acta Psychiatrica Scandinavica* concludes: "Our findings also suggest that conceptualizing mental disorder as a brain disease or a medical problem facilitates the acceptance of a medical professional solution for this problem. There has been a general increase in the belief that mental illness requires professional help . . . including psychiatric medication."

Thus, while the brain disease "illness like any other" anti-stigma campaign has been unhelpful in reducing stigma, this brain disease conceptualization has benefited two groups. This conceptualization has increased acceptance of the authority of medical professionals, and by increasing compliance with their treatments, which are increasingly medications, it has greatly benefited pharmaceutical companies.

For Spinoza, the explanations for human suffering offered by organized religion provided clergy with power over others, and it undermined freethinking and tolerance for diversity. Ecclesiastic authorities have a vested interest in promoting consensus realities that give them power, and this is the case for all authorities. The conceptualization of mental illness as an "illness like any other" gives authority to medical professionals to treat others. The idea that mental illness is a brain disease provides psychiatrists with more power than professionals who cannot prescribe medications. And obviously, this illness conceptualization is financially beneficial for pharmaceutical corporations. If a group's authority and profits are vested in a certain view of reality, those groups will likely attempt to ensure that alternative explanations not be given a fair hearing and that proponents of such alternative realities are marginalized.

There is extensive empirical support that the conditions that are viewed as serious mental illnesses, such as schizophrenia, are highly associated with childhood trauma. In 2012, *Schizophrenia Bulletin* published the review "Childhood Adversities Increase the Risk of Psychosis: A Meta-analysis of Patient-Control, Prospective- and Cross-sectional Cohort Studies." The review examined multiple studies on the relationship between traumatic childhood adversity (including sexual abuse, physical abuse, emotional/psychological abuse, neglect, parental death, and bullying) with psychoses such as schizo-phrenia. The analysis included thirty-six studies of different varieties, and re-searchers report: "There were significant associations between adversity and psychosis across all research designs . . . findings indicate that childhood ad-versity is strongly associated with increased risk for psychosis."

Given that the relationship between trauma and serious mental illness is now an uncontroversial one, conventional wisdom is that psychosocial stress can trigger schizophrenia. However, consensus reality remains that serious mental illnesses such as schizophrenia and other psychoses are *fundamentally* brain diseases—even though there is far greater empirical support for the re-lationship between trauma and psychosis than the relationship between any brain defect and psychosis (more in Chapter 10: "Brain Disease").

So, what would be more effective in reducing stigma?

Spinoza knew that humility in our judgments about normality can increase tolerance and reduce stigma, and so he cautioned us against arrogance in this regard: "So when something in Nature appears to us as ridiculous, absurd or evil, this is due to the fact that our knowledge is only partial, that we are largely ignorant of the order and coherence of the whole of Nature and want all things to be arranged to suit our reason." Spinoza would not jump to conclusions about disturbing, frightening, bizarre behaviors.

Not all that long ago, individuals who believed that homosexuality was nei-ther a sin nor a mental illness were forced to the fringes of society. Today, mar-ginalized are those who believe that hearing voices is not a symptom of illness but, like homosexuality, a normal human variation. Thus, also marginalized is the belief that the best way to destigmatize individuals who hear voices is to depathologize this phenomenon.

Toward the end of his life, Spinoza was saddened by the direction of the Dutch Republic, which he loved for its relative tolerance but which was be-coming less so, and so he would be happy to know that, in the twenty-first century, one of the most freethinking psychiatrists on the planet is a Dutch one, Marius Romme.

Romme has championed the idea that hearing voices is a normal, albeit un-usual, human variation, and he has challenged the notion that it is a character-istic of serious mental illness. Romme, along with ex-psychiatric patient Patsy Hage and journalist and psychiatry investigator Sandra Escher, pioneered the Healing Voices Network. This movement argues that the best way to destig-matize mental illness is to stop calling people mentally ill on the basis of their hearing voices, and to begin viewing what has been previously viewed as a symptom of serious mental illness as a meaningful human experience.

The idea that voice hearing is not a symptom of illness but a meaningful experience became a somewhat less marginalized perspective following a 2013 *TED* talk, "The Voices in My Head," presented by Eleanor Longden, which by 2021 had well over five million views on the *TED* website (and millions more views on other sites).

Longden tells us that after making the mistake of telling others about her voice hearing, "A hospital admission followed, the first of many, a diagnosis of schizophrenia came next, and then, worst of all, a toxic, tormenting sense of hopelessness, humiliation and despair about myself and my prospects." She recounts how a psychiatrist told her, "Eleanor, you'd be better off with cancer, because cancer is easier to cure than schizophrenia." At her lowest point, she reports, "I'd been diagnosed, drugged and discarded, and was by now so tormented by the voices that I attempted to drill a hole in my head in order to get them out." Ultimately, she rejected standard treatment and came to believe "that my voices were a meaningful response to traumatic life events, particularly childhood events, and as such were not my enemies but a source of insight into solvable emotional problems." Today, Eleanor Longden is a psychologist.

As an alternative to the failed "illness like any other" strategy, the Healing Voices Network aims to destigmatize by normalizing voice hearing. Part of how this can be accomplished is to show that hearing voices is more common than psychiatrists believe it to be, and that depending on how the voices are experienced, the voices may or may not be problematic. There has been a great deal of research examining just how common voice hearing is, and a major review of these studies ("A Comprehensive Review of Auditory Verbal Hallucinations: Lifetime Prevalence, Correlates and Mechanisms in Healthy and Clinical Individuals") was published in *Frontiers in Human Neuroscience* in 2013. The review analyzed multiple studies investigating the existence of voice hearing—termed by psychiatrists as auditory verbal hallucinations (AVH)—in the general population and concluded: "Epidemiological studies have estimated the prevalence of AVH to be between 5 and 28% in the general population." This review also concluded that among those who hear voices, the difference between those who enter medical treatment and those who do not is the "way in which each respective group processes their experiences." Specifically, the more that the voices are experienced negatively, the more likely a person seeks medical help, and the more likely that individual will be diagnosed with a serious mental illness. And so the reviewers recommended discovering ways to help people "interact with their voices in a less distressing manner."

Paralleling the Healing Voices Network is the unusual beliefs movement that, psychologist Rufus May explains, supports individuals with unusual beliefs, as opposed to labeling such beliefs as symptoms of serious mental illness and trying to eradicate these beliefs. This approach is based on the work of Tamasin Knight, a researcher and mental health human rights campaigner and author of *Beyond Belief: Alternative Ways of Working with Delusions, Obsessions and Unusual Experience* (2013). Knight found that individuals are better able to function if they are supported in accepting and coping with their unusual beliefs (including beliefs about spiritual possession, alien abduction, global conspiracy, and FBI persecution). Specifically, Knight found that in contrast to standard psychiatric treatment of labeling such beliefs as symptomatic of schizophrenia and attempting to eradicate them, if these beliefs are initially accepted, then fear is reduced and an individual is more capable of functioning and even rethinking these beliefs. Spinoza may well have seen this movement—in which individuals support one another's unusual beliefs rather than labeling them as delusions—as similar to what goes on in religious communities that take the Bible literally.

When conditions and behaviors are deemed as symptoms of illness, they become more frightening for both the individuals with those behaviors and for others—resulting in greater stigma. To the extent that an individual is frightened by their experience, this increases their likelihood of behaving irrationally and self-destructively, which in turn creates a vicious cycle of escalating fear. Individuals who are already frightened by the strangeness of their own condition and then experience fear about it from others will be even more fearful. For most people, the term "schizophrenia" has only alarming associations, and so if a person is diagnosed with schizophrenia, that person and their family will be frightened.

Spinoza would have seen the irrationality and inherent contradictions of people who try to destigmatize schizophrenia via "illness like any other" anti-stigma campaign but who, at the same time, advocate that schizophrenia is a serious brain disease that cannot be cured but only treated with medication (and who also believe that even when medicated, may still destroy the lives of afflicted individuals and their families). For Spinoza, it would have been obvious that if society wants to create greater tolerance and eliminate stigma, then efforts must be made so that individuals are no longer seen as frightening, and it would have been obvious to him that the more a phenomenon is seen as a normal human variation, the less frightening.

Those who need historic proof of such a proposition, need only look to individuals who were once stigmatized for their homosexual thoughts and behavior. In 1948, the courageous freethinker Gore Vidal published *The City and the Pillar*, the major message being that homosexual and bisexual behaviors are perfectly normal, and that it is society's attitude about human sexuality that is perverse. At the time, Vidal's book's message was so taboo that following its publication, the *New York Times* refused to accept advertising for it. In the 1950s and 1960s, many progressives sanctimoniously fought to transform homosexuality from being viewed as immoral and criminal to being seen as a mental illness, but Vidal knew that the mental illness attribution was just as stigmatizing as the immoral and criminal attributions.

History tells us that viewing homosexual thoughts and behaviors as a frightening condition to be treated did not reduce stigmatization. What has majorly reduced stigmatization of homosexual thoughts and behaviors is society viewing these as a normal human variation.

If we view hearing voices and unusual beliefs as symptoms of a brain disease, this creates stigma; but if viewed as a normal human variation, this reduces stigma. Logically, it follows that if hearing voices and having unusual beliefs, at least the "right ones," are viewed as better than normal, then the voice hearer and the unusual belief holder will be esteemed, perhaps even given prophet status. In the *Theological-Political Treatise*, Spinoza discusses the nature of the voices and beliefs that the prophets reported hearing and believing. Such voices and beliefs would certainly qualify for what are today labeled as auditory hallucinations and delusions. Spinoza points out: "With a real voice God revealed to Moses the laws which he willed to be enjoined on the Hebrews, as is clear from Exodus. . . . This clearly shows that God employed a real voice."

Would Moses have had enough political clout today so that psychiatrists would give him a "Hearing God's Voice Exclusion" and not diagnose him with a serious mental illness? For the 24 percent of Americans who believe that the Bible is the literal word of God, psychiatry grants them a "Biblical Belief Exclusion" and does not diagnose them with schizophrenia based on those beliefs; and somehow even with beliefs that fit psychiatry's definition of bizarre delusions, most of these people manage to function at their jobs and in the rest of their lives.

CHAPTER 10

BRAIN DISEASE

The American Psychiatric Association (APA) website states: "Schizophrenia is a chronic brain disorder that affects less than one percent of the U.S. population." In his popular 2017 book, *No One Cares about Crazy People: My Family and the Heartbreak of Mental Illness*, Ron Powers states: "Schizophrenia is a chronic and incurable disease of the brain."

These views are consensus reality, which presents a problem with respect to hopelessness, despair, and stigma. The idea that schizophrenia is chronic and incurable obviously results in greater hopelessness and despair, and studies (detailed in the previous chapter) show that a belief that serious mental illnesses are brain diseases is associated with greater stigma.

Thus, the question is: Do we need a "noble lie" that schizophrenia is *not* a chronic and incurable brain disease, or is a noble lie unnecessary because both reason and the empirical research reject the idea that schizophrenia is a chronic and incurable brain disease? I'll get back to this, but first, the strange bind that the institution of psychiatry finds itself in with regard to brain defect causality.

For the institution of psychiatry to survive, its general theory that serious mental illnesses such as schizophrenia are brain diseases needs to be accepted. However, if a specific brain abnormality is scientifically connected with a valid disease that can be reliably measured and scientifically treated, then psychiatry as an institution could be in jeopardy. For a brain abnormality, afflicted patients and their family members would want treatment from a medical specialty that has been trained to have a thorough knowledge of the brain's workings. That specialty is not psychiatry. It is neurology.

It might surprise most of the media and the general public, but schizophrenia, schizoaffective disorder, and bipolar disorder are not listed as brain diseases by health and medical institutions outside of psychiatry. The World Health Organization (WHO) website, on its page "What Are Neurological Disorders?", provides a lengthy list of brain disorders (including dementia, epilepsy, multiple sclerosis, neuroinfections, Parkinson's disease, stroke, and traumatic brain injuries). Not listed is schizophrenia, schizoaffective disorder, or bipolar disorder. WHO's 217 page report "Neurological Disorders: Public Health Challenges" lists no psychiatric illnesses. Similarly, the Brain Foundation's website of "A–Z of Brain Disorders" lists over seventy-five brain disorders but does not list schizophrenia, schizoaffective disorder, or bipolar disorder. And the National Institute of Health's website for the National Institute of Neurological Disorders and Stroke has an "All Disorders" list of over four hundred brain disorders that does not include schizophrenia, schizoaffective disorder, or bipolar disorder.

In 2019, in "Push Is On to Reclassify Schizophrenia as a Neurologic Disease," *Medscape Medical News* reported that a "mental health advocacy group [Schizophrenia and Related Disorders Alliance of America] has spearheaded a new initiative to reclassify schizophrenia as a neurologic, rather than a psychiatric, disease. The action is designed to reduce stigma and ultimately obtain more research funding from the Centers for Disease Control and Prevention (CDC)."

The problem for psychiatry is that if schizophrenia is classified as a neurological disease, then most individuals with this condition and their families would want treatment from a neurologist. For an actual brain disease, psychiatrists themselves would not want to be treated by a psychiatrist, as virtually all psychiatrists know that even the most inexperienced neurologist knows more about the brain than the most experienced psychiatrist.

Psychiatry exists because neurology makes no claim to brain-defect knowledge about individuals diagnosed with serious mental illnesses. Psychiatry exists to prescribe psychotropic medications to attempt to control disturbing behaviors. And psychiatry exists to legally coerce noncompliant patients into treatment—an unpleasant chore that neurology and the rest of medicine is happy to hand over to psychiatry (more in Chapter 12: "Coercion").

Psychiatry walks a tightrope. If a specific brain abnormality is scientifically connected with a valid disease that can be reliably measured and scientifically treated, then neurology takes over psychiatry's patients; but psychiatry's existence is in jeopardy if the idea of a general brain disease theory of mental illness is disproven.

The good news for psychiatry is that it has little to fear that its general brain disease theory will be disproven. As previously noted, if any specific brain defect theory is disproven—as is now the case with the rejection of the serotonin imbalance theory of depression and the dopamine imbalance theory of schizophrenia—psychiatry can turn to another brain defect theory. Given the large number of areas of the brain and the variety of chemical/electrical transmissions and circuitry, and given the larger number of combinations of these variables, it would be difficult to exhaust specific brain defect theories. So each time such a theory is scientifically disproven, psychiatry can simply move on to another biological theory. Ironically, to the extent that critics debunk any specific brain defect theory, they are doing the institution of psychiatry a favor by ensuring neurology doesn't take psychiatry's patients.

In scientifically examining the consensus reality that schizophrenia is a brain disease, the first problem is one of validity, and the second problem is reliability. Specifically, if a construct is not clearly a valid one, there is no scientific value in correlating it with other variables such as an area of the brain. And even if the construct is a valid one, if it cannot be reliably assessed, then again there is no scientific value in attempting to correlate it with other variables.

With respect to mental illness, validity means calling something a disease or illness that actually is a disease or illness. In every era, we see human conditions that are so disturbing, frightening, and enraging that they are labeled as either immoral, criminal, or a mental illness—and it is taboo to challenge these labels. The *DSM* criteria for schizophrenia consists of the following: the presence of two or more of the following behaviors with at least one of them being from the first three listed: (1) delusions; (2) hallucinations; (3) disorganized speech; (4) grossly disorganized behavior; and (5) negative symptoms (which include apathy, lack of emotion, poor social functioning, and difficulty following instructions). By 1968, it was obvious to psychologist Don Bannister that *DSM* criteria makes schizophrenia "a concept so diffuse as to be unusable in a scientific context." Specifically, it is possible for one individual to be diagnosed with schizophrenia based on two symptoms that are completely different than the two symptoms of another individual similarly diagnosed. Bannister put it this way: "The two people are now firmly grouped in the same category while not specifically possessing any common characteristics."

When critics of the construct of schizophrenia say that "schizophrenia doesn't exist," they don't mean that people with the above behaviors don't exist. Rather, they mean that the term "schizophrenia" is used as simply a wastebasket for disturbing behaviors, and it is not a scientifically valid construct. Thus it is no surprise for genuine scientists that schizophrenia cannot be reliably diagnosed, that brain structure correlates are not used for its diagnosis, and that standard treatment of it has been so ineffective.

Delusions, especially bizarre delusions, are a hallmark symptom of schizophrenia. However, as previously noted, culture and politics dictate a great deal of what is considered to be a bizarre delusion; and studies show that senior psychiatrists cannot reliably distinguish between bizarre and non-bizarre delusions. With respect to hallucinations, the other hallmark symptom of schizophrenia, as previously noted, many individuals hear voices that they are not troubled by, don't enter medical treatment, and find their voices to be meaningful parts of their lives.

Even if one ignores the problem of validity of the construct of schizophrenia, there is the undeniable scientific problem of the diagnosis of schizophrenia being an unreliable one. Recall that in the *DSM-5* field trials, the agreement between raters was established as poor to weak (with the kappa being .46).

Scientifically speaking, it's the end of the discussion. Without a scientifically valid construct that can be reliably measured, there is no scientific value in looking for brain defect correlates.

The Yiddish words *mensch* (a person with integrity and honor who is kind and considerate) and *schmuck* (a person who is foolish and contemptible) describe people; but we all have somewhat different ideas as to who is a *mensch* and who is a *schmuck*, which results in being unable to reliably measure the conceptualizations of *mensch* and *schmuck*. Thus, scientists cannot conduct scientific research associating *mensch* and *schmuck* with brain abnormalities. As previously noted, psychiatrist Allen Frances concluded that schizophrenia is not a disease, but that the term is useful for purposes of communication. In this sense, schizophrenia is no more useful than *mensch* and *schmuck*. All such terms are useful only in communicating how a person using those labels feels about the person being labeled.

One reason for psychiatry's past bigotry around homosexuality is the previously mentioned "Clinician's Illusion," in which mental health professionals come to conclusions about an entire population based on the troubled individuals from that population clinically seen. For example, prior to the 1960s, homosexuals that psychiatrists saw in their practices routinely sought treatment because they were troubled in some manner by their homosexuality in a society that did not welcome it; but if, in 1948, a psychiatrist would have been friends with the twenty-two-year-old, witty, self-confident, resilient, and unashamedly homosexual Gore Vidal, that psychiatrist may well have had much more dissonance about labeling homosexuality as a mental illness.

If my sole experience of people who had been diagnosed with schizophrenia was purely a clinical one, I too would be bigoted, and vulnerable to accepting the belief that the condition is a chronic and incurable disease. Working in a psychiatric emergency room, I saw many patients who were agitated and acting bizarrely, and who were dragged into the hospital by police and family and then diagnosed with schizophrenia or some other psychosis. There were many repeat customers, and so the idea that this condition is a chronic and incurable condition with periodic remissions appeared to be correct. However, unseen by most mental health professionals is a group of individuals who, though once diagnosed with schizophrenia or some other serious mental illness, at some point reject medication and no longer experience psychotic symptoms, and no longer have any contact with doctors. This is no small group, and I will discuss them in subsequent chapters.

This chapter, so far, might be exasperating for people convinced that schizophrenia is a chronic and incurable brain disease, as they may be frustrated about a lack of examination of the brain studies used by proponents of this idea. I will discuss this research, but I fully recognize that given the validity and reliability problems of the construct of schizophrenia and other conditions termed as serious mental illnesses, scientific thinkers would consider the following discussion a waste of time.

"The Brain in Schizophrenia" on the schizophrenia.com website offers colorful brain images that depict how different the schizophrenic brain is from a normal brain. Scrolling down, there are schizophrenic brain images and research regarding: "Significant Loss of Gray Matter of Brain (up to 25 percent in some areas)"; "Enlarged Ventricles"; and other "Neurological Abnormalities." There are especially compelling brain scan comparisons of "Early and Late Grey Matter Deficits in Schizophrenia," with mostly blue brains (that represent 0 percent deficit) compared to five years later lavender brains (that represent 20 percent deficits).

"The Myth of Schizophrenia as a Progressive Brain Disease" was published in *Schizophrenia Bulletin* in 2013, and lead authored by psychiatrist Robert

Zipursky. While Zipursky reports that brain scans do reveal a modest decrease in certain brain tissue volumes of some individuals diagnosed with schizophrenia, he concludes, "There is no direct evidence for a toxic effect of psychosis on brain tissue, and emerging evidence from human and animal studies suggests that these changes are in part consequent upon antipsychotic medication. Furthermore, there is evidence that cannabis, alcohol, smoking, stress-related hypercortisolemia, and low physical activity also contribute to the changes in cortical and ventricular volumes observed over the course of schizophrenia. Together with the effects of antipsychotic medications, these factors appear to account for the majority of the so-called 'progressive' brain changes."

Zipursky concludes, "Thus, the idea that schizophrenia is a progressive brain disease is not supported by the weight of longitudinal neuroimaging and cognitive studies, and it is not consistent with what is now known about the clinical course of schizophrenia."

A 2020 *JAMA Psychiatry* study on the effects of antipsychotic medications on brain structure showed that antipsychotic drugs are not only associated with brain damage but, by the use of a randomized controlled trial design, researchers were able to posit that the antipsychotic drugs *caused* the observed effect on the brain, concluding: "Unlike uncontrolled studies, our randomized, double-blind placebo-controlled clinical trial design provides potential evidence for causation: olanzapine [an antipsychotic medication whose brand name is Zyprexa] administration may cause a decrease in cortical thickness in humans."

In her 2019 book *Mind Fixers: Psychiatry's Troubled Search for the Biology of Mental Illness*, Anne Harrington concludes: "The infusion of new funds into still more impressive imaging technologies like functional magnetic resonance imaging (fMRI) failed, however, to move knowledge of mental illness forward in the definitive ways that so many psychiatrists had hoped. There were plenty of findings, but they varied across studies and proved hard to replicate and interpret."

"Above all," Harrington concludes, "the new neuroimaging work failed to have any appreciable impact on how the overwhelming majority of patients were diagnosed and treated." Neuroimaging is simply not considered valid and reliable for use in the diagnosis and treatment of schizophrenia, and thus is not covered by insurance companies. It's long been known that the brains of the majority of individuals diagnosed with schizophrenia are normal, and there are individuals who have no symptoms of schizophrenia but who have brain abnormalities that have been associated with schizophrenia.

Paralleling the serotonin deficit chemical imbalance theory of depression that was debunked by the 1990s, the dopamine surplus imbalance theory of schizophrenia has long ago been rejected by researchers and psychiatry. How did both of these chemical imbalance theories come into being? For some depressed individuals, serotonin-enhancing drugs are helpful, and for some individuals diagnosed as psychotic, dopamine-inhibiting drugs reduce symptoms. However, jumping to the conclusion that deficient serotonin was the cause of depression or that excessive dopamine was the cause of schizophrenia is no more logical than concluding that the cause of headaches is an aspirin deficit or that the cause of social inhibition is an alcohol deficit.

The dopamine imbalance theory as the cause of schizophrenia was debunked by the 1980s. In 1982, neuroscientist and physician John Haracz, in the *Schizophrenia Bulletin* ("The Dopamine Hypothesis: An Overview of Studies with Schizophrenic Patients"), examined the evidence from various sources such as dopamine metabolites in cerebrospinal fluid and brain tissues in autopsies. He concluded that with respect to unmedicated patients, "These findings do not support the presence of elevated dopamine turnover in the brains of schizophrenics."

Ironically and sadly, it is the antipsychotic drugs themselves that cause brain defects that are a likely source of relapse and chronicity. By blocking a significant portion of dopamine receptors, antipsychotic drugs create what's been called a "supersensitivity" to dopamine. This was first discovered by McGill University physicians Guy Chouinard and Barry Jones, who published several studies about this phenomenon in the 1980s. Specifically, if patients abruptly stop taking their antipsychotic drugs, owing to this induced supersensitivity, they are especially vulnerable to a dopamine assault on their body, which is highly distressing and can result in a psychotic state.

Thus, while research has not proven that brain or dopamine differences are causal for schizophrenia, research has shown that antipsychotic drugs are associated with brain abnormalities and can cause "supersensitivity" to dopamine, leading to severe distress with an abrupt withdrawal from such drugs resulting in relapse and chronicity.

There has never been a shortage of brain defect theories to explain schizophrenia, and the theory that Ron Powers embraced in his 2017 book is "synaptic pruning." Specifically, he tells us, "In its final development stage, the cortex must actually *lose* some of its prefrontal 'gray matter,' the clusters of nerve-cell bodies that formed transmission routes during infancy and childhood. This 'synaptic pruning' peaks in late adolescence and is necessary for a regrouping of the cortical connections. . . . It is normally during this period that a schizo-phrenia-inducing gene will activate." In the next chapter, I will discuss the possibility of a "schizophrenia-inducing gene."

For individuals such as Powers who assert that "Schizophrenia is a chronic and incurable disease of the brain," their biggest challenge is explaining away long-term outcome studies. Longitudinal follow-up studies on individuals di-agnosed with schizophrenia, Zipursky reports, "have consistently found that about 40% achieve social or functional recovery," which defies the notion that schizophrenia is essentially chronic and incurable.

Powers actually mentions one of the more well-known early outcome studies conducted by psychiatrist Courtenay Harding in 1985, the "Vermont Longitudinal Study of Persons with Severe Mental Illness." Harding followed up on the long-term outcomes of patients who had been diagnosed with schizophrenia, originally under the care of psychiatrist George Brooks, who were discharged from the hospital in the 1950s. Powers states, "The most amazing finding was that 45 percent of all those in Dr. Brooks's program no longer had signs or symptoms of any mental illness three decades later."

In fact, Harding states that "one-half to two-thirds of the sample had achieved considerable improvement or recovered." What Powers neglects to include is that Harding makes clear in her subsequent publications that the common factor shared by the best-outcome group was they had all success-fully weaned themselves off antipsychotic drugs.

So, how does Powers, with his knowledge of the outcome results in the Harding study, continue to maintain that "Schizophrenia is a chronic and in-curable disease of the brain"? He tells us, "It is important here to stress a point I have made before: Harding does not equate 'recovery' with 'cure,' though her criteria for the two conditions often seem nearly identical." Harding's defini-tion of recovery is "reconstituted social and work behaviors, no need for meds, no symptoms." For Powers, Harding's use of the term cure is *nearly* identical with recovery, but for others it is identical.

What would Spinoza make of Powers's refusal to let go of the notion that "schizophrenia is a chronic and incurable disease of the brain" despite his ad-mission of a significant number of individuals in *recovery*, which he agrees is nearly identical to *cure*? Powers reconciliation might well remind Spinoza of Maimonides's reconciliatory theism, which Spinoza "was thoroughly conver-sant with, and hostile to," notes Rebecca Goldstein. Maimonides's reconcilia-tory theism is described by Goldstein as such: "Since scientific truths are true and the Torah, too, is true, there is always a way to interpret the Torah so that it is consistent with science."

Even though Powers is aware of research that shows a large number of individuals once diagnosed with schizophrenia have "reconstituted social and work behaviors, no need for meds, no symptoms," reconciliatory theism dictates that this cannot be called *cure*. Reconciliatory theism here is: Since it must be true that schizophrenia is a chronic and incurable disease of the brain, there is always a way to interpret the facts of outcome studies so that it is consistent with this belief.

Today, the evidence from multiple outcome studies—not just Harding's—that contradicts beliefs about schizophrenia and recovery that are adhered to by Powers is so overwhelming that, in 2013, the National Institute of Mental Health (NIMH) director, Thomas Insel, reconsidered the consensus reality about schizophrenia and revised it. I will discuss his revision in Chapter 12: "Coercion," detailing even more compelling recent outcome studies showing that a significant number of individuals diagnosed as schizophrenic become symptom free, and that the best outcomes are among individuals who stopped taking their antipsychotic medication.

The brain disease conceptualization of serious mental illness, however, is a politically necessary one for psychiatry. Psychiatrists striving to maintain psychiatry's authority recognize that in today's world there is great faith in brain research and thus large funding for it. The 1990s "Decade of the Brain" resulted in bipartisan Democrat-Republican support for brain-research funding. In 2018, the National Institutes of Health (in which the NIMH is one of twenty-seven institutes) announced a "new round of awards for cutting-edge brain research . . . totaling over $220 million . . . to arm researchers with revolutionary tools to fundamentally understand the neural circuits that underlie the healthy and diseased brain."

There is ready money for researchers who study the brain, and since researchers need funding to survive, if funding for biological research is what is most available, researchers will focus more on biological areas than on psychological, social, cultural, and political variables. The current biological focus has become what Thomas Kuhn called "normal science," and it will take "revolutionary science" to go outside of this paradigm, because so doing is a career and financial risk.

The idea that mental illness, especially serious mental illness, is a brain disease is an idea that has large political ramifications. While psychiatry claims to have a "biological-psychological-social" model, the flow of dollars dictates bio-bio-bio research and treatment. Psychological, social, cultural, and political causes of emotional suffering and behavioral disturbance, while not denied by psychiatry, receive significantly less consideration. By paying scant attention to societal and political causes, the societal status quo is maintained, which benefits those at the top of the societal hierarchy.

Just as Spinoza criticized organized religion's view of God but believed strongly in a very different conceptualization of God, psychiatry critics reject the brain disease paradigm but fully recognize the brain's significance—that it is involved in all thoughts, feelings, and physical actions. As I choose words and type them, and as a reader reads and considers them, there are correlate brain activities. Spinoza needed no brain-imaging technology to intuit that the mind and body are not different substances. However, from this, he would not deduce a "mental illness brain disease" conceptualization.

Clergy in Spinoza's era and today declare—based purely on opinion—which thoughts, feelings, and behaviors are sins. And contemporary psychiatry—also based purely on opinion—declares which thoughts, feelings, and behaviors are symptoms of mental illness. While our thoughts, feelings, and behaviors are associated with brain activities, this does not mean we can label these thoughts, feelings, and behaviors as symptoms of illness.

In Spinoza's day, the manner in which God was defined was a hugely important political issue, as Spinoza's definition of God curtailed clergy power. For some thinkers today, Spinoza's equating God with Nature makes him a naturalist or even an atheist who cleverly disguised his atheism by equating God with Nature, however, Spinoza adamantly proclaimed that he did believe in God, and that God and Nature were one—and that most clergy simply had a wrongheaded idea of God.

A major component of Spinoza's mission was rescuing God from ecclesiastic authorities. If alive today, it is quite possible that Spinoza would feel a need to rescue the brain from psychiatry authorities.

CHAPTER 11

GENETICS

The twentieth-century eugenics movement resulted in the mass sterilization of individuals diagnosed with mental illness in the United States, as well as mass murder of this population in Nazi Germany. And so today, the word *eugenics* is taboo, but the theories that inspired the eugenics movement remain consensus reality in U.S. society.

Today, the consensus reality is that schizophrenia is a genetic brain disease triggered by environmental stressors. If such consensus reality is in fact reality, given recent history, if ever there was a case for a noble lie, then it would be about the genetic basis of mental illness. Specifically, history tells us that, should a society again turn to the type of fascism seen in Nazi Germany, we would likely see a return to these now taboo eugenics practices. To the extent that a nation's need for efficiency and productivity trumps toleration for individual differences, then such a nation will seek to eliminate inefficient, nonproductive, and tension-producing people. Thus, if the consensus reality of any society is that schizophrenia is rooted in genetics, and if such a society embraces fascism, history tells us what happens next.

However, perhaps a noble lie is unnecessary. Even if one ignores the previously discussed validity and reliability problems of schizophrenia that make all associations between it and any variables—including genetic ones—to be unscientific, both reason and empirical research cast doubt on the consensus reality of genetic causality.

While the general public may question genetic causality of some mental illnesses, most people do not question the genetic causality of schizophrenia and other serious mental illnesses. People diagnosed with schizophrenia create a great deal of tension, and the greater the tension a person creates, the more serious their mental illness is considered to be; and the more serious a mental illness is considered to be, the more it is seen to be a brain disease rooted in genetics.

The American Psychiatric Association (APA), as noted, tells us that "Schizophrenia is a chronic brain disorder," and while they remind us that "there is no cure for schizophrenia," they tell us that experts are "unraveling the causes of the disease by studying genetics" as well as conducting other research. The APA states: "Researchers believe that a number of genetic and environmental factors contribute to causation, and life stressors may play a role in the disorder's onset and course." Conventional wisdom is that for carriers of schizophrenia genes, similar to carriers of cancer genes, the manifestation of these diseases is triggered by environmental stressors.

Given the catastrophic intolerance created by the eugenics movement, Spinoza, who cared greatly about tolerance, might well today ask several questions: Does reason and science dictate that we must accept the idea of schizophrenia as a genetic disease? Or should we recognize that we are biased to labeling conditions that frighten us as serious mental illnesses, and biased to labeling such conditions as brain diseases with genetic causality? And so should we then recognize our fears and biases, take a deep breath, and examine the actual evidence for genetic causality of schizophrenia?

Spinoza may well start with a simple application of reason to the consequences of a shameful historic event. As previously detailed, the Nazis, first through sterilization and then through mass murder, did their utmost to rid Germany of any individual approximating serious mental illness. The obvious question for a freethinker is: What was the effect of Nazi eugenics policies on the subsequent prevalence and new incidences of schizophrenia in Germany? For some people, it is taboo to ask that question, as they equate it to asking about the results of a sadistic Nazi medical experiment. The reality is that this question has been asked and answered by researchers, but their findings have not been widely publicized, perhaps because they challenge consensus reality.

The Nazis were, if nothing else, obsessively thorough. An estimated 73 percent to 100 percent of individuals diagnosed with schizophrenia living in Nazi Germany were sterilized or killed, according to "Psychiatric Genocide: Nazi Attempts to Eradicate Schizophrenia," published in *Schizophrenia Bulletin* in

2010. As would be expected, owing to Nazi policies, immediately after World War II, in 1945, the prevalence of the population diagnosed with schizophrenia significantly decreased in Germany. However, a generation after the fall of the Third Reich, the incidence of new cases of schizophrenia in Germany was unexpectedly high.

The first postwar study indicating this high new incidence rate of schizophrenia in Germany was done by University of Heidelberg researchers led by Heinz Häfner, who examined this population in Mannheim, Germany, in 1965, twenty years after the last diagnosed schizophrenic had been sterilized or murdered. Häfner reported a schizophrenia incidence rate in Mannhein of 53.6 per 100,000, which was more than twice as high as the U.S. rate of 23.8 per 100,000 at that time.

Later, Häfner examined the incidence of people diagnosed with schizophrenia in Mannheim for each year from 1974 to 1980; and he discovered it ranged from 48 to 67 per 100,000 (averaging 59 per 100,000). Häfner compared this Mannheim average of 59 per 100,000 with eleven studies in the Netherlands, Italy, Denmark, Norway, Iceland, Australia, the United Kingdom, and the United States. In these eleven studies, the average was 24 per 100,000, less than half the schizophrenia incidence rate in Mannheim, Germany.

Thus, Nazi Germany sterilized or murdered 73 percent to 100 percent of individuals diagnosed with schizophrenia, yet the incidence of cases of schizophrenia in Germany from 1974 to 1980 was more than twice the incidence rate of the combined average rate of other Western nations. This one piece of evidence alone should, at the very least, bring into question the consensus reality of genetic causality of schizophrenia.

Most of psychiatry simply ignores this research. Ironically, the author of the *Schizophrenia Bulletin* article in which the above research is detailed is psychiatrist E. Fuller Torrey, who remains a strong advocate of genetic causality. Torrey concludes that the Nazi attempt to eradicate schizophrenia failed because it was "based upon a mistaken belief that schizophrenia was a simple Mendelian inherited disease in which a single gene, or small number of genes, is sufficient to cause the disease . . . the cause of schizophrenia involves dozens, and perhaps hundreds, of genes and includes common variants such as single nucleotide polymorphisms."

However, the logical question is, if 73 percent to 100 percent of individuals manifesting schizophrenia were sterilized or murdered and removed from the gene pool, if genetics has anything to do with the cause of schizophrenia, wouldn't that at least somewhat reduce this population of people manifesting this condition—not increase it?

Similar to Ron Powers's reconciliatory theism (his attempt to reconcile finding of long-term recovery rates for individuals diagnosed with schizophrenia with the belief that the disease is incurable) is Torrey's attempt to reconcile the data from Germany with his beliefs of genetic causality. With respect to genetic causality of schizophrenia, a modern version of reconciliatory theism goes something like this: since the genetic causality of schizophrenia must be true, there is always a way to interpret the data so that it is consistent with the belief in the genetic causality of schizophrenia. As noted, Spinoza was annoyed with reconciliatory theism, as freethinking scientists and philosophers such as himself reconsider beliefs when they discover facts that contradict them.

There is another fact that would have compelled Spinoza or any logical individual to question the consensus reality of genetic causality of schizophrenia: the population of people diagnosed with schizophrenia is increasing despite this group's significantly lower reproductive rates as compared to the general population. The increase in the number of people being diagnosed with insanity, schizophrenia, and serious mental illness has been documented by both Torrey (in his 2002 book *The Invisible Plague: The Rise of Mental Illness from 1750 to the Present*), and journalist and psychiatry critic Robert Whitaker (in his 2010 book *Anatomy of an Epidemic*). Coupled with this "plague" or "epidemic" are a large number of studies that confirm the commonsense expectation of a markedly lower reproductive rate in people diagnosed with schizophrenia as compared with the general population. Reported in *Behavioral and Brain Sciences* in 2006, the majority of fourteen studies on individuals diagnosed with schizophrenia and psychosis show that reproductive rates were less than 50 percent of the general population. This lower reproductive rate should ultimately decrease, not increase, the rate of schizophrenia if schizophrenia is a genetic disease.

Given the facts, a rational society would be asking the following questions about the idea that schizophrenia is genetically caused: Should we accept genetic causality as consensus reality when Nazi Germany systematically sterilized and murdered most of its diagnosed schizophrenics, yet a generation later this population was higher than other Western societies? And if the population of those diagnosed with schizophrenia is increasing despite this group's significantly lower reproductive rates as compared to the general population, what does that say about genetic causality?

This chapter, so far, is likely exasperating for genetic advocates who may well be frustrated that there has been, so far, no mention of the large body of research, including twin studies, that supports their view that schizophrenia is genetically based.

One of the earliest U.S. attempts to prove the genetic basis for serious mental illness was by psychiatrist Aaron Rosanoff in 1911. He reviewed the records of seventy-two patients who had been classified as insane, examining 1,097 of their relatives. He calculated that, according to Mendelian laws of genetics, 359 of the 1,097 relatives should be classified as seriously mentally ill, but he found that only forty-three of the 1,097 had ever been hospitalized for mental illness. Again, reconciliatory theism rescues the genetic theory. Rosanoff concluded that he had defined mental illness too narrowly for the relatives, and that just because they weren't hospitalized, they could still be considered mentally ill if they were, for example, "worried over nothing" or acted like "religious cranks." By expanding his criteria, his number of relatives viewed as mentally ill increased from 43 to 351.

In Germany, influential promoters of the theory that schizophrenia is a genetic disease included psychiatrists Ernst Rüdin, who joined the Nazi Party in 1937, and Franz Kallmann, a student of Rüdin and a pioneer of twin study research. Kallmann believed that it was necessary to not only sterilize schizophrenics themselves but also their healthy relatives because the gene for schizophrenia was a recessive gene that may not manifest itself (even some Nazi geneticists argued against this, pointing out that there were simply too many healthy relatives of schizophrenics). In 1936, Kallmann, because of his Jewish heritage, emigrated from Germany to the United States, where he continued his twin research.

In twin studies, *heritability* is a statistic found by comparing identical twins (monozygotic twins) to same-sex, non-identical/fraternal twins (dizygotic twins) with the intent of teasing out environmental influences. However, one scientific problem is that it is incorrect to assume that the environmental influence on identical twins and fraternal twins is equivalent, and so it is incorrect to assume that differences between them can thus be attributable to genetics. Specifically, the 1984 book *Not in Our Genes*, authored by evolutionary geneticist R.C. Lewontin, neurobiologist Steven Rose, and psychologist Leon Kamin, reports how identical twins—as compared to same-sex fraternal twins—are often treated more similarly by parents, peers, and teachers; have more similar friends; do more similar things; and spend more time with one another. In one study, 40 percent of identical twins reported that they usually studied together, compared to only 15 percent of fraternal same-sex twins.

What about research on twins reared apart? There are few studies of this kind. Much of what the general public has heard about twins raised apart have been anecdotal stories, and as psychologist Jay Joseph points out in his 2003 book *The Gene Illusion*, "Most pairs come to the attention of researchers and journalists *because* of their similarities. . . . Stories of similar reared-apart twins are news because they are interesting and compelling; stories about dissimilar twins are not."

It is difficult to find twins reared apart (TRA), and so it is especially difficult to find a sufficient number of TRA individuals diagnosed as mentally ill to study. In his 2015 book, *The Trouble with Twin Studies*, Jay Joseph details scientific problems with TRA studies. He points out that many of these pairs of twins in TRA studies are not exactly reared apart. All these twins share the same prenatal (intrauterine) environment, and many twin pairs experienced late separation, as they were reared together in the same home for several years. In twin researcher James Shields's 1962 study, some twins classified as TRA were separated as late as age nine or separated for only five years during childhood; and one of Shields's pair of twins classified as TRA was reported as "living next door to each other, brought up by different aunts."

The most well-known TRA study is the 1990 "Sources of Human Psychological Differences: The Minnesota Study of Twins Reared Apart" (MISTRA), lead authored by Thomas Bouchard. Joseph notes that Bouchard examined IQ, personality variables, and social attitudes; but that apart from anecdotal case reports, there were too few pairs with serious mental illness for conclusions specific to mental illness. What's most troubling about Bouchard's study is that, while it is standard in science for other scientists to be able to re-examine the original data of a study, Joseph points out, "In direct contrast, the MISTRA researchers have kept their original data secret, thereby rendering it inaccessible."

Behavioral geneticist Kenneth Kendler is one of psychiatry's most revered researchers (psychiatrist Peter Kramer, who helped popularize Prozac in his 1993 book *Listening to Prozac*, described Kendler as a "genius"). However, Kendler, in a July 2005 *American Journal of Psychiatry* article that reviewed the evidence for "gene action in psychiatric disorders," concluded: "Although we may wish it to be true, we do not have and are not likely to ever discover 'genes for' psychiatric illness."

Kendler's prediction has proven to be true. A 2020 study in *Schizophrenia Bulletin* reported that no genetic variants were found to predict schizophrenia, as no significant difference was found in the genetic variance of people with a diagnosis of schizophrenia and people without such a diagnosis. Similarly, examining mood disorders, a 2021 investigation published in the *Journal of Affective Disorders* (that included 5,872 cases and 43,862 controls, and examined 22,028 genes), reported that the study "fails to identify genes influencing the probability of developing a mood disorder" and "no gene or gene set produced a statistically significant result."

Thus, a noble lie appears to be unnecessary. The truth is that there is a great deal of evidence that challenges the idea that schizophrenia (or any other so-called serious mental illness) is a genetically caused illness.

The evidence that has been used to claim schizophrenia as a genetic disease is replete with scientific methodological problems. The hunt for a genetic cause has the same underlying scientific problems of validity and reliability as does the hunt for brain defects. Specifically, as previously detailed, even some high-level members of psychiatry see schizophrenia as a construct and not a disease; and some scientists view schizophrenia as simply a wastebasket category for disturbing behaviors rather than a scientifically valid construct. Moreover, research shows there is weak to poor reliability in assessing whether or not an individual has schizophrenia. To repeat, if a condition is not clearly a valid disease that can be reliably diagnosed, there is no scientific value in associating it with any variable, including genetic ones.

Furthermore, even if one ignores these validity and reliability methodological issues, as has been described, there are multiple inconsistencies and contradictions in the evidence routinely used for claims that schizophrenia and other serious mental illnesses are genetically caused.

Thus, given the catastrophic consequences of the twentieth-century eugenics movement, this hunt for genetic causality is not simply politically dangerous but foolhardy in a scientific sense. The good news is that noble lies are unnecessary. All that is necessary is the truth.

CHAPTER 12

COERCION

Coercion is defined as the attempt to persuade or control by use of force or by the threat of force. Coercion can be exercised through a variety of methods that include censorship, banishment, financial deprivations, incarceration, and execution.

The use of coercion is probably the most divisive issue among advocates and critics of psychiatry. Both advocates and critics agree that a significant role of psychiatry is a coercive one, but they disagree sharply about the value and impact of coercion.

The issue of coercion in society was of supreme importance to Spinoza. Both of his parents descended from *converso* families in Portugal, in which their Jewish ancestors had been forcibly converted to Catholicism and coerced to ostensibly practice Catholicism. Bento's ancestors privately maintained their Judaism, which they could only openly practice again upon their arrival in the Dutch Republic.

It was obvious to Bento that it is unwise for societal authorities—be they government, religious, or private—to attempt to suppress freedom of thought and expression. Spinoza knew that while coercive authorities might get many individuals to publicly comply, people will privately continue to think and express themselves freely, and at the same time, lose respect for such authorities and acquire resentment for them. Spinoza asserted that: "But it is far beyond the bounds of possibility that all men can be made to speak to order. On the contrary, the greater the effort to deprive them of freedom of speech, the more obstinately do they resist."

Early in his life, Spinoza recognized that civil authorities were not the only threat to freedom of thought and expression, as he experienced banishment from ecclesiastic authorities in his Jewish community. He understood, as Steven Nadler explains, "Ecclesiastic authorities of various persuasions and rogue sectarian groups will strive to stifle the expression of ideas they deem offensive and inconsistent with their political, religious and moral beliefs, not to mention those that they believe pose a challenge to their power and prerogatives. They will attempt, either directly or through manipulating the secular authorities, to suppress oral or written expression of unorthodox or offensive opinions."

Spinoza had respect for the religious moral teachings of justice and generosity, but he had contempt for the use of coercion by ecclesiastic authorities. He saw much of religious ceremonial law and rituals as not contributing to true morality but merely as tools for ecclesiastic authorities to control congregants.

For Spinoza, all people are guided by self-interest, but only those who are also guided by reason conclude that it is in their self-interest to act with justice and charity toward other people, so as to create a more cooperative community. He was a realist who recognized that, while all people are guided by self-interest, most people's ideas of self-interest are not guided by reason, and thus given such irrationality, they act in unjust and uncaring ways that create unsafe and hostile environments.

Truly rational people, for Spinoza, do not need laws to coerce them to act justly. He said, "Now if men were so constituted by nature as to desire nothing but what is prescribed by true reason, society would stand in no need of any laws." But from his experience, most people don't act rationally, and so laws are necessary, and a civil authority to enforce those laws is necessary. Spinoza concluded that, unfortunately, those people unguided by reason need to be afraid of negative consequences for disobedience to laws. However, the critical question for him was: what type of government creates the most just laws and just enforcement and thus creates the least resentment? His radical solution was democracy.

The use of coercion in psychiatry, as noted, is probably the most divisive issue among advocates and critics. Today, there are multiple ways that coercion is applied to individuals who have been diagnosed with serious mental illnesses such as schizophrenia and bipolar disorder. Through the use of force, punishment, or the threat of punishment, such individuals are coerced to comply with psychiatric treatment.

The American Psychiatric Association (APA) guide on "Ethics in Practice" states: "Involuntary psychiatric treatment is on occasion needed to ensure the safety of the public or the care and protection of patients. . . . Enforced treatment contains an inherent ethical tension among several values: respecting the individual's autonomy, providing care for that individual, and protecting the community. To exercise this coercion while balancing these competing values calls for great sensitivity on the part of the psychiatrist."

While some psychiatrists prefer to use the term *involuntary*, others explicitly use the term *coercion*. Psychiatrist Steven Sharfstein, a former APA president (2005–2006), wrote two articles about "caring coercion" that were published in 2005: "Individual Rights Must Be Balanced with 'Caring Coercion'" and "The Case for Caring Coercion."

Conventional wisdom in U.S. society is that the seriously mentally ill need medication for their own good and for the safety of society, and so that sometimes involuntary interventions are required to stop the downward spiral that results in the mentally ill being a danger to themselves and others. Coercive treatment advocates believe that those people in denial that they have a serious mental illness such as schizophrenia have an additional illness of *anosognosia*, a blockage of insight into self; and because of their anosognosia, they cannot voluntarily do what's best for themselves.

The use of coercion on people diagnosed with serious mental illness has steadily increased in society, and there are multiple coercive methods to compel individuals to comply with psychiatric treatment.

The least controversial coercion—though not uncontroversial—is forced involuntary hospitalization for individuals who have been assessed to be mentally ill and judged to be an imminent danger to themselves or others. More controversially, coercions are increasingly used on individuals diagnosed with serious mental illness who have been, in the past, psychiatrically hospitalized and have a history of noncompliance with medication but who are not judged to be in imminent danger to themselves or others—but whose family members and psychiatrists fear that they will become dangerous if they refuse to comply with psychiatric treatment. There are a variety of coercions used to force such people to comply with taking antipsychotic medications, with all such coercions using the threat of punishment if medications are refused.

Judges can order patients who have been diagnosed with mental illness and who have been arrested for minor offenses to comply with psychiatric treatment or else face jail. And through the use of outpatient commitment statutes, individuals can be ordered to comply with psychiatric medication treatments even if they have committed no legal offense and are not judged to be in imminent danger to themselves or others. Involuntary outpatient commitment ordered by a judge with the threat of involuntary hospitalization for noncompliance with their treatment orders is commonly referred to as "Assisted Outpatient Treatment" (AOT). For patients already hospitalized, the threat of continued hospitalization for medication noncompliance is used as a threat. In addition to the punishments of jail and hospitalization, the withholding of housing, job training, and other services is used as leverage to coerce medication compliance.

The rationalist Spinoza would immediately recognize the inherent contradictions and hypocrisies regarding the message society is sending about (1) hospitalization and (2) stigmatization.

The use of psychiatric hospitalization as a means of control and as a threat for medication noncompliance is an acknowledgment by psychiatry and society that psychiatric hospitalization is experienced as significantly "restrictive" and a punishment to be avoided. Once hospitalization is used as punishment to coerce compliance, it becomes Orwellian to consider it as "treatment." Society could more straightforwardly use jails and prisons—that are called *jails* and *prisons*—as threats for medication noncompliance; however, this would be more difficult to politically accomplish, as it would be less acceptable for society to use jails and prisons as punishment threats for people who have broken no laws.

Both advocates and critics of coercion to force treatment compliance agree on the following: what has persuaded the public to create these coercive laws has far less to do with caring about the patient than fear of violence committed by individuals with mental illness. This was made clear by one of the leading advocates for the use of coercion, D.J. Jaffe.

In Jaffe's "Remarks on Assisted Outpatient Treatment (AOT)," presented to the annual conference of the National Alliance for the Mentally Ill in 1999, he stated: "Laws change for a single reason, in reaction to highly publicized incidents of violence. People care about public safety. I am not saying it is right, I am saying this is the reality. . . . So if you're changing your laws in your state, you have to understand that. . . . It means that you have to take the debate out of the mental health arena and put it in the criminal justice/public safety arena."

By using the fear of violence as a tactic to procure the passage of coercive outpatient treatment laws, one is attempting to persuade the public that people diagnosed with serious mental illness are dangerous to society. Individuals such as Jaffe and organizations such as NAMI who use the fear of violence to get these laws passed but who also claim their major mission is to destigmatize the mentally ill are obviously working at cross purposes. It doesn't take Spinoza's brilliant rational mind to recognize that there is nothing more stigmatizing for those diagnosed with mental illness than to be viewed as potentially violent.

Another contradiction for promoters of coercive treatment is that, while they advocate for making psychiatric treatment more accessible, the potential for coercion once one enters treatment inhibits individuals from seeking help. An individual struggling with anxiety or depression might be afraid to seek treatment out of fear of being identified as needing coercive treatment. Such a fear is especially widespread among individuals who have already experienced coercive treatment or known others who have.

Society wants psychiatry to have a dual role: (1) policing certain frightening behaviors with the power of coercion, and (2) doctor/healer. However, the policing role undermines the doctor role. If individuals are fearful of expressing something that can be used to coerce them, they are going to be far more careful about what they express, and they are not going to be fully candid, which undermines therapy. Psychiatry, however, accepts this dual role because it is essential to its survival as an institution (more on this later).

Beyond these hypocrisies and contradictions with respect to how coercion creates stigma and undermines treatment, there is the empirical issue of whether or not coercive treatment actually helps individuals and reduces violence in society.

The most well-known advocate for AOT court-ordered treatment to ensure compliance is psychiatrist E. Fuller Torrey who, earlier in his career, during a more anti-authoritarian era, was an admirer of Thomas Szasz and, like him, was highly critical of psychiatric coercion. In Torrey's 1974 book *The Death of Psychiatry*, he stated, "As Szasz points out, a drunken driver is infinitely more dangerous to others than is a 'paranoid schizophrenic,' yet we allow most of the former to remain free while we incarcerate most of the latter." In that book, Torrey informs us that studies of psychiatric patients following their discharge "have almost unanimously shown a lower arrest rate than that of the general population," and he details two such studies. However, in 1998, Torrey created the Treatment Advocacy Center to lobby for laws—most famously Kendra's Law in New York (and similar such laws in most other states)—that "establish clear consequences for noncompliance," specifically noncompliance with respect to antipsychotic medication.

Torrey reports that research shows that applying AOT to the seriously mentally ill has been successful in reducing arrests, psychiatric hospitalizations, homelessness, and harmful behaviors. However, AOT includes not only coerced medication compliance but also a package of what is termed "enhanced services," which includes better access to housing and vocational services; and the research that Torrey claims supports the use of coercive treatment doesn't parse out the effects of coerced medication compliance versus these enhanced services. It may well be that access to better housing explains why there is decreased psychiatric hospitalization and homelessness. Torrey uses a *Psychiatric Services* 2010 study to support his assertion that AOT results in people "4X less likely to perpetuate serious violence." However Torrey neglects to mention that the authors of this *Psychiatric Services* study concluded that "these findings should be interpreted in terms of the overall impact of outpatient commitment, not of legal coercion per se. As such, the results do not support the expansion of coercion in psychiatric treatment."

A crucial question with respect to coerced antipsychotic medication is whether or not there is evidence of long-term effectiveness of such medications. In the acute phase of disruptive psychotic behaviors, tranquilizing antipsychotic drugs can be effective in reducing disturbing behaviors; but given how much resentment forced drug treatments cause, it is especially imperative that the evidence clearly shows that antipsychotic medication has long-term value.

However, there is a great deal of research that challenges the value of these medications for long-term use. And in 2013, based on two recent long-term studies, the director of the National Institute of Mental Health was convinced that for some people diagnosed with schizophrenia, "remaining on medication long-term might impede a full return to wellness." Before examining those two studies that convinced the NIMH director to rethink this issue, let's look at earlier studies that should have raised red flags.

In 1969, the World Health Organization (WHO) began tracking outcomes of patients diagnosed with schizophrenia in various countries, including three so-called "developing countries" (India, Nigeria, and Columbia) as well as the United States and five other "developed countries." The WHO reported that at the end of five years, the poorer developing countries had "considerably better course and outcome," as patients were more likely to be asymptomatic and have better social outcomes. Then in 1978, the WHO, looking at patients suffering a first episode of schizophrenia—diagnosed by Western criteria—in both developing and developed countries, found that after two years in developed wealthier countries, 59 percent became chronically ill, while in developing poorer countries, only one-third became chronically ill; only 16 percent of the patients in poorer countries had been maintained on antipsychotic drugs while 61 percent of the patients in wealthier countries had been so maintained. And in 1997, WHO researchers interviewed the patients from both of these previous studies, and found that patients from the poorer countries continued to do better.

From the WHO studies, it could not be clearly ascertained whether it was the absence of antipsychotic drugs or the presence of other social variables that improved outcome in the developing world. Journalist Ethan Watters, author of *Crazy Like Us* (2010), suggests that a major reason for the superior outcome in poorer developing countries was the absence of stigma for unusual behaviors, an absence that kept individuals within community. In general, the WHO studies raised a red flag about both drug use and stigma in developed wealthier countries.

Another study that challenged the value of long-term use of medication was the previously mentioned long-term outcome study on individuals diagnosed with schizophrenia that was conducted by psychiatrist Courtenay Harding in 1985. She showed that "one-half to two-thirds of the sample had achieved considerable improvement or recovered," and that the common factor shared by the best-outcome group was they had all successfully weaned themselves from antipsychotic drugs.

However, it was not the WHO or Harding studies that convinced the NIMH director to rethink the value of long-term use of antipsychotic medication, but two more recent studies.

Researcher Martin Harrow, in a NIMH-funded study, followed the long-term outcomes of patients diagnosed with schizophrenia. In 2007, he reported that at the end of fifteen years, among those patients who had stopped taking antipsychotic drugs, 40 percent were judged to be in recovery; this compared to only 5 percent in recovery among those who had remained on antipsychotic drugs. Those off medication fared better on every measure (including the presence of psychotic symptoms, relapse rate, anxiety level, cognitive functioning, and employment). At the 2008 APA annual meeting, Harrow reported: "I conclude that patients with schizophrenia not on antipsychotic medication for a long period of time have significantly better global functioning than those on antipsychotics." Harrow continued to follow up these individuals, and at twenty years, he reported: "While antipsychotics reduce or eliminate flagrant psychosis for most patients with schizophrenia at acute hospitalizations, four years later and continually until the twenty-year follow-ups, patients with schizophrenia not prescribed antipsychotics had significantly better work functioning. . . . The longitudinal data raise questions about prolonged treatment of schizophrenia with antipsychotic medications."

Given the consensus reality that medication compliance is necessary to prevent relapse, the major institutions of psychiatry initially simply ignored the Harrow study; and when challenged about it, dismissed it because it was not a randomized control trial (RCT). However, in a study published in 2013 in *JAMA Psychiatry*, RCT was applied to this issue by researcher Lex Wunderink. Specifically, 128 patients who had been assessed to have recovered from their first psychotic episode were randomly assigned either to standard medication treatment or to a program in which they were tapered off the drugs. At the end of seven years, the recovery rate for those who had been tapered off the antipsychotic drugs was 40 percent versus 18 percent recovery for those who remained on them.

Citing the Harrow and Wunderink studies, NIMH director Thomas Insel acknowledged in 2013: "It appears that what we currently call 'schizophrenia' may comprise disorders with quite different trajectories. For some people, remaining on medication long-term might impede a full return to wellness. For others, discontinuing medication can be disastrous."

It would not surprise Spinoza, however, that what most persuades the media and lawmakers is not science, reason, or NIMH directors. It is fear and anecdotal accounts.

AOT coercive treatment advocate Ron Powers, in his book *No One Cares About Crazy People*, offers a compelling account of how both of his sons were diagnosed with schizophrenia, but that one rejected treatment and died by suicide, while his other son was forced to comply with treatment and remains alive. Powers tell us that his youngest son, Kevin, "was prescribed oral antipsychotics by a series of psychiatrists over three years; he loathed taking them yet pretended not to; he went off them; eventually hiding the ones he assured us he'd taken; and destroyed himself in the midst of a psychotic break."

Powers tells us that his older son Dean, "some years and some resistance later, accepted the shrewdly constructed arguments of his psychiatrist, agreed to 'depot' injections of Haldol [long-acting injections of an antipsychotic drug used to counter noncompliance], and has lived, and has improved." For Powers, his youngest son was able to resist his antipsychotic medication and died of suicide, while his oldest son was unable to offer such resistance and remains alive.

The media and lawmakers hear many such emotionally-charged anecdotal accounts to support AOT coercive treatment, however, there are also emotionally charged accounts offered by critics of AOT. One such account is from attorney Elizabeth Rich about her son, Andrew, reported by Robert Whitaker and Michael Simonson in 2019. After Andrew Rich was found in a highly disturbed state—reported by 911 caller as a "naked man in the parking lot (of a golf course) howling like a wolf"—he was tased and handcuffed by police, and charged with disorderly conduct as well as resisting an officer. Rather than being tried on criminal charges, he was committed to a psychiatric hospital. After his hospitalization, Rich was discharged on an outpatient order that required him to get regular injections of an antipsychotic drug, and that order was later extended. At each extension hearing, his psychiatrist testified that Rich wouldn't admit that he was mentally ill in need of medication and thus court-mandated treatment was necessary. Whitaker and Simonson report, "After the last hearing, Rich's despair about being under state control deepened, and he began talking about suicide . . . [One month after the last hearing] he was found dead from an overdose of morphine and codeine." Andrew Rich's mother Elizabeth concluded, "Looking back on it, I made so many mistakes in how much faith I had in the mental health system to help my son."

Spinoza fully recognized how emotional-charged anecdotes are, for most people, more persuasive than reason and science. However, he would consider anecdotal evidence or random experience as "knowledge of the first kind," which results in inadequate ideas—confused and vague conceptualizations that are partially or completely false. He trusted reason.

Spinoza would deduce that if society tells someone that they have schizophrenia and that it cannot be cured but only treated with medications that have significant adverse effects—including weight gain, diabetes, constipation, drowsiness, sexual dysfunction, and tardive dyskinesia (uncontrollable movement of the tongue, lips, face, hands)—many such individuals will resist their diagnosis and treatment; and their noncompliance will frighten a society that believes these individuals without medication are a threat to them. It would also be clear to Spinoza that if society has been persuaded to enact AOT coercive treatment laws from the fear that untreated schizophrenics can become violent, then the stigmatization of individuals diagnosed with schizophrenia will be exacerbated, and such stigmatization will be damaging for their recovery.

The rationalist Spinoza would be interested in the deductions about the use of coercion in psychiatry by David Cohen, a professor of social welfare, in his 2014 *Mad in America* article, "It's the Coercion, Stupid!"

Cohen makes the case that coercion is the essential component of psychiatry, "The coercive element of psychiatry has persisted despite all changes in treatments. . . . This is the invariant part of psychiatry." While society has either mocked psychiatry or has had mixed feelings about its diagnoses and treatments, Cohen concludes that what society does appreciate about psychiatry is its coercive function, "That families and other people in crisis can call upon the police to restrain someone acting in a seemingly incomprehensible or dangerous way and have that person taken by force to a place run by psychiatrists is truly where psychiatry as a profession distinguishes itself."

What Spinoza would find most compelling about Cohen's analysis is that Cohen comes to similar conclusions about psychiatry that Spinoza came to as to why organized religion persists and maintains authority. For Cohen, because society so values psychiatric coercion, "society gives psychiatric theories a free pass. These theories never need to pass any rigorously devised tests (as we expect other important scientific theories to pass), they only need to be asserted." For Cohen, "knowledge is not supporting the power. The power to coerce is what excuses the lack of valid knowledge."

Spinoza knew that the major function of organized religion was to coerce obedience. And so he understood that it did not matter how well he made the case that the Bible was not sacred (not revealed by God and instead had many different human authors, and was full of factual inconsistencies that only humans could make). Spinoza knew that the sacredness of the Bible was so critical to the authority of clergy as a tool to coerce obedience, the Bible would get what Cohen calls a "free pass."

Spinoza would not be unequivocally opposed to the use of force and surveillance to keep individuals who are overwhelmed by their passions from doing harm to themselves or others. Recall that after the de Witt brothers were barbarically murdered, Spinoza had to be restrained from placing a placard near the site of the massacre reading *ultimi barbarorum*. He was held back by his landlord, Hendrik van der Spyck, who locked Spinoza in the house to prevent him from also getting slaughtered by the mob.

However, critical to Van der Spyck's intervention was Spinoza's relationship with him. "Spinoza seems to have had a friendly, even intimate, relationship with Van der Spyck's family," reports Nadler who adds, "They had many good things to say about their lodger to Colerus." Thus, Spinoza was restrained by a person whom he knew personally and believed cared about him. Nadler speculates that Van der Spyck might have also been concerned by the repercussions to himself and family if Spinoza had placed the placard; however, Spinoza would not have resented such a motivation, as he would not have wanted his actions to cause the Van der Spyck family any harm.

While Spinoza would not have opposed restraint and surveillance to keep someone overwhelmed by their passions from acting self-destructively or destructively to others, what would be critical for him is whether or not the restraint and surveillance resulted in resentment. Critical to whether resentment results from coercion is whether or not the coerced individuals have experienced caring from those controlling them; and critical to the experience of caring is the nature of the relationship between parties, including whether or not there is a history of mutual respect and affection.

In general, Spinoza fully recognized that since people behave irrationally, laws are required and a civil authority is necessary to enforce those laws. He believed that democracy, in which the governed have given consent to those who govern, creates the least amount of resentment. Given Spinoza's rational conclusion that democracy creates the least amount of resentment, he might well be interested in a more democratic alternative approach for people who have had psychotic reactions. One such approach is called Open Dialogue, developed in Western Lapland, Finland in the 1980s (more later about Open Dialogue in Chapter 15: "Pals and Peers").

In a rational society, the coercion debate would not be a "pro and con" one, but a "who, how, and why" one. Even among self-identified anarchists (which Spinoza was not) who advocate for a stateless society with mutual aid, there are those who accept the necessity for coercion in certain circumstances. Perhaps the most famous contemporary self-identified anarchist is linguist and political activist Noam Chomsky, who gives an example of justified coercion: "When you stop your five-year-old kid from trying to cross the street, that's an authoritarian situation: it's got to be justified. Well, in that case, I think you *can* give a justification."

There are other instances in history of famous individuals who were re-strained and surveilled when in irrational emotional states but who did not later resent such controls. In *Lincoln's Melancholy* (2005), his biographer Joshua Wolf Shenk reports that Abraham Lincoln experienced two major depressive breakdowns, which included suicidal statements that frightened friends enough that they formed a suicide watch. Shenk reports that, in the summer of 1835, "After several weeks of worrisome behavior—talking about suicide, wandering alone in the woods with his gun—an older couple in the area took him into their home." Lincoln's caretakers were Bowling Green, a second father to him, and his wife Nancy, who both watched over Lincoln for one to two weeks.

Whenever there is restraint and surveillance, for there not to be resent-ment, those being controlled must experience caring. That is what Lincoln felt from Bowling and Nancy Green. Shenk reports that seven years later, in 1842, at Bowling Green's funeral, when Lincoln tried to deliver his eulogy, he so sobbed that he could not proceed. We also can surmise that Spinoza ex-perienced Hendrik van der Spyck's locking him in the house to prevent him from getting torn to pieces by a mob as caring. Near the end of his life, Bento entrusted Van der Spyck to send his prized manuscripts, which included the *Ethics*, to Spinoza's publisher following his death.

In a rational and sane society, the goal should always be to eliminate re-sentment. Resentment results from the experience of uncaring control. Involuntary coercive psychiatric treatment routinely creates resentment for those so controlled because it is not routinely experienced as caring. Many individuals who experience coercive treatment believe that they are coerced only to meet others' control needs. Such individuals often believe that they posed no threat to themselves or others and that authorities over-reacted; and even if they recognize later that they were a threat to themselves and others, if they judge the motivation of authorities who coerced them to not be a caring one, there will be resentment. That would be obvious to Spinoza.

CHAPTER 13

MADNESS AND *SCIENTIA INTUITIVA*

The terms *mental illness* and *psychosis* were not used in Spinoza's time, however, in the *Ethics*, Spinoza discusses *madness*, including hallucinations. He did not romanticize madness, as he saw nothing romantic about the irrational, however, he saw hypocrisies in the determination of madness. Specifically, he observed: "For sometimes we see men so affected by one object that they think they have it before them even though it is not present. When this happens to a man who is not asleep, we say he is delirious or mad. . . . But when the miser thinks of nothing but gain or money, and the ambitious man of honor, they are not reckoned as mad. . . . But in reality avarice, ambition, lust etc. are kinds of madness, although they are not accounted as diseases."

Spinoza's goal was not to explain madness but to provide a rational path to freedom and happiness, however, he provides concepts that are helpful to understanding madness. These concepts include: his recognition that a third kind of knowledge, intuitive knowledge (*scientia intuitiva*), is superior to reason; his belief in monism as opposed to dualism; and his recognition of the force by which each thing perseveres in existing (*conatus*). Before explaining the relevance of these concepts to madness, some thoughts on why it is so difficult to understand madness.

One way to gain perspective about just how difficult it is to comprehend all aspects of our humanity—including what is now called serious mental illness and psychosis—is to consider our earliest experiences with art. Were there some musicians and painters whom you immediately connected with? However, do you also recall some music and paintings that other people resonated with and you did not, but that which later in life, you were able to acquire a genuine appreciation for?

When I was a teenager, musicians and painters that were overtly emotional, political, and heroic were most easily accessible for me. For example, even when very young, I could resonate with some of Beethoven's symphonies, though I was not able to connect with much of classical music. As a teenager, folk music was extremely accessible for me, as it spoke directly to my emotions and soothed them, and validated my sense of injustice in the world. Among painters, it was easy at an early age to connect with the overtly emotional Vincent van Gogh and Edvard Munch, and it was easy to understand overtly political paintings such as Pablo Picasso's *Guernica*. But I could not connect with much of abstract modern art and, similarly, most of jazz.

With each new understanding of reality, I could connect with that which I could not before. As a teenager, I thought that I had completely grasped oppression and freedom, but it was only a partial understanding, and that is one reason why I could not completely understand Spinoza, whose grasp of freedom was far deeper than mine. So too did jazz musician Miles Davis and abstract expressionist Jackson Pollock have a deeper understanding of freedom, spontaneity, and other aspects of the human condition than I had—and so only later were they accessible for me.

It is difficult to comprehend what is not readily accessible in art and human nature. Some of us simply stop thinking about what we cannot immediately understand. In contrast, some of us recognize that we need to grasp a thing or two more before we can connect with what we now cannot, and we accept that our mind might simply not be ripe for certain understandings.

As a teenager and young adult, I could easily resonate with many conditions that psychiatry calls mental illnesses but which seemed perfectly normal to me because my friends and I had experienced them and understood why. It was obvious to us that if one is forced to attend school and pay attention to that which did not interest us, then it was perfectly normal to become oppositionally defiant and inattentive. We thought that it made perfect sense to be anxious and depressed in a world where most adults appeared miserable at jobs that they only remained at for a paycheck, and in a world where politicians routinely lied about reasons for war.

I had the *DSM* symptoms that now qualify a person for oppositional defiant disorder, generalized anxiety disorder, and depression. I never had the symptoms for what psychiatrists call psychosis and schizophrenia, and so these states were not immediately understandable to me. However, because psychiatry had lost credibility with me in its other mental illness declarations, I trusted my reason and intuition that there was a good chance that psychiatry's ideas about psychosis and schizophrenia were wrong as well.

The human conditions that we have experienced and are most accepting of—and possibly even proud of—are those conditions that we are likely to consider as normal aspects of human nature, not defects or diseases. So, if we have defied authorities, refused to comply with their requests and rules, argued with them, been angry with them and lost our temper, been annoyed by them and deliberately annoyed them, and even been vindictive with them—and we are proud of our defiance—we see our reactions not as symptoms of a mental illness but as a normal rebellion against a perceived illegitimate authority. In contrast, individuals who have never behaved in this manner and who have only experienced the tension caused by individuals who have so behaved, see these reactions as symptoms of the current *DSM* mental illness called oppositional defiant disorder.

For many of us, it is easier to reconsider whether or not certain conditions are mental illnesses when we learn about well-known, successful people who not only experienced these conditions but recount how they were intrinsic to their success. Young Albert Einstein's contempt for authorities, as previously noted, resulted in problems for him in school. At twenty-two, he proclaimed, "A foolish faith in authority is the worst enemy of truth." Banesh Hoffmann, a physicist and Einstein collaborator, concluded about Einstein, "His early suspicion of authority, which never wholly left him, was to prove of decisive importance. Without it he would not have been able to develop the powerful independence of mind that gave him the courage to challenge established scientific beliefs and thereby revolutionize physics."

Einstein's biographer Walter Isaacson details how Albert's "cocky contempt for authority" led him to question conventional wisdom, and how Einstein himself believed that his slow verbal development allowed him to observe and wonder more about what others took for granted. Einstein concluded: "The ordinary adult never bothers his head about the problems of space and time. These are things he has thought of as a child. But I developed so slowly that I began to wonder about space and time only when I was already grown up. Consequently, I probed more deeply into the problem than an ordinary child would have."

Like the young Bento, the young Albert also became a Bible critic, a factor that resulted in both of them questioning consensus reality and conventional wisdom throughout their lives. Einstein recalled, "Through the reading of popular scientific books, I soon reached the conviction that much in the stories of the Bible could not be true. The consequence was a positively fanatic orgy of freethinking coupled with the impression that youth is intentionally being deceived by the state through lies; it was a crushing impression."

For some young people, their recognition of the deceit and irrationality of the adult word can result in not trusting anything, and they begin to have faith only in their own intuition. Beliefs uncritically examined can escalate into delusions and what is commonly called psychosis. This was the case with mathematician John Nash who, as previously noted, was a Nobel Prize winner in economics in 1994 and made famous by the film *A Beautiful Mind*. Like Spinoza and Einstein, John Nash was disdainful of authority and trusted his own mind, but Nash took an irrational turn on that Spinoza-Einstein road. Only later would Nash right himself with a rational disdain of authority and reason to counter what Spinoza would call his "inadequate ideas" (more later on his recovery in Chapter 14: "Icarus and Recovery").

The three concepts in Spinoza's philosophy that might provide us with fresh insights into what was once called madness and insanity—and what today is called psychosis, schizophrenia, and other serious mental illnesses—are intuitive knowledge (*scientia intuitiva*), monism, and *conatus*.

The concept of intuitive knowledge links Einstein to Nash but also differentiates them, and thus gives us insight into why Nash plunged into irrationality and delusions but Einstein did not. Recall that in the *Ethics*, Spinoza distinguishes three kinds of knowledge: (1) opinion, hearsay, imagination, and random experience; (2) reason; and (3) intuitive knowledge. While reason (unlike opinion, hearsay, imagination, and random experience) is a method to truly understand the truth of things, Spinoza concluded that intuitive knowledge is actually superior to reason; as through this third type of knowledge, we can attain the highest satisfaction. However, because Spinoza was not completely explicit in his definition of intuitive knowledge, Spinoza scholars struggle over its exact meaning and the nature of its superiority.

For Spinoza scholars, it is uncontroversial that Spinoza believed that intuitive knowledge is superior to reason, and they agree that intuitive knowledge "is grasped in a single act of apprehension and is not arrived at by any kind of deductive process," explains Spinoza scholar Blake Dutton.

Most dictionaries define *intuition* as the ability to understand something immediately without the need for conscious reasoning. Steven Nadler tells us that what Spinoza means by intuition is that "you come to know the essence of a thing not by some irrational insight but because . . . your intellect has so clearly perceived the way in which something relates to nature itself and its laws." For Nadler, intuitive knowledge "consists in an immediate, intuitive, noninferential grasp of the essence of a thing," and he explains that this form of knowledge is "a deep causal understanding" of things "that situates them in their necessary relationships to each other and, more important, to higher, universal principles."

Spinoza himself described intuitive knowledge this way: "This kind of knowledge proceeds from an adequate idea of the formal essence of certain attributes of God to an adequate knowledge of the essence of things." For Spinoza, God is Nature, and so when you grasp God/Nature—its laws, principles, relationships, and yourself as part of Nature—you can immediately intuit the nature of something without conscious reasoning.

Attempting to clarify intuitive knowledge and explain its superiority to reason, Spinoza scholar Sanem Soyarslan devoted her dissertation to this topic ("Reason and Intuitive Knowledge in Spinoza's *Ethics*: Two Ways of Knowing, Two Ways of Living," 2011). "Intuitive knowledge," she tells us, "starts where reason leaves us—with knowledge of God [Nature]."

> Unlike reason, it does not require any quasi-syllogistic operations with generalizations and their instances. . . . There is something that can be known by intuition—namely, the unique essences of things—that cannot be known by reason. . . . By grasping the knowledge that *I* am in God [Nature] and conceived through God [Nature], intuitive self-knowledge supplies a maximal understanding. . . . By attaining this superior form of self-knowledge, intuition also ascends to a higher level of affective power that reason cannot access. . . . Since one cannot achieve a complete change in perspective through reason alone, a person who has attained only rational knowledge will live a different life than someone who has achieved intuitive knowledge. . . . The lesson for Spinoza is this: the more we understand nature through reason, the more we become free and happy. However, it is only when we understand *ourselves* as a part of nature through intuition that we can reach the ultimate happiness.

Spinoza scholars agree that intuitive knowledge goes beyond the truths that reason alone provides, and that intuitive knowledge provides us with a true understanding of the unity of things, including the unity of the truth of ourselves as part of nature, which provides us with supreme joy.

While the nuances of intuitive knowledge are debated among Spinoza scholars, what's critical for the present discussion is that Spinoza—and many other well-known and not well-known individuals—conclude that we can acquire a kind of knowledge that is superior to the knowledge that we acquire through reason alone; and through this superior kind of knowledge, we will become connected with nature in such a way that results in the greatest experience of power and pleasure.

John Nash provides us with a window to a mind that has experienced a way of knowing that is superior to reason. In his autobiographical essay written for the Nobel Prize, Nash stated: "So at the present time I seem to be thinking rationally again in the style that is characteristic of scientists. However this is not entirely a matter of joy as if someone returned from physical disability to good physical health. One aspect of this is that rationality of thought imposes a limit on a person's concept of his relation to the cosmos."

Nobel Prize winners Albert Einstein and John Nash both highly valued intuition as a path to deeper and more profound truths. They recognized the value of both reason and intuition. However, just as our emotions can undermine reason when we are not truly connected with ourselves (for example, when we deny distorting passions such as the ambition for fame), we can confuse confidence of a true intuition of Nature with arrogance about imaginings which have no basis in reality—what we commonly call *delusions*.

Einstein said, "A new idea comes suddenly and in a rather intuitive way. . . . But intuition is nothing but the outcome of earlier intellectual experience." After Einstein was told by poet Saint-John Perse about the role played by intuition and imagination in creating a poem, Einstein responded, "It's the same for a man of science. . . . It is a sudden illumination, almost a rapture. Later, to be sure, intelligence analyzes and experiments confirm or invalidate intuition." While confident that he was capable of brilliant intuitions, Einstein retained humility that any of his intuitions could be invalid, while Nash did not.

In her biography of John Nash, journalist Sylvia Nasar concludes, "No one was more obsessed with originality, more disdainful of authority." Nash, like Einstein, had faith in his intuitions. Nasar tells us, "The flashes of intuition were non-rational. Like other great mathematic intuitionists. . . . Nash saw the vision first, constructing the laborious proofs long afterward. . . . Nash always worked backward in his head. He would mull over a problem and, at some point, have a flash of insight, an intuition, a vision of the solution he was seeking." A mathematician colleague of Nash's, Eli Stein, recalled, "Nash knew exactly what he wanted to do. With his great intuition, he saw that certain things ought to be true."

Prior to his breakdown, Nasar describes Nash this way: "His tolerance for solitude, great confidence in his own intuition, indifference to criticism—all detectable at a young age but now prominent and impermeable features of his personality—served him well." Unfortunately, stresses and pressures, self-imposed by his own ambition as well as from relationships, broke down his capacity to apply critical thinking to his intuitions.

It was only much later in his life that Nash received recognitions for his game theory work (now called the Nash Equilibrium concept), which he had developed at age twenty-one. At the time of his descent into bizarre delusions at age thirty, the world had not yet recognized the importance of his ideas and neither had Nash, and he was pained by his lack of accomplishment. Decades later, Nash stated that he believed what triggered his mental disturbance was his "possibly overreaching and psychologically destabilizing" attempt to resolve quantum theory. Moreover, he had been accustomed to a selfish existence, solely devoted to his own intellectual thought, but by his mid-twenties, he was forced to deal with his responsibilities to others. He had fathered a son when he was twenty-five but abandoned his responsibility to both child and mother, Eleanor, causing her to give the child up for foster care; and at the time of Nash's first psychiatric hospitalization, his wife Alicia was pregnant with his second child.

"Madness can be an escape," Nash determined. In a 2014 documentary about him, he concluded, "Things are not so good, maybe you want to imagine something better. In madness, I thought I was the most important person in the world. . . . To some extent sanity is a form of conformity. . . . I think mental illness or madness can be an escape."

Nash became, as Nasar put it, "beguiled by the idea of alien races of hyper-rational beings who had taught themselves to disregard all emotion."

"How could you," Harvard professor George Mackey asked Nash, "a mathematician, a man devoted to reason and logical proof . . . how could you believe that extraterrestrials are sending you messages? How could you believe that you are being recruited by aliens from outer space to save the world?" Nash answered him, "Because the ideas I had about supernatural beings came to me the same way that my mathematical ideas did. So I took them seriously."

Nash, Einstein, and many non-famous individuals sense the superiority of intuition as a way of discovering profound truths about connections and unity in the universe. That "sudden illumination, almost a rapture" described by Einstein can be intoxicating; and our emotions, life stressors, and other variables can prevent receptivity to the possibility of invalidating the intuition; and we can become delusional. When we recognize the human capacity for intuitive knowledge, we have a better understanding as to why those among us who sense its supremacy so crave it, and how this can make one vulnerable to intuitions that are not true at all.

When we grasp the essence of intuitive knowledge, we rethink the notion of the relationship between what is commonly called mental illness and what is commonly called creativity. In her book *The Insanity Hoax: Exposing the Myth of the Mad Genius* (2012), psychologist Judith Schlesinger re-examines the notion of the link between serious mental illness and creativity, a link that has been made popular by psychologist Kay Redfield Jamison and psychiatrists Nancy Andreasen and Arnold K. Ludwig. Schlesinger notes that creativity-mental illness research lacks a scientifically valid definition for both creativity and mental illness, and neither can be reliably measured. One invalid notion that much of the research in this area is based on is the false assumption that there are "creative professions" such as writers and scientists as compared to "noncreative professions" such as farmers and plumbers. The reality is that there are many writers who have never experienced the supremacy of an intuitive insight, and there are farmers who regularly experience it. Intuitive wisdom is not simply the flash seen by Nobel Prize winners such as Einstein and Nash, but also the intuitive flash for farmers that tells them which field will produce the highest yield for a specific crop. People from all walks of life—not simply Nobel Prize winners—have the capacity for "sudden illumination, almost a rapture"; and all human beings have the potential to attach themselves to illuminations that prove invalid and false.

Another important Spinoza concept that is relevant to understand madness is his belief in unity and a singular reality, or what some today call *monism*. Monism is the idea that all of reality is one. In Spinoza's monism, there is one and only one substance, which he identifies as God or Nature. For Spinoza, the singular, unified God/Nature is an infinite substance with infinite attributes. The only two attributes of God/Nature that the human mind can grasp are what Spinoza calls "thought" (which includes ideas) and "extension" (which includes physical entities).

Important with respect to understanding madness is Spinoza's rejection of the dualism of Descartes, who believed that the mind and body are separate things. There are radical anti-hierarchical consequences that result from Spinoza's belief that the mind and body are two aspects of the same reality.

Spinoza's belief leads to a rejection of a reductionist account of human beings that elevates either mind or body at the expense of the other. Specifically, Clare Carlisle, explains, "Descartes's mind-body dualism involves the claim that we are, in essence, thinking beings—that the intellectual should be privileged above the physical, reason above the body. Conversely, modern science often regards the human being as primarily a physical entity, and attempts to reduce mental activity to physical processes." In contrast, Spinoza's anti-hierarchical radical view declares, as Carlisle explains, it is "incoherent to attempt to explain the mental in terms of the physical, or vice versa. . . . They offer two alternative ways of describing and understanding our world, and ourselves, which are equally complete and equally legitimate."

For Spinoza, the mental and the physical are two aspects of a single reality. "Thus a thought," journalist and Spinoza explicator Matthew Gindin points out, "is one event which can be viewed two ways: as a neuron firing or as a conscious experience." The idea that there is a singular reality, which Spinoza calls God or Nature, is less common in Western thought than Eastern thought. Among Hindus, Gindin adds, "Some Vedantins, for example, assert that all of reality is one."

Einstein, like Spinoza, had an instinct for unity and singularity that propelled his attempt to construct a unified field theory in which electromagnetism and gravity would emerge as different aspects of a single fundamental field. He died before he was able to discover a single set of principles that could unify gravity and light—and be applied to diverse forces and particles in the universe. Einstein, Spinoza, and Vedantins have not been the only ones to intuit unity.

It is common for many individuals, including many young people, to experience the intuition of unity, connectedness, and oneness in the universe. This comes to some of us through reflection and meditation, and to others with the aid of psychedelic drugs. However, given society's attachment to the view of a separate self, this intuition of oneness can be both exciting and frightening, both mind-expanding and mind-blowing, and both a path to discovery and a path to psychosis.

Psychologist Paris Williams, in *Rethinking Madness* (2012), interviewed individuals who had been diagnosed with schizophrenia and other psychoses, and who could articulate their recoveries. Williams integrated this research with his analysis of prominent alternative explanations for madness (including those of John Weir Perry, Isabel Clarke, Irvin Yalom, Rollo May, and Ernest Becker). Williams synthesized his findings in what he calls a "Duality Unity Integrative Model." He concludes that there is "a nearly constant dance taking place between our experience of duality (our experience of ourselves as fundamentally *separate* from the rest of the world) and our experience of unity (our experience of ourselves as fundamentally *interconnected* with the rest of the world)."

Many people remain unaware of this unity and interconnectedness, and so it is no concern for them; and for some of those individuals who are aware, such as Spinoza and Einstein, this intuition of oneness and unity does not unravel them. However, there are other individuals who gain a degree of awareness of this unity and interconnectedness, and this results in a tension-producing crisis. The dilemma is, as Williams puts it, "the need to maintain the survival of a dualistic self within a world that is fundamentally nondual," and "the need to maintain a tenable balance between autonomy/individuation and connection with others." Williams concludes, "An overwhelming degree of dialectical tension can initiate psychosis."

We can integrate our sense of connectedness with our need for individuation, but this integration is not without tension. If along with this connectedness-individuation tension, there exists other tension-creating conditions such as trauma and relationship conflict, we can become overwhelmed by so much tension that we break down into immobilizing depression or psychosis.

This brings us to another major Spinoza concept important to understanding madness, which is *conatus*, the striving to persevere. Spinoza explains in the *Ethics*, "The *conatus* with which each thing endeavors to persist in its own being is nothing but the actual essence of the thing itself."

How then is *conatus*—this striving to persevere—important in understanding madness and psychosis? The flip side of striving to persevere is a fear of demise—a fear of death. Many individuals attempt to deny this fear of death or tranquilize it. However, some of us cannot deny or tranquilize this fear and become so consumed by terror that this results in being overwhelmed to the point of psychosis.

The fear of death includes a fear of biological death and a fear of existential death—what philosopher and psychologist Søren Kierkegaard called a "dread of non-being." As previously noted, Kierkegaard distinguishes *fear* from *anxiety*. Both are responses to perceived threats, but fear is triggered by a clear external threat while anxiety consists of feeling threatened by uncertainty—such as an awareness of freedom and becoming overwhelmed by possibilities. For Kierkegaard, anxiety, though painful, is not a symptom of mental illness but as, his biographer Clare Carlisle put it in *Philosopher of the Heart* (2019), is "a mark of spiritual nobility."

Philosophers, psychologists, and the existential psychiatrist Irvin Yalom have all come to the same conclusion that being overwhelmed by this fear of death can propel us into psychosis. Anthropologist Ernest Becker, author of *The Denial of Death*, is perhaps the most well-known proponent of the relationship between the fear of death and emotional problems. For Becker, to ensure our biological self-preservation, we need some fear of death, but if we become consumed by it, we can become so overwhelmed that we cannot function, and we can become psychotic.

For Kierkegaard, by depathologizing and ennobling anxiety, we won't be destroyed by it. Spinoza's solution for the fear of death was to simply accept it as unavoidable, but many people cannot implement Spinoza's logical approach. And so some people seek religious after-life belief solutions to reduce their fear of death, while other people who are overwhelmed by this fear of death seek release from it by what Becker called a striving for the heroic.

"The hero's journey," as termed by mythologist Joseph Campbell, may begin with a metaphorical death necessary to transform ourselves from an inauthentic existence to who we are truly meant to be. However, for some of us, trauma and fear can undermine this journey of transformation, and we can become attached to heroic delusions. Heroic delusions—such as John Nash's delusion that he had been recruited by aliens to save the world—are quite common in people who are diagnosed with psychosis.

Psychoses and modern art—two aspects of our humanity that earlier in my life I found difficult to comprehend—may have something in common that makes them incomprehensible for many people. This is the conclusion of psychologist Louis Sass, author of *Madness and Modernism: Insanity in the Light of Modern Art, Literature, and Thought* (1992). Sass concludes that many people diagnosed with schizophrenia share the following elements with modern art: a hyper-focus and a hyper-reflection about routinely ignored realities.

Specifically, a Jackson Pollock painting is incomprehensible for many people who focus on a certain conventional reality; but Sass notes that in, "Works like abstract expressionism . . . instead of accepting the conventions of using paint to depict some object like a landscape or a nude body . . . the paint itself and the surface of the canvass become the actual focus of the work."

Similarly, Sass sees many people diagnosed with schizophrenia as hyper-focusing and hyper-reflecting on realities that are conventionally disregarded. For example, someone diagnosed with schizophrenia may hyper-focus on the act of shaking hands with another person and become hyper-aware of the strangeness of, as Sass puts it, "sticking this lump of flesh out into the space between two human bodies and moving it up and down simultaneously in contact with that other lump of flesh coming from the other person." Ironically, with the advent of the coronavirus epidemic, it is no longer deemed "schizophrenic," "autistic" or "obsessive-compulsive" to hyper-focus—or even recoil—at persons disregarding revised convention and offering their hand in a greeting.

Critical to Spinoza's entire perspective (including his psychological, ethical, and political thought) is his conclusions about the essential nature of reality—what philosophers call *metaphysics*. Metaphysics has long been a major topic in the historic conversation among philosophers; however, psychiatry has essentially attempted to terminate this conversation by proclaiming certainty about what are departures from reality. This unphilosophical stance toward the nature of reality, according to contemporary philosopher and linguist Wouter Kusters, is a major reason why psychiatry cannot comprehend psychoses such as schizophrenia. Kusters, in the Dutch freethinking tradition of Spinoza and the psychiatrist Marius Romme, is the author of *A Philosophy of Madness: The Experience of Psychotic Thinking* (2020). "My basic proposition," he states, "is that philosophy and madness have everything to do with each other."

Through Kusters's own personal encounters—he had two experiences of psychosis for which he was psychiatrically hospitalized—and his philosophical and linguistic scholarship, he came to believe that such states, which are commonly called *psychosis*, are better understood philosophically than medically. For Kusters, "Being in a condition of madness means you are trying to resolve the most fundamental questions of existence but in an uncontrolled, wildly associative way. You want to know what it's all about, what good and evil are, what is at the very heart of existence: you want to know the meaning of life and the cosmos."

Kusters prefers the term *madness* to the term *psychosis* because he believes medicalizing the condition undermines understanding it: "So a term like 'philochosis' might be more appropriate in many cases than a term like 'psychosis' for referring to a person's deep-seated existential confusion, a confusion about the boundaries between the self and the world, language and concepts, finitude and infinity." For Kusters, there is a distinction between how the philosopher and the mad individual routinely approach these issues: "When the philosopher concerns himself with such great themes, he does so as a hobby or a profession, on paper or in academic dialogue. For the madman, however, dealing with these themes is a matter of bitter necessity in the struggle to simply hold his head above water and stay afloat." The philosopher knows how to deal with these issues in a socially acceptable way but, Kusters tells us, "For the madman, these profound questions can completely derail and dominate his life."

Such derailments can be a mixed bag of pain and pleasure for those who experience them; but for observers, including family members and even mental health professionals, these derailments can be absolutely terrifying—and fear undermines rational thought. With overwhelming fear and anxiety, family members and professionals are vulnerable to accepting erroneous beliefs about these derailments. With fear, all of us are vulnerable to invalid compartmentalizations, superstitions, unproven theories, and pseudoscience. We are vulnerable to delusions about other's delusions.

There are multiple tragedies that are created from our inadequate ideas about other's flights from consensus reality. Not only can we undermine other's re-integrations and recoveries, we lose an invaluable opportunity to understand more deeply about what it means to be a human being. Letting go of our fear of madness allows us to think more freely about it. Thinking freely about madness for both Sass and Kusters is not glorifying or romanticizing the condition. Such freethinking, however, can result in a radical enlightenment. Radical Enlightenment thinkers such as Spinoza, intoxicated by reason, refused to suppress their thinking so as to yield to the consensus. Such an intoxication can result in becoming a philosopher as bold as Spinoza or becoming a madman, or—as in the case of Wouter Kusters, Friedrich Nietzsche, and others—both.

CHAPTER 14

ICARUS AND RECOVERY

How did John Nash recover from his descent into irrationality and bizarre delusions, which began at age thirty, and for which he was diagnosed with paranoid schizophrenia?

In the 2001 film *A Beautiful Mind*, there is a scene in which Nash (played by Russell Crowe) is being assessed for his fitness to receive the Nobel Prize (awarded to him in 1994). He is asked how he recovered, and in the film he states, "I take the newer medications." This, as previously noted, is not true. Journalist Sylvia Nasar's biography of Nash, *A Beautiful Mind* (1998), documents that he stopped taking medication in 1970, and in 2009, Nash confirmed that the film was inaccurate about his taking medication.

In Nash's autobiographical essay for the Nobel Prize, he is candid about his departure from rationality, but he puts his psychiatric diagnoses within quotation marks and prefers to term his delusional state as a *mental disturbance*: "Now I must arrive at the time of my change from scientific rationality of thinking into the delusional thinking characteristic of persons who are psychiatrically diagnosed as 'schizophrenic' or 'paranoid schizophrenic.' The mental disturbances originated in the early months of 1959."

Nash is adamant that all his psychiatric hospitalizations were involuntary and that he fought against them, "I later spent times of the order of five to eight months in hospitals in New Jersey, always on an involuntary basis and always attempting a legal argument for release."

From the perspective of Nash and his wife Alicia, he recovered in spite of psychiatric treatment and not because of it. Throughout the 1960s, when Nash was in his thirties, life was hellish for him and his family. During his long-term stay at Trenton State Hospital, his treatments included insulin-induced comas for six weeks, five days a week—a now discarded treatment that is seen by psychiatry as an embarrassment (and seen by psychiatry critics as a recent example of barbarism). Nasar notes, "From the outset . . . Alicia drew the line at electroshock." Nash's sister Martha recalled, "We debated electroshock therapy. But we didn't want to mess with his memory."

In 1970, after his last hospitalization, Nash completely stopped psychiatric medications. Alicia, who had divorced him in 1963 (remarrying him later), felt guilty about her decision to force psychiatric hospitalizations, "Much of his past hospitalization I now feel was a mistake and had no beneficial permanent effects, rather the opposite." In 1970, Alicia agreed to allow John to move in with her, promising to not commit him to another forced hospitalization.

Alicia's support, Nasar concludes, was key to saving John's life. Nash was also lucky to receive tolerance for his eccentricities from a supportive Princeton academic community that continued to greatly admire him. Nasar concludes, "Princeton functioned as a therapeutic community. It was quiet and safe . . . human contact was available, but not intrusive. . . . Here he found what he desperately wanted . . . safety, freedom, friends."

Nash ultimately discovered, notes Nasar, "a growing awareness of the sterility of his delusional state and a growing capacity for rejecting delusional thought." He compared his self-help to dieting, Nasar reports, "It is a matter of policing one's thoughts, he has said, trying to recognize paranoid ideas and rejecting them, just the way somebody who wants to lose weight has to decide consciously to avoid fats or sweets."

In Nash's autobiographical essay, he states how gradually, "I began to intellectually reject some of the delusionally influenced lines of thinking which had been characteristic of my orientation. This began, most recognizably, with the rejection of politically-oriented thinking as essentially a hopeless waste of intellectual effort." Nash began to re-apply his mind to what was naturally stimulating, elsewhere stating, "I began to study mathematical problems and to learn the computer as it existed at the time."

Throughout Nasar's biography of Nash, there are several anecdotes about how Nash, prior to and during his breakdown, was selfish, arrogant, and abusive; but as he recovered, he made attempts to consider other people. His experience of being cared about and his attempts to care about others appear to have been vital to his recovery.

The facts of John Nash's life challenge the consensus reality that schizophrenia is a chronic brain disease that can only be treated with medication but not cured. Nasar is forthcoming about the facts of Nash's rejection of psychiatric treatment including medication, however, she terms his nearly three decades without being psychiatrically hospitalized—which by the time of his death in 2015 was more than four decades—as a *remission*, not *recovery* or *cure*. The *remission* word choice kept Nasar from being attacked by defenders of the consensus reality of schizophrenia as a chronic and incurable brain disease.

However, the facts of Nash's life suggest recovery and cure. Not only was Nash never again hospitalized after 1970, he also returned to mathematical work. Even more significantly, Nasar ends her 1998 book with the following description of Nash as he began his sixties: "The self-deprecating humor suggests greater self-awareness. The straight-from-the-heart talks with friends about sadness, pleasure, and attachment suggests a wider range of emotional experience. The daily effort to give others their due, and to recognize their right to ask this of him, bespeaks a very different man from the often cold and arrogant youth."

There are many more non-famous individuals who, like Nash, have descended into irrationality, bizarre delusions, and other symptoms of what psychiatry calls serious mental illnesses such as schizophrenia, schizoaffective disorder, and bipolar disorder, and who, like Nash, recover without psychiatric treatment. So as to maintain the consensus reality, in addition to the use of the word *remission* rather than *recovery* or *cure*, it is common for these individuals previously diagnosed with serious mental illnesses such as schizophrenia to be told that they must have been misdiagnosed, as schizophrenia is a chronic and incurable brain disease. Like Nash, their stories don't fit into consensus reality, and rather than reconsidering consensus reality, an attempt is made to reconcile the facts of their lives with consensus reality.

While the recovery by Nobel Prize winner John Nash was misrepresented in the film version of his life so as to fit consensus realty (and the film was acclaimed by mental health institutions and awarded an Academy Award for Best Picture), the recoveries of many other individuals that also challenge consensus reality are simply ignored and remain unknown to the general public.

In reaction to society ignoring these stories, the "Personal Story Project," supported by the human rights organization MindFreedom International, collected histories from thirty former psychiatric patients who self-identify as "psychiatric survivors" (some of whom term their previous condition as a "lived experience in an altered state"). They, like Nash, believe that their psychiatric labeling and most of their treatment caused them suffering and delayed recovery.

The "Personal Story Project" was created by Oryx Cohen, who is currently chief operating officer of the National Empowerment Center (NEC), which promotes an empowerment-based recovery model and is run by psychiatric survivors/ex-patients in recovery. In 1999, in his early twenties, Cohen had bizarre delusions, including a belief that his car could fly, and this resulted in a bipolar disorder diagnosis. One component of the project is to describe recovery methods for each individual. Cohen himself includes: the support of family and friends, social activism, spirituality, self-help (which includes diet, exercise, and regulating sleep), peer support of fellow former psychiatric patients, art and music, and "one good therapist." Others interviewed for this project included those same recovery methods and add others such as vigilance of signs that they are entering problematic states, getting a job, cooking, gardening, and being in nature/wilderness.

John Nash was a great admirer of the philosopher Friedrich Nietzsche and Nietzsche's book *Thus Spoke Zarathustra*. In Nash's Nobel Prize autobiographical essay, he includes the following: "A non-Zoroastrian could think of Zarathustra as simply a madman who led millions of naive followers to adopt a cult of ritual fire worship. But without his 'madness' Zarathustra would necessarily have been only another of the millions or billions of human individuals who have lived and then been forgotten."

In the Prologue of *Thus Spoke Zarathustra*, Nietzsche tells the reader that Zarathustra at age thirty, "left his home and the lake of his home and went into the mountains. Here he enjoyed his spirit and his solitude, and for ten years did not tire of it." Perhaps it is only a coincidence, but it was age thirty that Nash had what he called his mental disturbances that resulted in him being psychiatrically hospitalized. In *Thus Spoke Zarathustra*, Nash was exposed to Nietzsche's concept of the overman (*ubermensch*), the man who could transcend conventional morality to create his own values and discover a path to freedom.

Nietzsche, at forty-four, himself became incapacitated, and he was nonfunctional for the last twelve years of his life. The source of his breakdown remains controversial; once attributed to syphilis, more recently to meningioma, with others believing that it was connected to his philosophical thinking. Prior to his breakdown, Nietzsche had written: "All superior men who were irresistibly drawn to throw off the yoke of any kind of morality and to frame new laws had, if they were not actually mad, no alternative but to make themselves or pretend to be mad."

Just as the film *A Beautiful Life* hijacked Nash's life to fit the consensus reality of psychiatry, after Nietzsche's demise and death, his sister hijacked her brother's work, editing it to make it appear that Nietzsche promoted the Nazi ideology that he would have despised. Nietzsche was repulsed by nationalism and any ideology that denigrated the individual, and thus he would have been repulsed by fascism and the Nazis. Thus, ironically, Nash shares with his hero Nietzsche the fate of being used to promote ideas that they disapproved of.

It is common among individuals such as Nash who develop grandiose delusions and are diagnosed as psychotic to have a sense of uniqueness and superiority that allows them to rise above conventions. Transcendence from conventions can bleed over to arrogance and delusions of being exempt from natural law. This is why for many individuals who ultimately recover from serious mental disturbances, the Greek myth of Icarus is an invaluable lesson.

Icarus's father Daedalus created wings out of wax and feathers for an escape. Daedalus warned Icarus to neither fly too close to the sun nor too close to the sea or his wings would be destroyed. Icarus, however, made giddy—or what we call today *manic*—by the ability to fly, soared high and went too close to the sun, melting the wax and destroying his wings, causing Icarus to fall into the sea and drown. This myth is a valuable one for individuals who have experienced altered states and have lost a sense of the limitations of natural law, resulting in them not only defying consensus reality but defying actual reality, believing that whatever goes through their mind is true.

In 2002, the Icarus Project was created by former psychiatric patients, its name meant to convey that extreme mental states can be a gift but also potentially dangerous, causing one to fly too close to the sun, resulting in some kind of tragic outcome. One of its founders, Sascha DuBrul, in the 1980s began connecting with other young people in the punk-anarchist scene who were alienated from society and their families. In his early twenties, DuBrul recounts that he began to have "a messianic feeling like I was a bridge between worlds." In New York City, he was picked up walking the subway train tracks, psychiatrically hospitalized, and diagnosed with bipolar disorder. In 2002, DuBrul wrote an article in the *San Francisco Bay Guardian* about his own experience of madness. He discussed how he was "part of a group of people that has been misunderstood and persecuted throughout history, but meanwhile has been responsible for some of the most brilliant of history's creations." He received a huge response and then, along with artist Ashley McNamara, created the Icarus Project. The Icarus Project was further developed by Bonfire Madigan Shive, a musician-activist, and Will Hall, a counselor and host of Madness Radio. The Icarus Project provides a space, DuBrul notes, for "freaks and kids who feel really alienated and alone . . . and gives them a community to be a part of. Mad Pride is parallel to Gay Pride." By 2010, there were 10,000 people registered with the project, with local groups throughout North America.

One participant in the Icarus Project, Maryse Mitchell-Brody, has chronicled it in her chapter "The Icarus Project: Dangerous Gifts, Iridescent Visions and Mad Community" (in the 2007 book *Alternatives Beyond Psychiatry*). She notes that "many of us have found that labels like 'madness' and 'crazy' suddenly become imbued with new, more positive nuances. . . . A common thread through all of our work is our emphasis on creativity and beauty." In contrast to an illness-tragedy conceptualization, Mitchell-Brody declares, "We assert that this madness is an intrinsic part of the artistic spirit."

The double-edged nature of madness has both artistic and political implications. Theologian Reinhold Niebuhr explained that "a sublime madness in the soul" is, at certain historical points, politically essential and that "nothing but madness will do battle with malignant power and 'spiritual wickedness in high places.'" Niebuhr understood that this sublime madness is dangerous but vital. He recognized that traditional progressivism is a useless force in moments of extremity. Liberalism, Niebuhr said, "lacks the spirit of enthusiasm, not to say, fanaticism, which is so necessary to move the world out of its beaten tracks. [It] is too intellectual and too little emotional to be an efficient force in history."

There is no better example of such sublime madness than Harriet Tubman. It was daring enough for a slave to attempt escape, but to return to slave territory several times to help other slaves escape as Tubman did was courageous in the extreme. Tubman biographer Kate Clifford Larson concluded that Tubman directly helped approximately seventy to eighty slaves escape in thirteen trips. Yet today, Tubman would likely be labeled with serious mental illness. Specifically, Tubman announced that she heard God's voice and spoke to God; she had visions; she believed that she was her era's Moses; she camped outside a New York City anti-slavery office asking for donations; and she packed a revolver, claiming she needed it for protection against slave catchers as well as to threaten those who she was rescuing if they tried to turn back. Tubman "seemed wholly devoid of personal fear," was the observation of William Still, an African American abolitionist who chronicled the Underground Railroad. Tubman often spoke about "consulting with God" and had complete confidence that God would keep her safe. Abolitionist Thomas Garrett reported that he "never met with any person, of any color, who had more confidence in the voice of God, as spoken direct to her soul."

For Tubman's voice-hearing, for her belief that she was her era's Moses, and for her audaciousness, she would likely today—especially being an African American woman—get diagnosed with paranoid schizophrenia or bipolar disorder (and viewed as a threat to herself and others and subject to coercive treatment).

Because Tubman is considered today to be a heroine, it is conventional wisdom to attribute her voice hearing and her beliefs not to mental illness but instead to temporal lobe epilepsy resulting from being struck in the head by a heavy object thrown by an overseer. Today, it would defy consensus reality to see her voice hearing and her beliefs in the way that Tubman and those who knew and admired her saw it. Advocates of Tubman's "symptoms" being caused by brain damage ignore the reality that her brain functioned at a high level—she was a brilliant strategist who had astute judgment about the consequence of her actions and had no delusions about the dangers she faced on her missions, which is why she never got caught. In this regard, Tubman's intuitive knowledge was no less profound than Einstein's.

Tubman believed that her slave escape missions were completely protected by supernatural forces, a belief shared by many individuals diagnosed with psychosis. For Tubman, however, this belief was never disconfirmed. When we experience extreme oppression, as was the case with Tubman, visions, voices, and a belief that one is protected by God may well be our only antidotes to psychological powerlessness. This is obvious to many individuals who have recovered after being diagnosed with serious mental illness, though it is not routinely recognized by modern psychiatry. Also not routinely recognized is that, while altered states can lead to arrogance and tragic outcomes, there are other individuals who maintain prudence and control, resulting in what Niebuhr called sublime madness—"necessary to move the world out of its beaten tracks."

What happens when altered states and madness are not sublime but instead result in frightening behaviors and dysfunctionality? Psychologist Paris Williams, in *Rethinking Madness*, concludes, "If we consider psychosis to be essentially a process initiated by the psyche in an attempt to regain equilibrium within the self system after experiencing an overwhelming existential threat to the self, then we can see recovery as movement in the direction of regaining that equilibrium." Recovery is a process of reorganizing cognitive constructs that previously have been dramatically destabilized.

Consider the cognitive construct that one is an inferior human being who deserves to be a slave. As a young boy, Frederick Douglass instinctively questioned slavery, asking, "Why am I a slave? Why are some people slaves and others masters?" Through fortunate circumstances, a wife of his master assisted him in his learning the alphabet; and even after he was later forbidden to read, he secretly continued and discovered writings that confirmed his instinct that slavery was wrong. Douglass's reading validated his instincts, and he needed no voices from God to liberate him, and he escaped slavery. Tubman never learned to read.

It is common for individuals to have a cognitive construct of deep self-hatred that becomes radically destabilized by various auditory hallucinations or delusions. It is possible for such individuals, through a recovery process, to establish what Williams calls a "new equilibrium" and to gain self-acceptance. Interviewing individuals who recovered from psychotic states, Williams found that common factors that aid this recovery process include: finding hope; finding meaning; connecting with one's aliveness; and healthy relationships.

Hope of recovery can be an antidote to fear and despair. However, a belief in the possibility of recovery is routinely dashed by the consensus reality that serious mental illnesses, such as schizophrenia, are a chronic brain disease that can only be treated but not cured. Among the individuals Williams interviewed who recovered, he reports, "All expressed the importance of maintaining hope in the possibility of full recovery," and that most also found it helpful to arrive at a more hopeful understanding of their psychosis than one of a brain disease model. The idea of brain disease created a fear and mistrust of their own minds that hindered recovery. Fear of their condition worsened it. Hope as an antidote to fear is crucial.

Finding meaning is also crucial. Thus, for recovery, individuals found it necessary to reject conventional wisdom. Specifically, the message they had repeatedly heard in their standard psychiatric treatment was, Williams notes, "that someone experiencing long-term psychosis should abandon serious ambitions and devote their life to minimizing stress, remaining compliant with lifelong regimen of heavy psychiatric drugs, and strictly monitoring their 'illness' to reduce the risk of relapse." Williams discovered that individuals who recovered had rejected this message and developed rich and meaningful lives.

Another key component of recovery hindered by standard psychiatric treatment is what Williams calls "connecting with one's aliveness." Specifically, recovered individuals reported the "importance of fostering a deep connection with their aliveness—particularly their feelings, needs, and sense of agency." This connection is damaged by long-term use of heavily tranquilizing antipsychotic drugs. Long-term use of antipsychotics is very different than the short-term use to calm panic and reduce dangerous agitation.

Williams concludes that hope, meaning, and aliveness work together symbiotically. For example, the more that a connection with aliveness returns, the greater one's capacity for hope and meaning. What is also crucial for recovery is "the importance of cultivating healthy relationships," in which individuals can feel safe and supported.

Psychiatrist Daniel Fisher, currently the chief executive officer of the National Empowerment Center, is a prominent figure in the movement of radically enlightened professionals and former patients. Fisher is a rare psychiatrist in that he was diagnosed in his twenties with schizophrenia and hospitalized several times but now publicly discusses his own long-term recovery that includes having been a psychiatrist for approximately forty years.

Echoing Williams's findings, Fisher states: "One of the worst things that can happen is that people are told that they can never recover. That takes hope away, and without hope, there's no reason to get up, no reason to form a friendship . . . and people retreat into hopelessness." Fisher has found that people need hope, support, and what he calls "a culture of recovery" in which everyone who has contact with them—not just professionals—can play a role in generating hope. He reports that in NEC studies that examine the most important variables in recovery, the variable on the top of the list for most individuals is "having someone who believes in me." Fisher notes that hopelessness is highly correlated with suicidality, and his experience as both a patient and a professional is that standard treatment can take away hope.

Fisher also tells us that *love* is a word that much of his psychiatry profession is uncomfortable with, but from his experience, "Without love, there probably won't be very much recovery." Loving someone else, he believes, can be as important as receiving love. He recounts how when he was in utter despair, only the love of his cat kept him from acting on his suicidal thoughts—as this love gave Fisher concern about who would care for his cat if he killed himself. Fisher reports being criticized for "giving people false hope," to which he responds, "I think that's better than false hopelessness—that's what we're giving people right now."

When people enter into conditions in which they disconnect from consensus reality—whether we call it psychosis, madness, or an altered state—this can be frightening. It can be frightening for the person in that condition, and it is frightening for family members and friends. And so too can mental health professionals be frightened, though they may incongruently appear otherwise. For Spinoza, a life that is controlled by fear rather than informed by reason is a life of bondage. Thus, a key component in recovery is reducing fear and terror. Fear, for Spinoza, "engenders, preserves, and fosters superstition." Fear undermines critical thinking.

Human beings can tolerate only so much fear and terror before they become irrational. And when individuals behave in frightening ways, there is only so much fear and terror that others, including their family and mental health professionals, can tolerate before their only goal is ending their own fear and terror.

Given the reality that we can only tolerate so much fear and terror, an effort must be made to reduce fear and terror for all involved, but this must be done in a manner that takes care not to create permanent damage. Early in my training at an internship at the psychiatry services hospital emergency room, I saw this vicious cycle of fear. The patient acting crazy and disruptively was frightened; their family was frightened; and professionals were often frightened. We all often made each other even more frightened. There were a handful of talented therapists who, rather than wasting their time obsessing over a psychiatric diagnosis, put their energy into de-escalating fear, but such therapists were more the exception than the rule.

Unknown to most of the general public, there are options to standard psychiatric hospitalization and lifelong antipsychotic treatment. In 1968, at the National Institute of Mental Health (NIMH), psychiatrist Loren Mosher became chief of the Center for Schizophrenia Research, and in 1971, he launched an alternative approach for people diagnosed with schizophrenia called the Soteria House in Santa Clara, California. Helping to start and run Soteria House was social worker Voyce Hendrix (cousin of Jimi Hendrix), who had been a psychiatric technician in state institutions observing the outcomes of conventional treatment and had become disillusioned by this experience.

The Soteria staff was comprised of non-professionals who, Mosher reported, were "selected and trained to relate to and understand madness

without preconceptions, labels, categories, judgments of the need 'to do' anything to change, control, suppress or invalidate the experience of psychosis."
Heavily tranquilizing antipsychotic drugs were almost never used (and used
only on a voluntary basis and when more mildly tranquilizing benzodiaze-
pines, also rarely used, were ineffective in helping exhausted individuals to
sleep). The two-year follow-up results showed that Soteria participants had
superior outcomes (including independent living status) as compared to a
control group who had received standard psychiatric treatment.

Soteria results, produced by a non-professional staff and by significantly
limiting psychiatric drugs, challenged consensus reality, embarrassed establishment psychiatry, and displeased the pharmaceutical industry. By 1980, as
previously noted, pharmaceutical companies began to have increasing influence over psychiatry; and not surprisingly, Mosher was fired from his NIMH
position in 1980, and Soteria House lost funding, closing down in 1983.

I don't know any critic of standard psychiatry who is "anti-medication."
Neither dissident psychiatrists such as Loren Mosher nor Daniel Fisher nor
former patients and activists such as Sascha DuBrul (who himself has utilized
psychiatric drugs) are "anti-drug." Rather, this underground radical enlightenment movement is very much pro-informed choice. There is respect for each
individual's choice of whether or not to use medications, what type, and how
much.

Fear can make us irrational, and irrationality can make us even more terrified. To the degree that we can accept our fear without shame or anger, we
can become more rational. The approach that may be the most rational way
of all to reduce the cycle of fear is for helpers themselves to have experienced
altered states—and recovered. More on this in the next chapter.

CHAPTER 15

PALS AND PEERS

Historically, freethinkers of all types have been marginalized. For such individuals to have satisfying lives, it is crucial to have supportive relationships with other individuals who have similar values and have been similarly shunned. It can also be helpful for freethinkers to have supportive relationships with free-thinking individuals who have been marginalized in ways different than they have been—and so too can have respect and affection for outsiders.

Supportive relationships were critical for the surviving and thriving of Spinoza, as well as for other freethinkers and anti-authoritarian renegades throughout history who have had more satisfying lives. Supportive relationships and genuine community are critical for individuals who self-identify as "psychiatric survivors," as they are twice marginalized—first for their mental disturbance, then for their noncompliance with psychiatric authority.

Spinoza cared a great deal about friendship. He developed a close-knit community of friends, all of whom cared about freedom of thought and expression, tolerance, kindness, and justice. They shared philosophical ideas and helped each other survive and thrive. In the *Ethics*, Spinoza mentions friendship several times, including in this passage: "It is of the first importance to men to establish close relationships and to bind themselves together with such ties as may most effectively unite them into one body, and, as an absolute rule, to act in such a way as serves to strengthen friendship."

Recall Spinoza's concept of *conatus*, which he defines as "each thing, as far as it lies in itself, strives to persevere in its being." Similar to philosopher Thomas Hobbes, whose work Spinoza was familiar with, Spinoza was a realist who recognized that humans, like the rest of nature, are driven by self-interest and self-preservation. However, for Spinoza, enlightened self-interest and rational self-preservation means the rejection of a dog-eat-dog ethos of selfishness; and instead it means embracing friendship and reciprocal support.

The type of people who are mutually helpful for Spinoza are individuals who respect reason and freedom. He stated: "Only free men are truly advantageous to one another and united by the closest bond of friendship, and are equally motivated by love in endeavoring to benefit one another." Individuals who have shared values are most capable of harmony and enjoying friendship.

Spinoza scholar A. Wolf (in his introduction to Lucas's *The Oldest Biography of Spinoza*) stated: "He left Amsterdam for good in 1660, at the age of twenty-eight. The remaining sixteen years of his life were passed partly in Rijnsburg, near Leiden (1660–1663), partly in Voorburg, near The Hague (1663–1670), and partly in The Hague (1670–1677)."

In Lucas's biography of Spinoza, he tells us that Spinoza moved to Rijnsburg to acquire greater solitude and to devote himself to philosophy: "For two years he stayed in this retreat, where, although he took precautions to avoid all intercourse with his friends, his most intimate friends went to see him from time to time, and only left him again with reluctance." Bento was a popular guy.

Spinoza lived in The Hague until his death. "He had many friends in The Hague," according to his other early biographer, Colerus, "some in the military, others of high position and eminence, who often visited and discoursed with him." His recent biographer Steven Nadler notes that there is one report from an acquaintance that, while living in The Hague, Spinoza was visited by "all types of curious minds, and even by upper-class girls [*filles de qualité*], who prided themselves on having a superior mind for their sex." None of his biographers report Spinoza having any close friendships with women.

Spinoza had a rich circle of lifelong friends dating back to his early years in Amsterdam. Some were initially business acquaintances from the Amsterdam mercantile exchange. Several of his friends attended Collegiant gatherings, which were Sunday biweekly worship/study sessions. Collegiants were Christians from the more dissenting sects, and were routinely disaffected Mennonites, Remonstrants, and Quakers. The Collegiants, as Nadler put it, "sought a less dogmatic and nonhierarchical form of worship. . . . Anticlerical to the core" and with no official theology. It is possible that Spinoza attended some of these Collegiant meetings.

All of Spinoza's friends were committed to religious tolerance and freedom of thought. One of Spinoza's closest longtime friends was Jarig Jellesz, whom Spinoza met at the Amsterdam mercantile exchange. Jellesz had been a wholesaler and retail grocer and was possibly a customer of the Spinoza family import business. Jellesz sold his business when he was a young man. Similar to Spinoza, money-making was dissatisfying for Jellesz who sought to pursue truth and wisdom. Like Spinoza, he was very much anti-authoritarian, rejecting organized religion and dogma, and he helped Spinoza get his works published.

Another devoted friend and great admirer was Pieter Balling. Balling published anonymously *The Light upon the Candlestick* (1662), which was critical of organized religion for placing dogma at its center, and he argued for tolerance and a more personal approach to worship.

Among his other close friends was Simon de Vries, born into an upper middle-class merchant family and who, as noted, attempted to ensure that Spinoza would have no financial worries by providing him with a stipend (a commitment that was honored by De Vries's sister and brother-in-law after De Vries's death).

Lodewijk Meyer was another valuable Spinoza friend. Meyer was a free-thinking physician with a broad humanist interest in philosophy, literature, and drama, who served as the director of the Amsterdam Municipal Theater. Meyer was a major figure in Spinoza's radical underground movement, authoring anonymously *Philosophia S. Scripturae Interpres* in 1666, which created a great furor and was mistakenly attributed by many people during that era to Spinoza. Meyer, notes Nadler, "more than anyone else was responsible for bringing Spinoza's writings to publication, both while Spinoza lived and after his death with the posthumous publication of his collected works."

Spinoza's courageous publisher Jan Rieuwertsz was another important member of Spinoza's supportive circle. Prior to Spinoza's death in February 1677, Spinoza requested from his landlord, the painter Hendrik van der Spyck, that after his death, his writing desk be shipped to Rieuwertsz. Locked inside the desk was the *Ethics* (along with other unpublished manuscripts and personal letters). Rieuwertsz, with the help of Spinoza's other friends, then orchestrated publication of Spinoza's works (more on this in Chapter 18: "Bento's Conclusions").

Those anti-authoritarians who manage to overcome societal assault and marginalization so as to have enjoyable lives have, more often than not, communities of loyal and supportive friends. Another example is Henry David Thoreau, often mischaracterized as a loner, perhaps because his book *Walden* celebrates solitude and self-reliance. However, Thoreau had many friends, most famously Ralph Waldo Emerson, who introduced Thoreau to unconventional and eccentric writers and thinkers in Concord, Massachusetts. This group included Bronson Alcott, the father of Louisa May Alcott, and Ellery Channing, who would become perhaps Thoreau's best friend and often travel companion.

Among the most marginalized individuals in U.S. history have been anarchists who, like Spinoza, were anti-authoritarians; however, unlike Spinoza, they reject being governed by any imposed authority, including the state. While Spinoza was not an anarchist, he would fully understand anarchists' resentment over coercion and their anger over legal and financial assaults on them. Philosophical and political beliefs can be a vehicle for a support group that provides opportunities to connect with friends and lovers, and that was the case with Emma Goldman, perhaps the most famous anarchist in U.S. history. Crucial for Goldman, and those other anarchists who had more satisfying lives, was what anarchists called "mutual aid." Historians Paul Avrich and Karen Avrich, in *Sasha and Emma* (2012), capture these anarchists' rich communities in the late-nineteenth and early-twentieth century. In major U.S. cities, there existed a network of informal mutual assistance among anarchists that provided, in addition to human contact and friendship, housing and other necessities.

Through serendipity, I connected with mutual-aid communities of former psychiatric patients—some of whom termed themselves "psychiatric survivors." They too oppose authoritarianism, hierarchy, and coercion, and promote mutual aid, which they term as *peer-to-peer support*. My initial encounter occurred in 1994, after a "letter to the editor" of mine was published in a magazine and spotted by a major organizer in the psychiatric survivor movement, David Oaks, then director of Support Coalition International (which morphed into MindFreedom International). Oaks telephoned me, and informed me of the existence of a subculture of dissident mental health professionals and of the Mad Pride movement of psychiatric survivors.

Thus, by chance, I have had the opportunity to encounter some very different individuals who have received psychiatric treatment than most mental health professionals come into contact with. Professionals at their jobs in hospitals and clinics often see people who have been diagnosed with serious mental illness and have stopped taking their medication and then become psychotic. Such professionals do not routinely see individuals who may have had psychotic episodes but recovered—and no longer have contact as patients with mental health professionals. Through serendipity, I escaped the previously mentioned "Clinician's Illusion," in which clinicians' ideas about a population are biased by the skewed subpopulation whom they encounter.

A disdain for coercion, a passion for freethinking, and tolerance for eccentricity are the norms in the anti-authoritarian groups that I have studied, as well as in groups which I am personally familiar with. Similar temperaments inhabit all these groups: Spinoza's Dutch pals in the 1650–1670s; Thoreau's Concord buddies in the 1840–1860s; Goldman's anarchist comrades in New York City and elsewhere in 1880–1920; and modern psychiatric survivor communities.

An early activist, organizer, public speaker, and educator in the psychiatric survivor movement was Judi Chamberlin, author of *On Our Own: Patient-Controlled Alternatives to the Mental Health System* (1978). At age twenty-one, in 1966, she had become significantly depressed and, following the advice of her doctor, agreed to be hospitalized, but she was then involuntarily committed. Chamberlin became incensed by the violation of her civil liberties and those of her fellow patients; and this became the impetus for her becoming an activist in the psychiatric survivor movement. She joined the Mental Patients Liberation Front in 1971, and later became Director of Education of the National Empowerment Center.

In Chamberlin's chapter "User-Run Services" (in *Models of Madness*, 2004), she explains why programs run by individuals who themselves have been diagnosed with serious mental illnesses and recovered are routinely more helpful than those run by professionals. Her experience is that professionals act more out of fear, demanding compliance with treatment, and this creates resentment that prohibits many patients from being honest, and turns off many other individuals from returning for help.

Chamberlin describes several peer-run programs, and the basic philosophy in all of them, she notes, is that "people who have been labeled as mentally ill have the capability to help themselves and one another." In self-help groups, individuals get to experience a different role, Chamberlin points out, "A person who has been seen—and has always seen him or herself—as needy and dependent responds dramatically when he or she has the opportunity to help another member." Their self-image changes when they experience appreciation for help.

It is common for participants in user-run services, Chamberlin notes, "to report that they received more practical help in such groups than they ever found within the mental health system." Chamberlin points out that it is a myth that self-help groups condemn psychiatric medication, as some members choose to use psychiatric drugs. What's crucial is choice and an absence of coercion.

While anarchists use the term *mutual aid* and Chamberlin used the term *user-run services*, today many former psychiatric patients who are helping one another use the term *peer-to-peer support*. One of the pre-eminent peer-to-peer support organizations is the Western Mass Recovery Learning Community (RLC) in Holyoke, Massachusetts. In reaction to the failure of standard psychiatric treatment to help many individuals, the state of Massachusetts, seeking innovative methods in the early 2000s, provided grants for peer-based programs run by former psychiatric patients.

RLC and its longtime director Sera Davidow received attention in 2017, when Davidow was the subject of an interview in the magazine *The Sun* ("An Open Mind: Sera Davidow Questions What We Think We Know About Mental Illness"). Davidow, at age twenty-two, was committed to a psychiatric hospital and monitored as a suicide risk. Beginning in her teens, she had accumulated approximately a half-dozen psychiatric diagnoses and had been prescribed several different psychiatric drugs. But these treatments only made her feel worse. Eventually, Davidow rejected both her medications and psychiatry's theories for her malaise, and she took control over her life. She came to attribute much of her emotional suffering to trauma, including sexual, physical, and emotional abuse. Today, in addition to directing RLC, Davidow is a writer, filmmaker, and mother of two.

Rather than using terms such as *serious mental illness* or *psychosis*, many former patients in peer-to-peer support find it more helpful to use terms such as *extreme states* to describe extreme emotional distress, hearing disturbing voices, having suicidal thoughts, and other conditions that can be extremely frightening, especially for those who have never experienced them. Davidow concludes that the absence of professional authorities allows individuals to define their own experiences, "We should be open to many answers, even ones that sound strange. Who cares if someone believes the voices they hear are coming from aliens, as long as their life is working for them?"

RLC is different from the mainstream mental health system because as, Davidow points out, "Everyone who works as an employee of the RLC has moved through some sort of life-interrupting challenge: trauma, homelessness, problems with substance use, psychiatric diagnosis." Davidow explains how peers can use the knowledge they have gained through their personal experience, "We know how the mental health and other societal systems can help as well as how they can hurt. We share those lessons with others, we're curious about people's stories, and we also just listen. Too often when no one listens, people are lost."

Professionals may want to be helpful, but they, as Davidow notes, "because of liability concerns, have been trained to take responsibility for people who have a psychiatric diagnosis and to make decisions for them. . . . The demands placed on clinical providers are intended to keep people safe, but the fact is they drive many providers to take action when they should be listening."

When an individual comes to RLC talking about suicide, peers—not being doctors—are liberated from liability fears that can make professionals ineffective. Davidow describes how different such an encounter is at RLC: "We ask what's going on for them—not what's 'wrong' with them or if they have been given a diagnosis. . . . If they talk about voices, visions, suicidal thoughts, or injuring themselves, we meet this with calm curiosity. We've found that what helps people move through such feelings is being able to talk openly about them. Unfortunately many people don't talk openly in clinical environments for fear that alarms will be sounded." In discussions with peers, it is easier for individuals experiencing extreme states to, as Davidow puts it, "talk about taboo topics without the threat of hospitalization or scaring away friends."

In mutual-aid, user-run services, and peer-to-peer support, a key value is self-determination. Davidow concludes, "If someone believes his or her distress is caused by something biological, or by past trauma, or by a spiritual emergency—or some mix of all three, or anything else—who are we to disagree? It doesn't matter whether we fully understand their beliefs. What matters is how their beliefs affect their life."

RLC provides multiple peer-to-peer support services, including a "peer respite" alternative to hospitalization called Afiya House, where someone can stay up to a week. There are no doctors at Afiya House and, as Davidow describes, "Unlike in a clinical environment, there's no expectation that a person will be up at any particular time of day," and it is not uncommon for people to simply want to be left alone and sleep. Afiya House has a small capacity, and there are few other such peer respites.

Sera Davidow, similar to Judi Chamberlin and most other individuals advocating for alternatives to standard psychiatric treatment, are not psychiatric drug abolitionists but believe in informed choice. Davidow concludes, "It's not our job to tell people what they should or shouldn't do, or what does or doesn't work for them. . . . Rather than saying that someone has a disease and then prescribing drugs that 'treat' that disease, we could just accept that drugs sometimes make people feel or function better, even if only for a period of time."

There are psychiatrists who agree with Davidow, including Joanna Moncrieff, author of *The Myth of the Chemical Cure* (2008) and co-chairperson of the Critical Psychiatry Network. In a 2010 interview, Moncrieff explained how psychiatric drugs, rather than correcting a defective brain or curing a disease, can have tranquilizing effects on anyone, "What psychiatric drugs essentially do is like using alcohol for social anxiety. Alcohol can be helpful for social anxiety, but that's not because people have an alcohol deficiency." Individuals feel improved for a wide variety of reasons, including through the use of chemical substances, and so while Moncrieff is clear about the dangers of alcohol use, she elsewhere acknowledges, "One patient I knew commented that the effects of alcohol had shown him how to overcome his shyness or social anxiety, such that he then learnt to socialize without it (of course, sometimes, alcohol used in this way can become a problem in its own right)."

Alcohol, of course, is ultimately nonproductive and even counterproductive for many people; and this is also the case for standard psychiatric drugs, which has resulted in society and psychiatry increasingly turning elsewhere and embracing psychedelics (such as psilocybin, LSD, MDMA). Here again, Moncrieff recommends not drug abolitionism but critical thinking. In a 2021 article ("Psychedelics—The New Psychiatric Craze"), Moncrieff points out that while "some people might learn important things about themselves through experiencing the effects of psychedelic drugs," transformative experiences can occur in all kinds of ways, including safer ones such as immersing oneself in nature. With respect to psychedelics, she cautions that similar to what has occurred with previous drugs used in psychiatry, "The current craze for psychedelics also means the adverse effects are being minimized or overlooked." Moncrieff reminds us that the context of a drug-induced experience is critically important. In contrast to the use of psychedelics with trusted friends within a genuine community, Moncrieff notes that "a clinical situation might be a highly alienating experience and might even induce a bad trip for some people."

While *community* is honored in modern society, this concept has been co-opted to mean something very different than *genuine community*. In *The Careless Society: Community and Its Counterfeits* (1995), sociologist and community activist John McKnight describes genuine community and how very different it is from what is commonly called community. In a genuine community, individuals (1) claim the power to decide what is a problem; (2) claim the power to decide how to solve the problem; and (3) become themselves the key actors in implementing the solution.

In a genuine community such as RLC, the members themselves define and solve problems. In what McKnight refers to as the "counterfeit" version of community, the professional provider in effect says: "I, the professional servicer, *am the answer. You* are not the answer. *Your peers* are not the answer" (McKnight's emphasis). In genuine community, there is informality, which means that relationships are not managed and controlled by professionals. Genuine community, McKnight observes, use stories rather than "the foreign language of studies and reports" to maintain its culture.

Highly relevant to the value of peer-to-peer support, McKnight notes, "While institutions and professionals war against human fallibility by trying to replace it, cure it, or disregard it . . . [genuine communities] incorporate both the capacities and the fallibilities of citizens." Many professionals and institutions, McKnight observes, actually preempt and destroy genuine community: "Human service professionals with special expertise, techniques, and technology push out the problem-solving knowledge and action of friend, neighbor, citizen, and association. As the power of profession and service system ascends, the legitimacy, authority, and capacity of citizens and community descend." McKnight concludes, "Modern heretics are those professional practitioners who support citizen competence and convert their profession into an understandable trade under the comprehensible command of citizens."

An example of professionals supporting citizen competence is the previously mentioned Open Dialogue, developed in Western Lapland in Finland in the 1980s. Rather than diagnosis and treatment imposed by a psychiatrist authority, Open Dialogue is decidedly more democratic, as there are regular meetings allowing the person who is the focus of concern, that person's family members, and their extended social network to have input and be part of the decision making. There is transparency so that all decisions made about treatment (including medication) are discussed in front of the person, with that person's input. The major role of professionals is to facilitate dialogue, thus professionals use ordinary language absent of professional jargon so that all can understand and be part of the decision making. Two of its developers, psychologist Jaakko Seikkula and psychiatrist Birgitta Alakare, in their chapter "Open Dialogues" (in *Alternatives Beyond Psychiatry*, 2007), report superior outcomes in a variety of areas (including fewer relapses and hospitalizations and greater employment) in two-year and five-year follow-ups of Open Dialogue as compared to standard treatment.

There are other professionals who, as McKnight put it, "support citizen competence." Among these professionals, some have been former psychiatric patients, including psychologist Ronald Bassman, author of *A Fight to Be: A Psychologist's Experience from Both Sides of the Locked Door* (2011) and, as previously noted, psychologist Eleanor Longden and psychiatrist Daniel Fisher. There are also mental health professionals who, though not former psychiatric patients, self-identify as "dissident professionals" and feel an obligation to expose fictions—promulgated by their profession—that disempower individuals with emotional difficulties.

The historian, philosopher, and social theorist Michel Foucault, in *Madness and Civilization* (1961), *Discipline and Punish* (1975), and other works, recognized that there is not simply a connection between knowledge and power, but that knowledge and power merge into one entity. Specifically, if the knowledge of anyone about their experience is silenced ("subjugated knowledge"), that individual has no power. In contrast, if the knowledge of former psychiatric patients about their condition and recovery is taken seriously, this automatically gives them more power and reduces the power of authorities lacking such knowledge. Foucault, similar to Spinoza, cared a great deal about freedom, and he recognized that only by winning a political battle to get one's knowledge taken seriously will one have the power necessary for freedom. This knowledge-power-freedom dynamic, for Foucault, is an inherent and never-ending struggle.

Among Spinoza's friends, the one who most reminds me of many modern psychiatric survivor activists and professional dissidents is Adriaan Koerbagh. This commonality is not only with respect to contempt for illegitimate authority but in Koerbagh's ire over jargon used by professionals to control people. For the same reason that many psychiatric survivors and professional dissidents seek the abolition of the term "mental illness," Koerbagh rejected the concept of "heresy." Jonathan Israel, tells us that for Koerbagh, "The idea of 'heresy' is . . . intrinsically an 'abuse of power' whereby churchmen appropriate jurisdiction to which they are not entitled."

Adriaan Koerbagh's rashness in criticizing organized religion resulted in him being hounded by authorities for blasphemy, but Adriaan was more than simply Spinoza's reckless radical friend who, after becoming a fugitive, was ratted out and died young in prison. Adriaan was approximately the same age as Spinoza but, unlike Bento, had an extensive university education, nine years in all, which included degrees in medicine and law. Adriaan published a dictionary of legal terms designed, as Israel explains, "to enlighten the people by showing how lawyers dupe them, and how to free themselves from thraldom to 'legalese,' helping them master the workings of the law." Then with his brother Johannes, Adriaan authored *A Flower Garden of All Kinds of Loveliness without Sorrow*; and here, "Fired with zeal to enlighten the populace," Israel tells us, "they charged all the ecclesiastical, legal, medical, and academic élites with contriving heaps of obfuscating terms and expressions to veil truth and reserve zones of specialized knowledge exclusively for the charmed circle of those equipped with the requisite professional training." Three hundred years prior to Foucault's work, the knowledge-power-freedom dynamic was obvious to Adriaan and Johannes Koerbagh, and it is equally obvious to contemporary psychiatric survivor activists.

While today, Spinoza is a famous figure, his radical underground community consisted of other significant freethinkers including Adriaan Koerbagh, who historian Jonathan Israel and philosopher Steven Nadler have brought attention to. Similarly, in the modern radical enlightenment movement with respect to psychiatry, while psychiatrist Thomas Szasz and journalist Robert Whitaker have received societal attention, there are significant figures within this underground community who are, for the most part, unknown to the general public.

The nonhierarchical nature of peer-to-peer support is threatening not simply to those at the top of mental health professional hierarchies. To the extent that any nonhierarchical organization is successful as well as pleasurable for participants, it serves as an attractive model for *everyone*, and the notion of a nonhierarchical organization can become contagious. In other words, the success and participant satisfaction of peer-to-peer support doesn't simply threaten psychiatric hierarchy but societal hierarchy, just as the success and participant satisfaction of nonhierarchical organization in the workplace—for example, a workplace cooperative—threatens hierarchical organization of society in general.

Those atop hierarchies would rather people not even consider the idea of nonhierarchical organization, and so *any* such nonhierarchical organization that is successful as well as satisfying for participants is a threat to those with power atop hierarchies. Thus, aligned against peer-to-peer support is not simply mental health professional hierarchy but others who are threatened by any nonhierarchical model of success and participant satisfaction.

CHAPTER 16

FREEDOM FROM BONDAGE

There is nothing more important to Spinoza than freedom—both *freedom from* and *freedom to*. *Freedom from* ecclesiastic authorities, state tyranny, and mob violence. *Freedom to* philosophize and express oneself. Those are freedoms that Spinoza celebrates in his *Theological-Political Treatise*. However, he recognized that even with those freedoms, we will remain enslaved if we do not free ourselves from self-imposed bondage. He describes this bondage in the *Ethics* and provides antidotes for it.

Early in life, in his first work, the *Treatise on the Emendation of the Intellect*, Spinoza committed himself to see "whether, in fact, there was something whose discovery and acquisition would afford me a continuous and supreme joy to all eternity." For Spinoza, such joy means freedom from the bondage of externalities. This freedom liberates us to act on our essential nature. In his second work, the *Short Treatise on God, Man, and His Well-Being*, probably completed by 1662, Spinoza sketched out a philosophy that he would present comprehensively in his magnum opus the *Ethics*, which took Spinoza over a decade to finalize and was the culmination of a lifetime of thought about how one could attain supreme joy.

Spinoza understood how our thoughts are tied to our emotions in ways that could make us more or less miserable. As I will later discuss, Spinoza is often seen as having much in common with both Stoicism and modern cognitive-behavioral therapy. There are also Spinoza concepts such as "blessedness"—the highest state of being—that strike some observers as similar to concepts in transpersonal psychology. And some historians believe that

Sigmund Freud appropriated Spinoza's concept of *conatus*—the drive to persevere (the Freudian terms *libido* and *Eros* are today associated with sexual drive, but these terms also have been used to mean a "life instinct," which is similar to *conatus*). Freud's theory of the unconscious would not strike Spinoza as novel, as it was obvious to Spinoza that we are routinely unaware of forces controlling us.

Spinoza, as previously noted, described three types of knowledge, the first type consisting of opinion, hearsay, imagination, and random experience, all of which results in inadequate ideas. It is likely that Spinoza would ascribe the type of knowledge used to judge both *mental illness* and *mental health* to be in this first category, thus resulting in inadequate ideas that do not reveal essential truths.

The modern concept of *mental health* would likely be seen by Spinoza as based on opinions assessed through hearsay and random experience, and thus an inadequate idea—a confused conceptualization that is partially or completely false. According to the World Health Organization (WHO), *mental health* is "a state of well-being in which the individual realizes his or her own abilities, can cope with the normal stresses of life, can work productively and fruitfully, and is able to make a contribution to his or her community." Common modern definitions of *mental health* use words such as *coping, adjustment, productive, equilibrium, harmony*, and *flexibility*. In modernity, mental health is largely ascribed to individuals who adjust to their circumstances and do not create tension for society. For most of society, including mental health professionals, individuals considered to be mentally healthy are those who accommodate to their family, workplace, school, and society; and if they have negative reactions to any circumstances, most people would react similarly to such circumstances.

Spinoza may well conclude that the solution for contemporary psychiatry's crisis is a therapy that he provides in the *Ethics*. He believed that by reading it, Clare Carlisle tells us, "people would gradually retrain their minds." For Carlisle, the *Ethics* "is not just a philosophical treatise, but also a kind of training manual for the philosophical way of life—and therefore reading it is a transformative spiritual exercise. As readers attain a deeper understanding of the text, their own activity of thinking should come to replace passive acceptance of prevailing superstitions and prejudices."

In his five-part structure of the *Ethics*, he applied reason to: (1) the nature of God/Nature; (2) human beings and how they acquire knowledge; (3) the nature of emotions; (4) human bondage by the emotions; and (5) freedom from such bondage.

Applying reason to detect the essence of reality can prevent a great deal of suffering. In the first part of the *Ethics*, Spinoza applies reason to understand the essence of God, and he concludes that God—or as he puts it, God or Nature—is all of reality and its laws. Thus to fear such a God, as clergy preaches, would be irrational, ridiculous, and harmful. If God is Nature and the singular substance that is reality, it is rational to attempt to understand increasingly more of God/Nature. The more we understand, the more we experience empowerment and pleasure.

While the God of Spinoza is a source of power and pleasure, this power and pleasure is through greater understanding of God/Nature—not through the inadequate false idea that we can manipulate God with prayers to win the lottery or get a hot date. In other words, we can love God to our benefit, but God cannot be manipulated to love us.

The essential component in nature, Spinoza concludes, is *conatus*, a drive toward self-preservation, and this drive or striving is the actual essence of humans. As Rebecca Goldstein explicates: "*Conatus* is simply a thing's special commitment to itself. It is its automatic concern about its own being and its intent to do what it thinks it takes in order to further its well-being." Increasing the perfection of one's essence and experiencing that accompanying increase in power is, for Spinoza, *virtue* and core to his ethics.

Conatus should not be equated with uncaring selfishness. Enlightened self-preservation means caring about harmonious relationships serving "the common advantage of all." "Therefore," Spinoza concluded in the *Ethics*, "nothing is more advantageous to man than man. Men, I repeat, can wish for nothing more excellent for preserving their own being than that they should all be in such harmony in all respects that their minds and bodies should compose, as it were, one mind and one body, and that all together should endeavor as best they can to preserve their own being, and that all together they should aim at the common advantage of all."

The task for Spinoza in the *Ethics* was elucidating how we enslave ourselves and how we can free ourselves from bondage so as to achieve happiness. In the Preface of Part III of the *Ethics*, "Concerning the Origin of the Nature of Emotions," Spinoza tells us that he will attempt to understand the emotions in the same way as everything else, which is by reason: "I shall, then, treat of the nature and strength of the emotions, and the mind's power over them . . . and

I shall consider human actions and appetites just as if it were an investigation into lines, planes, or bodies [solids]."

Given that *conatus* is our essential nature, we pursue that which we believe to benefit us. What benefits us is to understand more of the essence of reality, which is to understand more of God/Nature. This includes an understanding of ourselves, as we are part of God/Nature. Such an understanding provides us with more power to become more of ourselves, which provides us even more power and pleasure. Understanding the essence of reality creates more freedom and thus more power, which translates to pleasure. *Pleasure* or *joy* is simply the experience of moving from a lesser to greater state of perfection, becoming more of our essence and making us more powerful. *Pain* or *sadness* is the opposite, the experience of the moving to a lesser state of perfection and diminished power.

Conatus, pleasure, and pain, for Spinoza, are the fundamental concepts from which all our emotions are derived. *Love* is simply pleasure accompanied by the idea of an external cause that creates the passage to greater perfection and makes us more powerful. *Hatred* is simply pain accompanied with the idea of an external cause that creates the passage to a lesser state of perfection and makes us less powerful. The experience of *hope* is one of an externality, yet uncertain, which may bring about pleasure; and *fear* is the experience of an externality, also yet uncertain, which may bring about pain. To the extent we become more certain of future pleasure, we experience *confidence*; and to the extent we become certain of future pain, we experience *despair*.

For Spinoza, our emotions are not bad in themselves but can hinder *conatus*, creating roadblocks and false paths that result in us not pursuing our essential being and thus being unable to experience pleasure and increased power. Spinoza termed emotions that are passively experienced because of external causes as *passions*—think "passive." By passions, he means that we are passively experiencing them rather than actively applying reason to understand them. This results in reacting to externalities in ways opposed to *conatus*; in other words, reacting in a way that does not benefit our well-being and that decreases our power. This is bondage and unhappiness.

Spinoza's ideas about bondage are explained by Bertrand Russell in this manner: "We are in bondage in proportion as what happens to us is determined by outside causes, and we are free in proportion as we are self-determined."

When we understand Spinoza's view of bondage and misery, we can see why ecclesiastic authorities were so problematic for him. Spinoza believed that if we passively accept religious dogma about an anthropomorphic God who rewards us with heaven for obeying and punishes us with hell for disobeying, the passions—or passive emotions—of fear and hope will prevent us from actively using reason to detect what truly does benefit us. This results in bondage. Passively accepting ecclesiastic authorities' inadequate ideas about God creates irrational fear and hope: fear that if we don't act on dogma we will go to hell; and hope that if we do comply, we will go to heaven.

Such an inadequate idea of God is self-destructive (anti-*conatus*), resulting in irrational behaviors against our self-interest. For example, if a person complies with clergy so as to be judgmental of a supportive friend because that friend rejects religious dogma, this may well result in destroying the friendship. In contrast, reason would result in an adequate idea of God that results in truly ethical behavior of tolerance and kindness, which furthers this supportive friendship, which increases our power.

Spinoza's ultimate goal in the *Ethics* was to be a therapist for those capable of reason. He recognized that life is filled with external events that we have no control over and that diminish our power and do not contribute to *conatus*. We can have a physical ailment, as he did with his respiratory illness, or we can learn that our good friend was imprisoned and died in prison, such as was the case with his good friend Adriaan Koerbagh. Throughout life, we will experience many losses. Thus, similar to the Stoics, Spinoza provided ideas about the wisest ways to deal with unpleasant externalities beyond our control.

Most Spinoza scholars note similarities between Spinoza's ethical philosophy and Stoicism. At the very end of Part IV of the *Ethics*, "Of Human Bondage, or the Strength of the Emotions," Spinoza tells us that we can bear what happens to us that is contrary to our advantage, "if we are conscious that we have done our duty and that our power was not extensive enough for us to have avoided" disadvantageous external events. If we understand that "we are part of the whole of Nature whose order we follow," and if we understand that "the better part of us" is to desire nothing other than "that which must be," we can find contentment in understanding and accepting the truth. To the extent that we understand the truth of Nature, we are "in harmony with the order of the whole of Nature," and that is a source of pleasure.

Spinoza's solution of acceptance, at first glance, might appear to be a fatalistic one, but it is not so. The confusion stems from the fact that he does advocate to "desire nothing but that which must be," promoting contentment in the truth of reality—the acceptance of God/Nature and the deterministic reality of the universe. However, as Spinoza biographer Matthew Stewart points out, "The stance he adopts is not 'fatalism,' but something more like what Nietzsche describes as '*amor fati*'—the love of fate."

Spinoza was fond of Stoicism, owning books by the ancient Stoics, and his philosophy has some of its therapeutic ideas. In the *Ethics*, Spinoza tells us, "For a man at the mercy of his emotions is not his own master but is subject to fortune, in whose power he so lies that he is often compelled, although he sees the better course, to pursue the worse."

"Spinoza's ethical theory," notes Steven Nadler, "is to a certain degree, Stoic, and recalls the doctrines of thinkers such as Cicero and Seneca." Similar to Stoicism, Nadler tells us that "Spinoza's 'free person' is one who bears the gifts and losses of fortune with equanimity and does only those things that he believes to be 'the most important in life.'"

Stoicism is very much about overcoming destructive emotions and accepting the logic and determinism of reality and nature. Individuals who become overwhelmed by their rage or fear so as to not think rationally about what must be accepted are seen by Stoics—as they were by Mr. Spock in *Star Trek*—as uncool. The Stoic philosopher Seneca the Younger had been the Emperor Nero's tutor, and when Nero became a tyrant and ordered Seneca's death, Seneca's reaction was an unemotional acceptance, already having recognized the reality of how irrationally violent Nero had become; Seneca simply killed himself in the least painful way.

Susan James describes Spinoza's view as "neo-Stoic": "He thinks that as you come to understand yourself and your relation to nature and the way that everything works, then you take delight in that kind of understanding and the power that it gives you, and that pleasure is actually far greater and more stable and more sustaining ultimately than the kind of pleasure you can get from this fretful Biblical God who is not to be relied on at all."

Cognitive-behavioral therapy (CBT) shares similarities with both Stoicism and Spinoza. Stoicism, Spinoza, and CBT all conclude that irrational thinking creates unnecessary suffering, and all seek liberation from the bondage of problematic emotional reactions. All recognize that we cannot control every externality from occurring, but we can control our evaluations of these externalities, and depending on the nature of our evaluations (our beliefs), we will—or will not—experience emotions that tyrannize us and cause us suffering. Stoicism, Spinoza, and CBT are all rationalistic and deterministic.

CBT, like Spinoza, recognizes that when we react to externalities, we will be enslaved by them. One of the most well-known conceptualizations in CBT is called the ABC paradigm. In this paradigm, "A" is short for an "activating event"; "B," short for "belief" about that activating externality; and "C," short for the "consequences" (the emotional reaction to one's belief). Therapy consists of the patient becoming aware that it is *not* A (the activating externality) that causes C (the problematic emotion); but that it is B, the belief about A (the externality) that caused C (the problematic emotion). For example, if the presenting problem is one of debilitating anxiety about public speaking, CBT directs the patient to recognize that the cause of anxiety is not public speaking, but rather the belief about public speaking; and therapy involves various techniques for transforming that belief.

While CBT and Stoicism have commonalities with Spinoza, there are also differences. According to Bertrand Russell, "Spinoza does not, like the Stoics, object to *all* emotions; he objects only to those that are 'passions,' i.e., those in which we appear to ourselves to be passive in the power of outside forces." Most importantly, Spinoza differs from both CBT and the Stoics in his contention that a problematic passion cannot be overcome simply by reason, but instead can only be overcome by a stronger emotion, an "active emotion." My guess is that Spinoza would see contemporary CBT as "almost getting it."

There is a great deal of empirical research examining the effectiveness of CBT, including many studies comparing the effectiveness of CBT to antidepressant medication. One such major comparison was a meta-analysis, published in 2015 by *BMJ* (formerly *British Medical Journal*), of eleven randomized controlled trials that included 1,511 patients with major depressive disorder. Its findings were: "Meta-analyses found no statistically significant difference in effectiveness between second generation antidepressants [that include SSRI antidepressants such as Prozac] and CBT."

The fact that CBT does as well as antidepressants for major depression should be nothing for CBT advocates to get excited about. As cited earlier, in drug company dice-loaded studies, antidepressants only slightly edged out a placebo in a manner that was described as "clinically negligible." Thus, the fact that CBT works as well as antidepressants does not mean that these treatments are, in a scientific sense, all that effective (but rather that they work about as well as a placebo and the passage of time).

The rationalist Spinoza, without any knowledge of empirical studies, would deduce that CBT lacks a powerful ingredient to make it truly effective. For Spinoza, a problematic passion can only be overcome by a stronger emotion.

While CBT is often effective in assisting patients to understand how their irrational beliefs are creating problematic emotions, CBT can lack the power necessary for patients to truly transform their irrational beliefs. It does not logically follow that because patients know that an irrational belief is causing them to panic, they can easily change that belief. Spinoza knew that. As Nadler puts it, "What matters, according to Spinoza, is not just what you know but also how powerful that knowledge is." Spinoza understood that for liberation from problematic passions such as anxiety or despair so as to achieve happiness and joy, something more potent and more enduring is required than CBT techniques.

Similarly, without seeing the previously described long-term studies on antidepressants, Spinoza may well have been able to deduce the downside of these drugs and all psychotropics (drugs that affect one's neurotransmitters). Spinoza drank beer and wine and he smoked tobacco, and thus was familiar with the effect of psychotropics, and so he may well have deduced that the body develops a tolerance to these drugs; and so if one is using a psychotropic to take the edge off emotional pain, increasingly higher dosages would likely be necessary for it to be effective, which can result in a bondage to a drug that, at some point, no longer sufficiently takes the edge off of emotional pain.

So, what was Spinoza's more potent and enduring therapy? It might surprise people who view Spinoza as purely a dispassionate rationalist to discover that Spinoza's more potent and enduring therapy demands *love*, specifically the "intellectual love of God," which can also be read as the "intellectual love of Nature." This is a critical component of Spinoza's therapy. However, it is not easy for many of us to comprehend why an intellectual love of God/Nature provides us with power over problematic passions.

Donald J. Robertson is a unique psychotherapist and author, having studied CBT, Stoicism, and Spinoza. In his 2019 *Medium* article "Spinoza's Philosophical Psychotherapy: Rational Techniques of Emotional Therapy in Spinoza and the Stoics," he concludes: "Spinoza famously labels the fundamental emotion, which man experiences when he accurately perceives the essence of universal Nature, *Amor Dei Intellectualis*, the 'intellectual love of God.' . . . I cannot emphasize enough that contrary also to those who would miscast Spinoza, and philosophy in general, as arid intellectualism, Spinoza's therapy is essentially founded upon a philosophy of love, one of the dominant themes in the *Ethica* [*Ethics*]. Spinoza argues that the ultimate human emotion is an active, rational, love of existence itself."

"Spinoza argues," notes Nadler, "that the mind's intellectual love of God *is* our understanding of the universe, our virtue, our happiness, our well-being and our 'salvation.'"

Attaining this intellectual love of God/Nature is the attainment of the third kind of knowledge in which, Blake Dutton points out, "the mind passes to the highest state of perfection that is available to it." As a result of the mind's achieving this intellectual love of God, it experiences the greatest level of joy. "When such a love dominates one's affective life," Dutton continues, "one attains the serenity and freedom from passion that is the mark of wisdom." For Spinoza, a person who has attained this love possess true peace of mind. This is blessedness.

In the *Ethics*, Spinoza uses the term *blessedness* several times but not in the way that it is routinely used in organized religion. In the book's final proposition, he tells us: "Blessedness is not the reward of virtue, but virtue itself. We do not enjoy blessedness because we keep our lusts in check. On the contrary, it is because we enjoy blessedness that we are able to keep our lusts in check." For Spinoza, we don't get blessed by God or some clergy interpreter of God for being good boys and girls; rather, if we have achieved blessedness, we are not enslaved by our passions.

In Spinoza's deductive proof of this final proposition he tells us: "Blessedness consists in love towards God, a love that arises from the third kind of knowledge, and so this love must be related to the mind insofar as the mind is active; and therefore it is virtue itself." In other words, through the third and highest form of knowledge—intuitive knowledge—we can achieve blessedness by grasping God/Nature at a deep intuitive level. The more our mind understands the totality of God/Nature, which includes ourselves and our relationship to God/Nature, the more power the mind has over our emotions. For Spinoza, it is "the mind's enjoyment of this divine love or blessedness" that gives our mind the power over our problematic passions.

In Spinoza's earlier *Short Treatise on God, Man, and His Well-Being*, he uses the word *love* several times, proclaiming that "one love may be extinguished by another which is greater." He asserts: "Reason has no power to lead us to the attainment of our well-being," as such attainment only comes through intuitive knowledge or "a direct revelation." For Spinoza, it is this direct intuitive knowledge that evokes love of God/Nature. He concludes, "So that when we get to know God after this manner . . . we must necessarily become united with him. And only in this union . . . does our blessedness consist."

Since we are part of God/Nature, loving God/Nature includes self-love. For Spinoza, only this self-love, along with a love of all of God/Nature—and not a mere CBT technique—can provide the power to overcome problematic passions. While CBT appears reasonable, my clinical experience is that Spinoza had it right. CBT is often too weak to counter powerful passions. Love is required. Love of Nature, which includes love of self and others, who are part of Nature.

Spinoza did not conduct family therapy or couples counseling, but I have. In practical terms, when a child's irresponsible and selfish actions create anger and resentment resulting in emotional abuse by a parent, a CBT technique such as the ABC one (whereby the parent recognizes that the child's actions didn't cause the abuse but it was the parent's belief about the actions that did) only works when the parent has self-love and truly loves the child. Similarly, a husband who receives anger management therapy after physically abusing his wife can learn CBT techniques and may successfully practice those techniques on his beloved dog after the dog chews up his shoes, but if that husband does not truly love his wife, the technique will not prevent his perceived spousal slights from resulting in anger, resentment, and ensuing abuse.

Spinoza knew that problematic compulsive behaviors that are driven by powerful passions cannot be overcome by an insight into causality alone, but only by a more powerful emotion. Spinoza would be struck by the glaring omission of *love* from virtually all modern psychiatric and psychological treatments. He knew that only by the experience of love of Nature—a love of what is—can one experience the kind of pleasure that is a more powerful emotion than passions that fuel compulsive behaviors.

In a Spinozist cognitive therapy, an example of a more powerful active emotion resulting from the intellectual love of Nature is *curiosity*, which results in empowerment and liberation from the tyranny of one's passive reactions (passions) to externalities. For example, rather than being controlled by the externalities of selfish behavior and reactively becoming angry and resentful, a love of Nature can compel the active internalized emotion of curiosity; for example, reflecting on why an individual is behaving in a certain manner. Such internalized curiosity can be a more powerful emotion than the passions of anger and resentment. Spinozist cognitive therapy informs us that when we are not passively reacting to externals but actively intellectually loving Nature and being curious, our responses will be more reasoned and wiser.

Spinoza's recognition of the power of the love of God/Nature was why, in large part, he thought so highly of Jesus. Spinoza certainly did not think highly of any organized religion, including Christianity; and he did not believe that Jesus was born of virgin birth and was the son of God or had supernatural gifts such as the ability to perform miracles that violated Nature/God. Instead, what impressed Spinoza about Jesus was that he, more than anyone, had complete confidence in his intuitive knowledge of God/Nature, and with that supreme confidence came his supreme capacity to teach people to love God/Nature, which includes loving oneself and one's fellow human beings.

While not arrogant, Bento was extremely self-confident, believing that he intuitively "got it" about God, Nature, love, and justice. In 1675, he received a vitriolic letter from Alfred Burgh, who was perhaps one of Spinoza's ex-pupils and the son of a wealthy friend. Alfred, having converted to Catholicism, accused Spinoza of using "diabolical cunning" in the *Theological-Political Treatise*, and he challenged Spinoza as to how he could be so sure that he had found the best philosophy of all. Spinoza responded: "For I do not presume to have found the best philosophy, but I know that what I understand is the true one. . . . I know it in the same way that you know that the three angles of a triangle are equal to two right angles."

For some Spinozists—though not all—the idea of supreme happiness through unity with God/Nature gives Spinoza a mystical element. Philosopher Neal Grossman, author of *The Spirit of Spinoza* (2014), tells us that intuitive knowledge and the intellectual love of God is a "mystical insight" that "involves the conscious awareness of our mind as a part of the Mind of God, and it is in this awareness that salvation, or blessedness, consists." In transpersonal psychology, the sense of self extends beyond—or transcends—the individual to encompass wider aspects of humankind, reality, and the universe; and this results in peak experiences that some thinkers have associated with Spinoza's "blessedness" and the intellectual love of God.

The term *mysticism*, for some Spinozists, conveys a sense of blissful unity with all of nature, and so for them, Spinoza is part of the mystic tradition. But for other Spinozists, the word *mystical* conveys a sense of spiritual mystery, awe, and religious feelings, and so they reject the attribution of mystical to Spinoza, as they view Spinoza's conceptualization of God/Nature as one that is not mystical at all, but accessible to understanding by reason; and so they also reject the idea that Spinoza's concept of blessedness is a mystical notion.

Spinoza's understanding of emotional tyranny and how we free ourselves from bondage and gain wisdom, happiness, and blessedness are not easy to immediately comprehend. And even when one finally understands these concepts, it is no easy matter to attain. Such difficulties were acknowledged by Spinoza in his last paragraph of the *Ethics*: "If the road I have pointed out as leading to this goal seems very difficult, yet it can be found. Indeed, what is so rarely discovered is bound to be hard. For if salvation were ready to hand and could be discovered without great toil, how could it be that it is almost universally neglected?"

Then, in the final sentence of the *Ethics*, Spinoza states what has become perhaps its most famous line: "All things excellent are as difficult as they are rare."

CHAPTER 17

TRACTATUS PSYCHIATRICO-POLITICUS

While the *Ethics* is routinely considered Spinoza's most significant work, his *Theological-Political Treatise* (*Tractatus Theologico-Politicus*) was stunningly radical when it was published in 1670. This treatise declares that democracy is the best of all forms of government, and that the best societies are organized to create the greatest freedom and security for all rather than to maintain the power of monarchs and clergy.

Spinoza wrote the *Theological-Political Treatise* because he was troubled by the control that religious authorities had over civil society. Specifically, he was concerned by the power that ecclesiastic authorities had to impede and prohibit what he cared most about—freedom of thought and expression. Tolerance for free thought and expression, he believed, was vital not only for the well-being of individuals but also for society.

The connection between theology and politics was clear for Spinoza. A belief in the divinity of the Bible results in a God-ordained social hierarchy, which results in the obedience to the ecclesiastic authority of interpreters of the Bible. And if ecclesiastic authorities have leverage over civil authority, then freedom of thought and expression for the entire society is curtailed.

Today, for the majority of society, a "psychiatric-political treatise" makes little sense, as psychiatry is seen as an apolitical medical specialty that treats people with mental illness. A generation ago, however, the apolitical nature of psychiatry was not as widely accepted. Back then, there was a visible group of high-profile thinkers who wrote about the political implications of psychiatry. But today, this camp, similar to Spinozists in the seventeenth and eighteenth century, has for the most part gone underground.

Not that long ago, it would not have been all that radical to ask the following political questions about psychiatry and psychology—questions that Spinoza, if alive today, would likely consider: (1) Are psychiatrists and psychologists being used by authorities to compel individuals to adjust to a society that is unjust and dehumanizing? (2) Are biological theories of mental illness diverting attention from societal ills that cause emotional suffering and behavioral disturbances? (3) Are psychiatrists and psychologists being used to pathologize dissenters so as to marginalize them? (4) Are mental health professionals undermining mutual aid and other forms of nonhierarchical organization and democracy?

Until his death in 1980, Erich Fromm was a high-profile psychoanalyst and social psychologist who wrote about the political implications of psychiatry. He occupied a prominent place in U.S. society (interviewed by Mike Wallace on network television two years after the publication of Fromm's best-selling 1956 book *The Art of Loving*).

In 1941, Fromm published *Escape from Freedom* in reaction to the spread of authoritarianism and fascism in Europe. Spinoza, given his love of freedom, would have been very much interested in *Escape from Freedom*. In it, Fromm provides an analysis of how in modernity, with the end of the order of medieval society and with the advent of capitalism, greater freedom followed; however, along with this greater freedom there has also been greater insecurity, which creates fear, tension, and discomfort—so much so that many individuals flee freedom for authoritarianism and conformity. Fromm concluded that freedom from medieval traditional bonds, "though giving the individual a new feeling of independence, at the same time made him feel alone and isolated, filled him with doubt and anxiety, and drove him into new submission and into a compulsive and irrational activity."

Similar to Spinoza, Fromm regarded the Bible as literature. Fromm noted the following about God's prohibiting Adam and Eve's eating from the tree of knowledge: "Acting against the command of authority, committing a sin, is in its positive human aspect the first act of freedom. . . . The act of disobedience as an act of freedom is the beginning of reason." Both Fromm and Spinoza would have seen the political nature of oppositional defiant disorder (ODD), which first came into existence in *DSM-III*, published in 1980, the year that Fromm died.

In Fromm's *The Sane Society* (1955), he offers a political perspective that today would result in his being marginalized by the mainstream media, but a perspective that Spinoza would be curious about. Fromm was very much concerned about the political nature of mental health professionals, stating: "Today the function of psychiatry, psychology and psychoanalysis threatens to become the tool in the manipulation of man. . . . Yet, many psychiatrists and psychologists refuse to entertain the idea that society as a whole may be lacking in sanity."

Fromm observed in *Escape from Freedom* that "the person who is normal in terms of being well adapted is often less healthy than the neurotic person in terms of human values. Often he is well adapted only at the expense of having given up his self in order to become . . . the person he believes he is expected to be. All genuine individuality and spontaneity may have been lost."

Psychiatry as an institution has long had a political role. While psychiatry promotes the abolition of the stigma of mental illness so that people feel more comfortable seeking psychiatric treatment, psychiatry's societal role of assessing people as mentally ill and dangerous—and then essentially policing them—provides psychiatry with societal status. An individual who has committed no crime but who frightens family or other societal members can be forced by psychiatrists into a hospital or coerced into medication compliance. For its policing role, psychiatry is no less appreciated by much of modern society than the rabbis who issued a *herem* banishing Spinoza were appreciated by the frightened Amsterdam Jewish community. Obvious to Spinoza would be that, just as state authorities use clergy's coercive power to maintain the societal status quo, the political use of psychiatry is also irresistible for societal authorities.

In the old Soviet Union, political dissidents were routinely psychiatrically diagnosed (most famously with "sluggish schizophrenia") and hospitalized. While, in some cases, this occurred because Soviet psychiatrists were attempting to curry favor with the Soviet KGB, the truth behind this abuse of psychiatry is even darker, according to psychiatrist Walter Reich who detailed this in his 1983 *New York Times* article, "The World of Soviet Psychiatry." While there were deliberate misdiagnoses of Soviet political dissidents, Reich concludes that in most cases, psychiatrists and many members of society genuinely believed these dissidents were mentally ill. "In the context of Soviet society," Reich concludes, "dissidents constitute a deviant element. They behave and speak in ways that are different from other Soviet citizens, and, for that reason, they come to be seen as strange. After all . . . isn't it strange when someone openly does and says things that, under the conditions of Soviet political life, everyone knows to be dangerous?"

Soviet dissidents reported that they experienced being viewed as strange by KGB and other Soviet officials for lecturing them about their rights under the Soviet Constitution. "The sense that someone is strange," notes Reich, "is not infrequently followed by the suspicion that the strangeness may be due to mental illness." Reich points out the following about the Soviet psychiatrists who diagnosed the dissidents: "They grow up in the same culture, are affected by the same political realities and develop the same social perceptions. And since the way in which a psychiatrist goes about determining whether a person is ill depends to a great extent on the psychiatrist's assumptions about what is usual and expected in his society, he may, upon coming into contact with the dissident, have the same sense of strangeness felt by the KGB agent—and may go on to suspect that the defendant may be ill." Reich concluded that "at least some of those healthy dissidents [were] sincerely seen to be mentally ill, not only by the psychiatrists and the KGB but by much of the population of that historically wounded land."

The practice of psychopathologizing political dissidents is certainly not exclusive to the old Soviet Union. In the United States, the practice of psychopathologizing dissidents began at the very beginning of the nation. Benjamin Rush, as noted, is well-known among psychiatrists as "the father of American psychiatry." In 1805, Rush diagnosed those rebelling against the newly centralized federal authority as having an "excess of the passion for liberty" that "constituted a form of insanity," which he labeled as the disease of *anarchia*.

More recently, in *The Protest Psychosis: How Schizophrenia Became a Black Disease* (2010), psychiatrist and sociologist Jonathan Metzl describes systemic racism that labels "threats to authority as mental illness," and how this process increases the likelihood that African Americans will be diagnosed with schizophrenia. In an interview, Metzl stated: "The main story of my book is about Black Power activists in Detroit who were swept up into the mental health system after protesting. They ended up in psychiatric hospitals and diagnosed with schizophrenia. Political protest in the '60s became coded as mental illness."

In U.S. history, there have been episodes of political abuse by psychiatry and psychology that have come to the public attention and have been embarrassments for these professions.

Perhaps the most publicized and embarrassing political use of American psychiatrists and psychologists in the twentieth century is the now infamous Project MK-Ultra, the Central Intelligence Agency (CIA) program of experiments on human subjects. MK-Ultra, beginning in the early 1950s, used drugs (including LSD) and other procedures (including sensory deprivation and electroshock) to attempt to weaken and break an individual. MK-Ultra was documented by the U.S. Congress's Church Committee investigations (1975) and detailed in *The Search for the "Manchurian Candidate": The CIA and Mind Control: The Secret History of the Behavioral Sciences* (1979) by former State Department officer John Marks. There was widespread involvement in MK-Ultra by at least eighty institutions (including universities, pharmaceutical corporations, and prisons) and 185 researchers, including some of America's leading psychiatrists such as Louis Jolyon "Jolly" West and leading psychologists such as Henry Murray.

In the twenty-first century, the most egregious political abuse by U.S. psychologists was enabling interrogations that employed torture. Following the events of September 11, 2001, the American Psychological Association nurtured relationships with the CIA and the Department of Defense; and this secret collaboration was used by the George W. Bush administration to bolster legal and ethical justifications for the torture of prisoners. The *New York Times* in 2015 reported, "The involvement of health professionals in the Bush-era interrogation program was significant because it enabled the Justice Department to argue in secret opinions that the program was legal and did not constitute torture, since the interrogations were being monitored by health professionals to make sure they were safe."

Psychologists and psychiatrists have also been used for political purposes in ways that these professions are proud of. A powerful political force compelling the end of American involvement in Vietnam was U.S. soldiers' refusal to cooperate with the military; however, more recently, psychologists and psychiatrist have made such resistance more difficult. Reported in the *New York Times* in 2009, the former president of the American Psychological Association, Martin Seligman, consulted with the U.S. Army's Comprehensive Soldier Fitness positive psychology program. In one role-play utilized in this program, a sergeant is asked to take his exhausted men on one more difficult mission, and the sergeant is initially angry and complains that "it's not fair"; but in the role-play, his "rehabilitation" involves reinterpreting the order as a compliment.

According to the *Military Times* in 2013, one in six U.S. armed service members were taking at least one psychiatric drug, many of these medicated soldiers in combat zones in Afghanistan and Iraq. In the Vietnam War, many soldiers, as part of a general noncooperation, used illegal psychotropic drugs, which alarmed U.S. government officials who were afraid of unleashing illegal-drug using veterans on American streets. Today, however, psychotropic drugs ubiquitously prescribed in the military co-opt the once rebellious culture of psychotropic use, and this legal prescription practice enables the U.S. military to deny concerns of drug dependency and adverse effects.

The United States has increasingly relied on psychiatric drugs to control discarded and potentially disruptive populations. By 2011, antipsychotic drugs had grossed over $18 billion a year in the United States, making antipsychotics at that time the highest grossing class of drugs. Much of this growth is attributable to the prescribing of these drugs to nonpsychotic people in marginalized populations, attempting to control them as inexpensively as possible. A 2021 New York Times investigation, "Phony Diagnoses Hide High Rates of Drugging at Nursing Homes," reported that at least 21 percent of U.S. nursing home residents are on antipsychotic drugs. Other marginalized populations include foster children and inmates in prisons and jails where, as is the case in nursing homes, antipsychotic drugs are a relatively inexpensive way to subdue and manage.

There are other uncared about and potentially disruptive U.S. populations also managed by drugs. Among U.S. veterans, a 2014 study showed that 1.85 million veterans were using at least one psychiatric drug, with 30 percent of them having no psychiatric diagnosis. For unhappy and potentially rebellious women in the 1960s and 1970s, rather than taking seriously societal reasons for their malaise, millions were prescribed the tranquilizer Valium, commonly known as "Mother's Little Helper." In 2011, the CDC reported that 23 percent of women ages 40–59 were taking antidepressants (compared to 11 percent for all American adults).

In Spinoza's day, monarchies and ecclesiastic authorities had a mutually beneficial—or symbiotic—relationship. Clergy enjoyed extensive power, which was used to control individuals to accept the societal status quo of hierarchy, which included the divine right of kings. It is axiomatic that those atop any hierarchy will reward a professional class that legitimizes that hierarchy and that diverts societal members from considering whether their suffering is a result of social and economic injustices that are caused by those atop the hierarchy.

In the mid-1980s, the view that the increasingly biological focus of psychiatry had political implications was an idea that had not yet been pushed completely to the margins of society. The 1984 book *Not in Our Genes: Biology,*

Ideology, and Human Nature was co-authored by prominent intellectuals: evolutionary geneticist R.C. Lewontin, neurobiologist Steven Rose, and psychologist Leon Kamin. They make clear the political ideology implicit in the individual defect theory of biochemical/genetic determinism: "Biological determinism (*biologism*) has been a powerful mode of explaining the observed inequalities of status, wealth, and power in contemporary industrial capitalist societies. . . . Biological determinism is a powerful and flexible form of 'blaming the victim.'" At the time of its publication, *Not in Our Genes* received praise from well-known public intellectuals such as anthropologist Ashley Montagu and paleontologist Stephen Jay Gould (who had similarly criticized the pseudoscience behind hereditary determinism of intelligence in his 1981 book *The Mismeasure of Man*).

If a population believes that emotional suffering and disturbing behaviors are caused primarily by nonsocial and nonpolitical variables—be it God's will; noncompliance with religious dogma; defects in biochemistry; or noncompliance with psychiatric treatment—rather than by socioeconomic variables, then the belief in nonsocial and nonpolitical variables can be as powerful in maintaining the status quo as a heavily armed police force.

The majority of Americans are unaware that socioeconomic variables are far more clearly associated with emotional suffering and behavioral disturbances than any biochemical defect. Results from a 2013 national survey, issued by the U.S. government's Substance Abuse and Mental Health Services Administration (SAMHSA), included socioeconomic correlates of serious mental illness and suicidality (serious suicidal thoughts, plans, or attempts). The survey results provide extensive evidence that unemployment, poverty, and involvement in the criminal justice system are highly associated with serious mental illness and suicidality.

Specifically, the unemployed were more likely than those who were employed full time to have serious thoughts of suicide (7 percent for the unemployed vs. 3 percent for the employed); to make suicide plans (2.3 percent vs. 0.7 percent); and to attempt suicide (1.4 percent vs. 0.3 percent). Among adults diagnosed with serious mental illness, the percentage who were unemployed was 6.6 percent compared to 2.7 percent full-time employed. Among those having a major depression episode, the percentage of those who were unemployed was 9.5 percent compared to 5.3 percent full-time employed. Similarly, family income below the Federal poverty level as well as involvement in the criminal justice system (such as being on parole or probation) are highly correlated with suicidal thoughts and serious mental illness diagnoses. Acknowledging these realities means recognizing that social policies such as preventing unnecessary involvement with the criminal justice system (for example, marijuana legalization and drug use decriminalization), may well be more powerful antidotes to suicidality and serious mental illness than medical treatment.

While correlation is not the equivalent of causation, the political question is: Why is U.S. society focusing far less on socioeconomic variables, which actually are associated with serious mental illness and suicidality than on variables such as chemical imbalances that are not even correlates?

Far more important to emotional suffering than any biochemical defect variable is trauma, including the trauma resulting from adverse childhood experiences which, in part, are related to a society's political realities.

In the late 1990s, the Adverse Childhood Experiences (ACE) Study revealed a powerful relationship between childhood trauma and later adult emotional difficulties and physical health problems. The ACE Study connected adult emotional and physical health status with an individual's childhood traumatic experiences. Physician and researcher Vincent Felitti (head of Kaiser Permanente's Department of Preventive Medicine in San Diego) and researcher Robert Anda (at the CDC) surveyed the adverse childhood experiences of 17,431 Kaiser Permanente patient volunteers. Since the average study participant was fifty-seven years old and their adult health status was known, Felitti and Anda could correlate their self-reports of adverse childhood experiences—for example, emotional/physical abuse and neglect—with adult health status decades later. They found that a high number of adverse childhood experiences is associated with significantly greater likelihood of later physical and emotional difficulties such as suicidality, alcohol abuse, and injecting illegal drugs.

In her 2018 book *Trauma and Madness in Mental Health Services*, psychologist Noël Hunter, documents the following: "Adverse experiences, particularly in childhood (such as physical and sexual abuse, parental separation, bullying, parental death, foster care, neighborhood violence, poverty, racism, etc.), have been demonstrated to have a direct and dose-response relationship (meaning the more adversity, the greater the risk) with adult mental health issues like hearing voices, suicidality, drug abuse, experiencing altered states of consciousness, extreme and intense emotions, fragmented sense of self, obesity, depression, paranoia, beliefs in conflict with consensus reality, anxiety, and more."

Most biological-defect theorists simply ignore the link between serious mental illness and the nature of modern society. However, one leading biological-defect theorist acknowledges the linkage but attempts to biochemically explain it. Psychiatrist E. Fuller Torrey, in his 1980 book *Schizophrenia and Civilization*, states, "Schizophrenia appears to be a disease of civilization. . . . Between 1828 and 1960, almost all observers who looked for psychosis or schizophrenia in technologically undeveloped areas of the world agreed that it was uncommon." Torrey disputes the contemporary narrative of psychiatry that schizophrenia occurs in the same prevalence in all cultures and is not a disease of civilization. He reports research in New Guinea that he himself had conducted, "There was over a twentyfold difference in schizophrenia prevalence among districts; those with a higher prevalence were, in general, those with the most contact with Western civilization." How does Torrey square his ideas that mental illness is due to biological factors when his own research shows that schizophrenia is highly associated with European-American civilization? For Torrey, "Viruses in particular should be suspect as possible agents." Torrey's suspected virus agents have never been found.

The focus on biochemical causality rather than socioeconomic/trauma variables is a political win for several groups: (1) pharmaceutical companies; (2) drug prescribers; (3) mental illness institutions whose survival is tied to biochemical causality; (4) researchers funded to do biochemical research; (5) those atop the societal hierarchy who prefer social and economic causes for emotional difficulties and behavior disturbances be unexamined; and (6) individuals convinced that there are only two options—biochemical causality or personal blame—to explain their own and family members emotional suffering and behavioral disturbances, and because they are unaware of the third option—the nature of society and trauma—prefer biochemical causality rather than personal blame.

It was a political battle to bury realities about cancer, and a political battle to expose these realities. Specifically, though cancer is very much a biochemical reality that can be seen in biopsies, it is in large part caused by inhaling, ingesting, and absorbing carcinogenic products and byproducts of industrial society, which social policy can increase or decrease. It has also been a political battle to bury societal causes of emotional suffering and disturbing behaviors. Biochemicalizing and depoliticizing emotional suffering buries the reality that society is designed less to meet fundamental human needs than to meet the financial needs of those at the top of the societal hierarchy.

Erich Fromm, in *The Sane Society*, reminds us that the term *alienation* was once used to denote an insane person, and that "This alienation and automatization leads to an ever-increasing insanity." Fromm was a democratic socialist who was sharply critical of both capitalism and communism: "They both are thoroughly materialistic in their outlook. . . . Everybody is a cog in the machine, and has to function smoothly."

Gallup polling in 2013 and 2017 show that approximately 70 percent of Americans were disengaged from what they do for a living. Even in occupations that are higher paying and generally viewed to have more inherent meaning, there is great dissatisfaction. A 2018 Wisconsin Medical Society survey reported "Physician Burnout in Wisconsin: An Alarming Trend Affecting Physician Wellness." Surveying 1,165 Wisconsin physicians, it was found that more than half of them evidenced at least one sign of burnout. Reported by physicians as major sources of burnout are the loss of autonomy, the demands of electronic health records, lack of a supportive practice environment, and poor work/life balance. When these physicians were asked if they would recommend their careers to others, only 40 percent said "Yes."

Modern economic systems imbue individuals with feelings of insignificance and powerlessness. Individuals experience alienation, disconnection, and estrangement on multiple levels—from the products of their labor; from other people as employers and as employees; and as customers who are merely objects to be used. Individuals are alienated from their own self, as they are compelled to objectify their own personality as something to be sold in the marketplace.

In the current era of domination by transnational corporations, alienation, anxiety, insignificance, powerlessness, helplessness and resulting depression, resentment, and rage have all been further exacerbated. There is greater job insecurity and even less opportunity for meaningful employment. In the Amsterdam of Spinoza, it is estimated that there were four hundred bookstores run by owner operators who selected the books for sale and who knew their customers. Today, we have Amazon, which by 2020 had approximately 900,000 employees, most of whom scurry around giant warehouses moving boxes, alienated from products, customers, and themselves.

For quite some time in U.S. society, there has been a breakdown of confidence in major societal institutions. In a 2020 Gallup poll "Confidence in Institutions," the percentage of Americans who reported a "great deal/quite a lot" of confidence in the following institutions that govern their lives are as follows: big business, 19 percent; criminal justice system, 24 percent; newspapers, 24 percent; television news, 18 percent; public schools, 41 percent; health maintenance organizations, 19 percent; Congress, 13 percent; the presidency, 39 percent; Supreme Court, 40 percent; banks, 38 percent; church/organized religion, 42 percent; and the medical system, 51 percent. The only institution that Americans had a great deal of confidence in was the military, at 72 percent.

The breakdown of a society's confidence in its ruling institutions, and the ever-increasing experience of alienation, anxiety, insignificance, powerlessness, helplessness, depression, resentment, and rage create adults who, in their interactions with children, have little frustration tolerance. This lack of frustration tolerance makes abuse and trauma of children more likely, resulting in adverse childhood experiences, which, as noted, studies definitively link to later emotional suffering and behavioral disturbances.

To not take seriously the nature of modern society as a causative agent in emotional suffering and behavioral disturbances would be, for Spinoza, simply irrational.

Another psychiatric-political issue is whether or not mental health professionals are undermining mutual aid and democracy. In democracy and in genuine community, as previously noted by John McKnight, it is individual citizens as a group—not authorities above them in a hierarchy—who have the power to decide what is a problem, how to solve that problem, and who implements solutions.

The issue of professionalization versus peer-to-peer support is clearly a political issue for individuals seeking recovery from emotional suffering and behavioral disturbances. Important for all societal members, as previously noted, the more that a society discards mutual aid in favor of hierarchical institutions, the more difficult it is for genuine democracy to take place in other parts of that society. Hierarchy becomes increasingly normalized, and people no longer even grasp that democracy does not simply mean voting for the lesser-of-two-evils candidate in an election; it means that power is truly vested in the people.

In summary, the relationship between society and emotional suffering is one major political issue, and another important political issue is hierarchy versus egalitarianism (specifically, professionalization versus peer-to-peer support). With respect to these issues, there are three camps in psychiatry.

The first camp, which includes most of psychiatry and the majority of society, has simply ignored the effects of societal policies. While psychiatry proclaims a "biological-psychological-social" model, the reality of research funding and treatment is a "bio-bio-bio" model. This first camp sees no alternative to professionals being on top of a hierarchy in charge of emotional suffering and behavioral disturbances.

The second camp is critical of psychiatry's poor performance, *DSM* validity, theories of mental illness, and believes in moderate reforms, for example seeing value in peer-to-peer support as long as this doesn't reduce professional authority. This second camp does not, however, challenge the legitimacy of psychiatry or that of other major societal institutions and their place in societal hierarchy.

The third camp, in the tradition of what Jonathan Israel terms the *radical Enlightenment*, sees the need for radical change. This means a complete break with past tradition, which includes: eliminating the power that the American Psychiatric Association (APA) has over civil society through its mental illness declarations; abolishing institutional hierarchies in which individuals with extensive experience in recovery but lacking professional degrees have little or no power; and prioritizing societal variables and social policies that affect emotional well-being.

CHAPTER 18

BENTO'S CONCLUSIONS

In his community, Spinoza was called Bento, which is short for the Portuguese name Benedito. His Hebrew name was Baruch, and he also would use its Latin equivalent Benedictus. Benedito, Baruch, and Benedictus all mean the blessed one. His family name Spinoza—also written as Espinosa and Espinoza—derives from *espinhosa*, which in Portuguese means thorny. Every radical Enlightenment requires a blessed one with thorns, a person who afflicts the comfortable and comforts the afflicted—afflicting those who are comfortable with irrational, intolerant, and unjust institutions, while comforting those afflicted by the pain of such institutions. For radical Enlightenment thinkers, Baruch de Spinoza—in his lifetime and since—has been a blessed thorn; but for those not in this camp, he has been a cursed prick.

The conclusion to Spinoza's life entailed a struggle that appears bittersweet, but more precisely, it is one of sweetness overcoming bitterness.

When it became known to the world that Spinoza was the anonymous author of the *Theological-Political Treatise*, following its publication in 1670, he became a notorious national and international figure—"a focus of general indignation, anxiety, and surveillance," notes Jonathan Israel who reports, "His every move was monitored by secular and especially ecclesiastical authorities." These authorities were worried that his radical ideas would not only be taken seriously by philosophers and intellectuals but would become understood by the general public and penetrate society.

Between 1661 and 1674, on and off, Spinoza had worked on the *Ethics*, his magnum opus. His select group of trusted friends had read much of it, and by 1675, Spinoza was ready to publish it. However, by the summer of that year, it became increasingly clear to him that his life's work might not be published during his lifetime, and that he would have to depend on his loyal friends to publish it following his death.

In the summer of 1675, we know that Spinoza left his home in The Hague for a visit to Amsterdam to attempt to get the *Ethics* published. After he concluded that it was too dangerous for it to be published, we know how he felt from a letter he wrote to Henry Oldenburg, the first secretary of the Royal Society and founding editor of the *Philosophical Transactions of the Royal Society* (considered to be the first scientific journal).

Spinoza's correspondence with Oldenburg dates back to 1661, and the following pained letter by Spinoza was written to Oldenburg in September, 1675. "Intending to put into print the book," which he had previously mentioned to Oldenburg, he tells Oldenburg that he learned that "a rumor became widespread that a certain book of mine about God was in the press, and in it I endeavor to show that there is no God. This rumor found credence with many. So certain theologians, who may have started this rumor, seized the opportunity to complain of me before the Prince and the Magistrates." The Prince referred to by Spinoza is the Prince of Orange, who was indebted to the Calvinist clergy for ensuring his rise to power. Spinoza then adds, "Having gathered this from certain trustworthy men who also declared that the theologians were everywhere plotting against me, I decided to postpone the publication I had in hand until I should see how matters would turn out, intending to let you know what course I would then pursue. But the situation seems to worsen day by day, and I am not sure what to do about it."

A deeply disappointed Spinoza could have spent what turned out to be the last eighteen months of his life feeling sorry for himself. He could have bitterly reflected upon the decline of tolerance in the Dutch Republic. He could have become depressed, overwhelmed by grief over the loss of so many people he loved and admired: the imprisonment of his good friend Adriaan Koerbagh in 1668 and his death in prison a year later; Adriaan's radical brother, Johannes, also a friend of Spinoza's, released from prison but a broken man and dead three years later, in 1672; the de Witt brothers savagely murdered by a mob in 1672; and his freethinking mentor, Franciscus van den Enden, after plotting to establish a free republic in Normandy, France, arrested and hanged in front of the Bastille in 1674. Add all this to his previous losses, which included the death of his great friends Simon de Vries and Pieter Balling, along with his own worsening chronic respiratory problems.

However, rather than self-pity, Spinoza worked on his final book, the *Political Treatise*, continued to meet with others, carried on correspondences, read, and sketched with charcoal and ink (Colerus reported that Spinoza taught himself to draw, and that he owned a collection of Spinoza's drawings, but this collection has never been found). Spinoza died in The Hague on February 21, 1677. Immediately after his death begins the sweet story of the publication of the *Ethics*.

Before dying, Spinoza had asked his landlord Hendrik van der Spyck, following Spinoza's death, to immediately and secretly send his writing desk that contained his unpublished manuscripts (which, in addition to the *Ethics*, included his other yet unpublished works as well as his personal letters) by barge to Amsterdam to his ally friends who then began, Israel tells us, "the complex business of saving and deploying his philosophical legacy."

Spinoza had written in the *Ethics* about the "good that follows from mutual friendship and social relations," and this proved true. He had wisely selected his friends. Not only did they have deep affection and respect for Bento but were themselves highly capable, and they formed a talented crew.

After receiving the manuscripts, his friends formed a team to edit, translate, publish, and distribute them. Along with his publisher Jan Rieuwertsz, the team included his close friends Jarig Jelles and Lodewijk Meyer, as well as Jan Glazemaker, Johannes Bouwmeester, Georg Schuller, and Petrus van Gent. Knowing the authorities were determined to prevent publication, the team had to move rapidly, making quick decisions as to how best to get Spinoza's work out to the world. They boldly decided to publish both a Latin and a Dutch edition of all Spinoza's unpublished works. Israel deduces that Meyer, Bouwmeester, and Van Gent, all skilled Latinists, were entrusted with the Latin edition, while Rieuwertsz, Jelles, and Glazemaker worked on the Dutch edition, with Schuller working in a "secondary capacity." In addition to this core team of Spinoza loyalists, Israel reports, "A sizeable group, including copiers and printers, knew of the undertaking organized by Rieuwertsz in Amsterdam, and that in itself posed a security risk."

It was not only Dutch authorities who were afraid of Spinoza's works. International authorities were threatened by them. Cardinal Francesco Barberini, the Pope's nephew, wrote Johannes van Neercassel, the Vicar Apostolic of the Dutch Catholic Church, that an atheist work by Spinoza could seriously harm the "purity of our Holy Catholic Faith," and he instructed Neercassel to prevent publication. Neercassel organized a task force to pressure informants to provide information about where the book was being published, and in December of 1677, he confronted Rieuwertsz. When Neercassel asked Rieuwertsz if he was in possession of unpublished work by Spinoza, Rieuwertsz brazenly lied. For Spinozists then and now, if ever there was a "noble lie," Rieuwertsz told it.

Before the end of 1677, the *Ethics* and the rest of Spinoza's previously unpublished works were published in a collection titled *Opera Posthuma*, with the author being identified only with Spinoza's legendary initials: B.D.S. By early 1678, the *Opera Posthuma* was in distribution, and almost immediately, a Dutch edict banned it, laying down severe penalties for printers and booksellers who defied the ban. Neercassel complained that the edict had produced "scarcely any other fruit . . . than to increase the renown and prices of Spinoza's books."

Israel reports, "The illegal sale of Spinoza's texts could not be stopped. . . . There was a ready market for such books and much profit to be made from selling them." While the banning did not prevent the curious from acquiring Spinoza's works, the outlawing of them was important in shaping societal attitudes about Spinoza for many years by "laying down legally the separation between radical and moderate Enlightenment which," Israel notes, "within a few years, was to extend across the whole of Europe."

Owing to Spinoza's devoted friends, we know about his final philosophical, psychological, and political conclusions. Given what we know about Spinoza and his thinking, what then would he likely conclude about psychiatry's practices and conceptualizations?

It was self-evident—axiomatic—for Spinoza that conflicts of interest, including financial ones, had a corrupting influence on philosophy and science, so it would not be an exaggeration to say that he would be appalled by what psychiatry considers to be ethical. The idea that researchers and practitioners receive financial remunerations from drug companies—whose profits increase to the extent that more human conditions are pathologized and more drugs are prescribed—would, for Spinoza, discredit the claims of such researchers and practitioners. Just as it was obvious to Spinoza that monarchs and ecclesiastic authorities had symbiotic relationships that gave each greater power, he would see the partnership between psychiatry and drug companies as symbiotic, providing each of them with greater power. As an advocate of democracy, Spinoza would reflexively recoil at any symbiotic relationship between powerful authorities, recognizing that this likely reduces the power of other members of society.

We know that Spinoza loathed dogmatism and arrogance about preconceived notions of the nature of Nature. He recognized that people often make false attributions about natural phenomenon because of their prejudices. In the *Ethics*, he tells us, "So when they see something occurring in Nature at variance with their preconceived ideal of the thing in question, they believe that Nature has then failed or blundered and has left that thing imperfect. So we see that men are in the habit of calling natural phenomena perfect or imperfect from their own preconceptions rather than from true knowledge."

Spinoza cared deeply about the validity of conceptualizations. He recognized that the discovery of truths can only happen if there is freedom of thought and expression. He cared about tolerance for all opinions, and so he cared about the nature of authority in society. He knew that the freedom to philosophize about the nature of reality and happiness can be impeded by authorities who need certain conceptualizations and ideas to maintain their power.

Consensus reality, Spinoza knew, is not necessarily reality. He spent a lifetime questioning and challenging consensus realities of his society and its institutions so as to discover essential reality. He rejected the consensus reality that the Bible is the divine word of God, and he rejected the consensus reality of the nature of God. He rejected the conceptualization of God as an entity that performs miracles by violating natural law; for Spinoza this would be a violation of God and Nature, which were one and the same. And he rejected the idea of a God who would answer prayers and reward and punish with heaven and hell, as it was obvious to Spinoza that this type of conceptualization is useful for theologians to control people.

In Spinoza's rational analysis of any conceptualization, he put great effort into considering whether it was, in his words, an *adequate* or *inadequate* idea. Adequate ideas provide one with the essence of reality, while inadequate ideas are confused and vague conceptualizations that are partially or completely false. Many of the ideas held by individuals in his day and today are acquired by what Spinoza described as the first kind of knowledge: opinion, imagination, hearsay, and random or anecdotal experience—all resulting in inadequate ideas.

Spinoza would certainly be curious as to what kind of knowledge is used today to declare that a human being is suffering from a mental illness. In the *Courtier and the Heretic*, Matthew Stewart reports that a powerful bishop, Pierre-Daniel Huet, proclaimed Spinoza to be "that insane and evil man, who deserves to be covered with chains and whipped with a rod." Throughout history, *insane* is commonly ascribed to individuals who frighten and enrage, and Spinoza was unquestionably frightening and enraging for that bishop.

If Spinoza were to hear someone call another *insane, mad,* or *seriously mentally ill*, this would tell him far less about the person being labeled than about the person doing the labeling. It would tell him that the person labeling another as insane, mad, or seriously mentally ill is frightened or enraged by that individual. Some people called Spinoza insane and evil, while others called him blessedly rational. What he was called informed him what others felt about him, not who he was.

Given that Spinoza and most of his friends were oppositionally defiant with authorities, it is a safe bet that Spinoza would have chuckled about the *DSM* diagnosis of oppositional defiant disorder (ODD). Given the number of people who took the Bible literally in his day, he would be unsurprised that there remains today many people who accept the Bible as literally true. Spinoza would also be unsurprised that the belief that Joshua could stop the sun and other such delusions of those who accept the Bible as literally true are not considered symptoms of mental illness. It would not surprise him to discover that delusions believed by a large enough group are treated differently than delusions that few individuals believe in. Spinoza knew that political power dictates which delusions are considered symptoms of madness.

In the *Ethics*, Spinoza discusses how hypocrisies determine *madness*, and so we can surmise that he would be vigilant for hypocrisies determining *serious mental illness*. Spinoza points out that, while his society considered hallucinating individuals to be mad, his society did not consider the miser who thinks of nothing but money to be mad. For Spinoza, the reality is that avarice is a kind of madness, but not considered so by society. The opinion of his society—which remains the consensus reality of contemporary society—that an individual who already has more money than 99 percent of the world but spends all their waking time trying to acquire more money so as to be the richest individual on the planet is either ambitious or, at worst, greedy and power hungry but not mad or seriously mental ill; for Spinoza, such an individual is acting as irrationally as an individual with hallucinations, and extreme irrationality is madness.

Spinoza would recognize that, given the values of his society, his opinion of madness was not the same as his society's opinion. He recognized that declarations of madness were based on opinion, and he would today see declarations of mental illness also based on opinion. Spinoza would view the conceptualization of mental illness as a value-laden one about individuals whose behaviors are experienced by others as disturbing, frightening, and dangerous. It would be obvious to Spinoza that the concept of mental illness is derived by the first kind of knowledge that involves opinion, which means it is an inadequate idea—a confused and vague conceptualization that is partially or completely false.

Concluding that the conceptualization of mental illness is merely an opinion, Spinoza would see psychiatric diagnoses as "opinions about opinions." Since clerical authorities in his day often had different views on theological dogma, he would be unsurprised by studies showing significant disagreement (poor reliability) among mental health professionals in their mental illness diagnoses—in their opinions about an opinion.

Since it was fundamental to Spinoza's philosophy that the mind and body are not different substances, Spinoza would be unsurprised that brain-scan technology shows correlates between brain activities with our thoughts and emotions. However, from these correlates, he would not deduce a "mental illness brain disease" conceptualization. While our thoughts and emotions are associated with brain activities, this does not tell us anything about the essential nature of those thoughts and emotions.

Given how much he cared about tolerance for minority beliefs, we can be fairly certain that Spinoza's tolerance-intolerance lens would be an important one that he would use to evaluate the practices of psychiatry and other mental health professions. Spinoza would not be satisfied with mere proclamations of tolerance; he would probe deeper to see if practices did in fact actually promote tolerance for individual differences.

Without the need for empirical research, Spinoza could have reasoned that the conceptualization of serious mental illness as a "chronic brain disease that can be treated and not cured" would result in greater stigma, not less. It would be obvious to Spinoza that the attribution of a brain disease to those individuals who create tension sets those individuals more apart from others—and makes them more vulnerable to stigma. It would be obvious to him that the attempt to destigmatize via the "an illness like any other" campaign would fail because of societal fear of individuals diagnosed with serious mental illness; and so the idea that such individuals suffer from a brain disease requiring medication for life to prevent dangerous behavior is an idea that would compel people to stay away from such a person. If Spinoza was shown the empirical research confirming this reasoning, he likely would be outwardly polite but privately think that only those with little capacity to reason would need this empirical research.

Fear, for Spinoza, is a dangerous fuel. He knew that fear makes people vulnerable to irrational beliefs such as superstitions, and that these beliefs provide ecclesiastic authorities with power over people. He knew that fear makes individuals vulnerable to handing over power to power-seeking demagogues, and so he would be wary of any authority who inflames fear. It would be obvious to him that one could not truly be an advocate for abolishing the stigma of mental illness if one is using fear of those diagnosed with mental illness to promote laws legalizing coercions to ensure compliance with psychiatric treatment.

Spinoza would deduce that if society tells people they have a serious mental illness that cannot be cured but only treated with medications that have unpleasant adverse effects, many such individuals will resist their diagnosis and treatment; and their noncompliance will frighten a society that believes these individuals, without medication, are a threat. It would be clear to Spinoza that if society has been persuaded to enact coercive treatment laws out of a fear that untreated schizophrenics can become violent, then the stigmatization of individuals diagnosed as schizophrenic will be exacerbated, and that this stigmatization will be damaging for their recovery.

Spinoza took a break from finishing the *Ethics* in order to publish the *Theological-Political Treatise* because he was concerned that the explanations for suffering offered by ecclesiastic authorities gave them power over everyone else and undermined freethinking and tolerance for diversity. Ecclesiastic authorities have a vested interest in promoting conceptualizations that give them power, and this is the case for all authorities.

The conceptualization of mental illness as a brain disease and an "illness like any other" gives medical authorities power, and it reduces the power of individuals who are not doctors. Spinoza would immediately recognize the political implications of these conceptualizations for peer-to-peer support. Since peers cannot treat brain diseases, their status, power, and funding are reduced to the extent that brain disease conceptualizations are the consensus reality.

Spinoza would also not need the empirical research that shows that the brain disease conceptualization facilitates acceptance of medical professionals as authorities, resulting in greater compliance with professional treatment, including medication. It would be clear to Spinoza that the brain disease focus provides more power to medical professionals and drug companies.

Given that political power rests on brain disease conceptualizations, Spinoza would recognize that there is a motivation to suppress the reality that many individuals diagnosed with serious mental illness have completely recovered without medical treatment, becoming fully functioning for the remainder of their lives; and he would recognize the need to suppress the value of peer-to-peer support for such recovery. The idea that peer-to-peer support should have greater status, power, and funding than medical professionals sounds irrational if the consensus reality of society is such that serious mental illnesses are brain diseases, but this idea is quite rational from the perspective of alternate paradigms and models.

Spinoza cared deeply about every aspect of freedom, including freedom from mob violence. Both his life experience and knowledge of history told him that people can behave irrationally and dangerously, and so he believed that laws—though unnecessary if all people behaved rationally—are required; and that a civil authority is necessary to enforce those laws. However, he believed that it was critical that laws are created democratically, which means with the consent of the governed, as without such consent there will be great resentment.

Thus, though Spinoza was clearly an anti-authoritarian with a deep love of freedom and an advocate of mutual aid, he was not anti-state, and so he cannot be considered an anarchist. However, Spinoza flows with anarchists "in the broad river of anarchy towards the great sea of freedom," in the language of historian Peter Marshall. Marshall views William Godwin (1756–1836) as "the first to give a clear statement of anarchist principles," and Marshall concludes, "Godwin's position resembles Spinoza's description of a free man as one who lives according to the dictates of reason alone."

The theoretical endpoint of Spinoza's political philosophy—though not his practical endpoint—is anarchism, notes philosopher Daniel Garber. Specifically, Garber observes, "Spinoza is often presented as the philosopher of democracy. . . . In a certain sense he can also be regarded as the philosopher of anarchy because the more rational we become the less we will need external constraints. So at the limit when we are all perfectly rational . . . there will be no need for government whatsoever." Theoretically, if all citizens in a society acted rationally, then there would be no need for an external government; as by virtue of reason, individuals will act justly and cooperatively because they understand that this is in their self-interest. While the theoretical endpoint for Spinoza is anarchism, Garber notes that Spinoza concluded it is unrealistic to expect that level of rationality in a society. However, among Spinoza's group of friends who were fully committed to reason, there was an anarchist sensibility characterized by a love of freedom, the practice of mutual aid, and an absence of hierarchy.

For Spinoza, resentment is a corrosive force for individuals and society, and while he would not have opposed restraint to keep someone overwhelmed by their passions from acting irrationally self-destructive or destructively to others, it would be obvious to him that resentment is highly dependent on whether or not the restrained individual experiences caring. It would be obvious to him that the nature of the relationship between parties is critical. From his own experience, he knew that resentment ensued when he was coerced by authorities who were only meeting their own needs and not his. It would be obvious to Spinoza that as long as society relies on impersonal authorities to police individuals, there will be resentment. Spinoza would deduce that what would serve society best is genuine community. In such genuine community, it would be more likely that individuals behaving irrationally and dangerously who required restraint and surveillance will conclude that such restraint and surveillance is for their benefit as well as for others, rather than only meeting the control needs of others.

Spinoza cared about the freedom to philosophize and express oneself, so he cared about a society that was least oppressive and most tolerant. He cared very much about friendship, happiness, and even bliss, all of which require freedom from different types of bondage, which includes the bondage of authorities and the bondage of one's own irrational passions.

Spinoza would take note of the fact that suicide is now the second leading cause of death in the United States among individuals ages ten to thirty-four. In the *Ethics*, he discusses suicide at length and concluded, "Therefore nobody, unless he is overcome by external causes contrary to his own nature, neglects to seek his own advantage, that is, to preserve his own being. Nobody, I repeat, refuses food or kills himself from the necessity of his own nature, but from the constraint of external causes." Thus, Spinoza would ask what kind of society is producing the "external causes" that are causing so many young people—individuals in their prime physical health—to violate the instinct for self-preservation and to kill themselves. For Spinoza, it would be obvious from the suicide statistics of young people that there are exceedingly oppressive externalities in society. It would be obvious to him that to the extent that a society is rational, it would attempt to detect those externalities and change them.

Spinoza was not anti-religion, as he recognized that many people find their particular religious practices to be helpful; and so he would not be anti-psychiatry, as it would be clear to him that many people find psychiatric treatment helpful. What he opposed was religious authority having any power over civil society, and this is why he challenged the sacredness of the Bible, which is the source of ecclesiastic authority. Thus, it is likely he would feel compelled to challenge the DSM, psychiatry's bible, which psychiatry's authority over civil society rests upon. Just as religious authorities realized that Spinoza's critique of their dogma was a threat to their power and thus attempted to marginalize him, psychiatry authorities today recognize that critiques of their dogma threaten their power.

Spinoza would not have opposed psychotropic drugs, as he himself drank wine and beer and smoked tobacco. While he would not be averse to on occasion using psychotropic drugs for pleasure, given that his goal was freedom from bondage from externalities and that his method of liberation depended on reason, he would be averse to using any substance that hindered his thinking.

Spinoza recognized that most people are not rational freethinkers but are controlled by their passions, especially fear, and this makes them vulnerable to the dogma and superstitions promoted by power-seeking authorities who gain control by exploiting fear. Spinoza had no fantasy that he was capable of helping irrational fear-based people to become otherwise. He wished only to have the freedom to express himself to rational freethinkers.

Spinoza is a therapist for rational freethinkers, and he would be interested in modern talk therapies from Freudian psychoanalysis to cognitive-behavioral therapy, but he would likely view them as lacking potency. He emphasized that problematic passions, such as despair and resentment, can only be overcome by a stronger emotion. He recognized that intellectual insights are not sufficient, and what is required is something more powerful, specifically an intellectual love of God/Nature. Spinoza's therapy, suited only for rational thinkers, is aimed at helping them understand and love God/Nature; and given that human beings are a part of God/Nature, helping them understand and love themselves. He knew that an intellectual love of God/Nature that compels a robust curiosity can overcome problematic passions such as despair and resentment, and is a powerful force that can produce "continuous and supreme joy."

It surprises many people to discover that the psychiatrist Thomas Szasz, routinely characterized as an anti-psychiatrist, vehemently denied that he

was an anti-psychiatrist; and Spinoza too would not likely be a psychiatry abolitionist. Both Szasz and Spinoza were advocates of freedom and consensual
activities.

Spinoza was wary of political revolution, as he knew that, without the nature of society changing, one tyrannical government is likely to simply be re-
placed by another. When Spinoza was a young adult, the English ruler Oliver
Cromwell (who died in 1658), was well-known internationally. Cromwell
defeated King Charles I to take power, but he would himself become Lord
Protector, essentially a King and military dictator. Cromwell invaded Ireland,
and, for his atrocities there, he remains today a hated figure among many
Irish Catholics. After Cromwell's death, the English monarchy was restored.
In Spinoza's discussion of how societies can change governments without
abolishing tyranny, he specifically refers to Cromwell without mentioning
him by name: "A sad example of this truth is provided by the English people,
who under the form of law sought grounds for removing their monarch. . . .
After much bloodshed they resorted to hailing a new monarch by a different
name." Spinoza, on a personal level, had a special reason to dislike Cromwell,
as during his rule, English ships confiscated goods from Dutch merchant ships,
which was a significant reason for his father's financial difficulties. Spinoza
would not have been surprised by the ascendancy of cruel dictators such as
Robespierre and Stalin following revolutions.

Spinoza would recognize that psychiatry as an institution arose from
societal conditions and is maintained by them. These conditions include: an
absence of genuine community; societal fear of the unusual; a passion for
eradicating this fear and thus a vulnerability to an authority that proclaims
itself capable of eradication; and an absence of a critically thinking population capable of examining the source of its fears and the consequences of its
controlling actions. Spinoza would recognize that psychiatry is maintained by
such societal conditions, and that if those conditions remain unchanged, then
an authority that replaces psychiatry may well be no improvement.

In Spinoza's day, there were philosophers who, rather than using their intelligence to seek essential truths, used it to reconcile undeniable aspects of
reality with religious beliefs. For example, since God had to be viewed as all
powerful and all good and the creator of the "best of all possible worlds," then
that which occurred that was horrific was explained as human beings' inability to grasp the big picture—in other words, tragedies and atrocities for some
individuals were part of a master plan for good. Such a view was mocked by

Voltaire via his *Candide* character Dr. Pangloss, a parody of Leibniz, who today is called "God's Lawyer" by some philosophers, and though viewed as a brilliant thinker in many areas, including in mathematics, with respect to God, is seen as a practitioner of reconciliatory theism.

Spinoza and radical Enlightenment thinkers had no use for reconciliatory theism. For them, the freedom to philosophize did not mean compromising between the truth and acceptable beliefs. For Spinoza, if reason makes clear that any conceptualizations—and this would include the conceptualizations of psychiatry—are inadequate ones resulting in models and paradigms being based on confused and false ideas, then he would not have compromised his position for the sake of maintaining an institution. That is what made him a key member of the radical Enlightenment.

As radical as Spinoza's politics were for his time, if alive today, he may well conclude that at least some of his ideas, especially about democracy, stopped short of being completely reasoned and thus were not radical enough. In his unfinished *Political Treatise*, after completing his chapters on monarchy and aristocracy, he began a chapter on democracy, which he believed to be the superior form of government. He never finished that chapter. On the last pages of that unfinished chapter on democracy, he offers a discussion of who has the right to vote in the supreme council and hold state offices, and he excludes women.

Given European society in his era, even his lengthy consideration of whether or not to include women is relatively radical, although his conclusions are not. In what turned out to be the last days of his life, Spinoza considered whether it is mere convention or reason that dictates that women should not be viewed as equal to men. He mentions Amazon women who once held rule; but ultimately, based on his limited knowledge of history and his observed but unpracticed experience of relationships between men and women, he concludes that women should not be given equal status with men. It is one of Spinoza's most poorly reasoned arguments, replete with opinion, hearsay, and random experiences; and perhaps in his last days, his respiratory problem had worn him down.

Despite his conclusions *about* women, among Spinoza scholars who *are* women—who take into account the times that Spinoza lived in (women did not receive the right to vote even in the United States until 1920), the entire body of his work, and how he conducted his life—many not only cut him some slack but have expressed deep affection and respect for him. The novelist, poet, translator George Eliot (the pen name of Marian Evans, born in 1819) translated the *Ethics*. Clare Carlisle, who edited Eliot's translation for publication in 2020, concludes that "some readers have found in her novels literary 'translations' of Spinozism, accomplished through character and narrative."

I have quoted Spinoza scholars Rebecca Goldstein, Beth Lord, Susan James, Sanem Soyarslan, and Clare Carlisle, all of whom have deep affection and respect for Spinoza, and it would be a safe bet that if Spinoza could see how these women have penetrated his thinking, and how clearly they have explicated him—making him accessible even to men who have had their minds muddled by theological and psychiatric dogma—Bento would rethink his views on women.

Were Spinoza's poorly constructed arguments about women the product of his own personal biases with respect to women, or were these opinions influenced by his desire to be taken seriously? We cannot be sure. In Spinoza's day, the idea of democracy was radical enough, and the idea of the inclusion of women as equals in a democracy would have been perhaps as outlandish as it would be today proposing the following: The abolition of current institutional hierarchies in which individuals with extensive personal experience in recovery but who lack professional credentials have little or no power; and proposing instead that peer-to-peer support get greater status, power, and funding than medical professionals.

It is to our benefit to acknowledge the possibility that even Baruch de Spinoza, who prided himself on being uncompromising in the quest for truth, was not perfect. The value of acknowledging Spinoza's imperfection is to compel us take into account that, no matter how certain we are of our commitment to the uncompromising pursuit of truth, in our desire to be taken seriously, we all are vulnerable to compromises.

As radical a thinker as Spinoza was in his day, there is nothing in what he said about theology and politics that today is considered by progressive thinkers to be *too* radical. In fact, modern progressive thinkers actually view Spinoza as not progressive enough in some matters—his views on women being an obvious area. This should provoke psychiatry critics to consider the possibility that as radical as their views about contemporary psychiatry are considered today, in the future, these views may well be seen as not progressive enough.

Finally, what would Spinoza do in today's world if his publisher asked him to make the talk show rounds?

Spinoza, though a strong believer in democracy as the best form of government to ensure greatest freedom and least resentment, did not believe that most people are guided by reason, and he made it clear that he did not want to be read by people unguided by reason. In the preface to his *Theological-Political Treatise*, he states: "Indeed, I would prefer that they disregard this book completely rather than make themselves a nuisance by misinterpreting it after their wont." Thus, if his publisher asked him to make the talk show rounds, my guess is that his immediate reflex would be to refuse. But what if his publisher, after putting his freedom and finances on the line to publish and distribute Spinoza's work, asked Spinoza to do media interviews so as to at least break even financially? The loyal Spinoza might reconsider.

We can imagine the question that Spinoza would have faced repeatedly about the *Ethics*: "Now be honest with me, do you believe in God or are you an atheist?"

Initially, he may have responded cautiously, "Yes, I know God to be true." Or less cautiously, he may have responded, "Tell me what you mean by God." However, having to answer this question repeatedly would have annoyed him, and he may well have gotten more pointed and responded, "Apparently you have not read the *Ethics* or you have not understood it. I do not invite people who are not seriously committed to reason and discovering the truth to read my work. In fact, I'd rather they spend their money on something else."

If Spinoza was alive today and wrote a psychiatry treatise, it is a safe bet that he would want it to be read only by freethinkers guided by reason, not by people emotionally attached to defending or attacking psychiatry who make themselves "a nuisance by misinterpreting it after their wont."

NOTES

For quotations from Spinoza's works (*Treatise on the Emendation of the Intellect*; *Short Treatise on God, Man, and His Well-Being*; *Theological-Political Treatise*; *Ethics*; *Political Treatise*; and *The Letters*), the edition used is *Spinoza: Complete Works*, trans. Samuel Shirley, ed. Michael L. Morgan (Indianapolis: Hackett Publishing Company, 2002).

Chapter 1: Introduction

2. **"America's psychiatrist in chief"**—Gary Greenberg, *The Book of Woe: The DSM and the Unmaking of Psychiatry* (New York: Blue Rider Press, 2013), 351.
2. **"Whatever we've been doing"**—Ibid.
3. **"As early as fall 1661"**—Steven Nadler, *Spinoza: A Life* (Cambridge: Cambridge University Press, 1999), 182.
3. **Homosexuality was called a mental illness by psychiatry until 1973**—"The A.P.A. Ruling on Homosexuality," *New York Times*, December 23, 1973, https://www.nytimes.com/1973/12/23/archives/the-issue-is-subtle-the-debate-still-on-the-apa-ruling-on.html.
4. **boarding schools, called residential schools**—Mary Annette Pember, "Death by Civilization," *Atlantic*, March 8, 2019, https://www.theatlantic.com/education/archive/2019/03/traumatic-legacy-indian-boarding-schools/584293.
4. **"Kill the Indian in him, and save the man"**—Colonel Richard H. Pratt, "The Advantages of Mingling Indians with Whites," 1892 Speech, available at the Upstand Project, https://upstanderproject.org/firstlight/pratt.
4. **forced assimilation for Native Americans continued into the**

1970s—"Boarding Schools," The Northern Plains Reservation Aid, Native Partnership, http://www.nativepartnership.org/site/PageServer?pagename=airc_hist_boardingschools.

5. oppositional defiant disorder (ODD)—American Psychiatric Association, *Diagnostic and Statistical Manual of Mental Disorders: Diagnostic and Statistical Manual of Mental Disorders, DSM-III* (Washington, D.C.: American Psychiatric Association, 1980).

5–6. "He was not yet fifteen years"—Jean-Maximilian Lucas, *The Life of the Late Mr. De Spinoza* (probably completed 1678, published in 1719), in *The Oldest Biography of Spinoza*, ed. A. Wolf (New York: The Dial Press, 1927), 42.

6. "That he knew the gravity"—Ibid., 50.

6. "In my story"—Antonio Damasio, *Looking for Spinoza: Joy, Sorrow, and the Feeling Brain* (Orlando: Harcourt Books, 2003), 264.

6. "In controversy he was courteous"—Bertrand Russell, *History of Western Philosophy* (New York: Simon & Schuster, 1945), 574.

6. "the noblest and most lovable of the great philosophers"—Ibid., 569.

7. "The peculiar combination"—Matthew Stewart, *The Courtier and the Heretic: Leibniz, Spinoza, and the Fate of God in the Modern World* (New York: W. W. Norton & Company, 2006), 38.

7. "monster of arrogance"—Rebecca Goldstein, *Betraying Spinoza: The Renegade Jew Who Gave Us Modernity* (New York: Schocken, 2006), 35.

7. "I sat in Mrs. Schoenfield's class"—Ibid., 47.

7. "a wit so well seasoned"—Lucas, *The Life of the Late Mr. De Spinoza*, 73.

7. Spinoza spells out how laughter—*Ethics*, Part IV, Proposition 45, *Spinoza: Complete Works*, 344.

7. "But in reality avarice, ambition"—*Ethics*, Part IV, Proposition 44, Ibid., 344.

7. treatments that include medication to treat their defiance—Mark Olfson, et al., "National Trends in the Office-Based Treatment of Children, Adolescents, and Adults with Antipsychotics," *Archives of General Psychiatry* (now *JAMA Psychiatry*) 69, no.12 (December, 2012): 1247–1256.

8. a chronic and incurable disease of the brain—Ron Powers, *No One Cares about Crazy People: My Family and the Heartbreak of Mental Illness* (New York: Hachette Books, 2017), xv. Also schizophrenia termed as a "chronic brain disorder" on American Psychiatric Association website, https://www.psychiatry.org/patients-families/schizophrenia/what-is-schizophrenia.

9. "How much do I love that noble man"—Max Jammer, *Einstein and Religion: Physics and Theology* (Princeton: Princeton University Press, 1999), 43.

9. "But you sit there in the back row"—Walter Isaacson, *Einstein: His Life and the Universe* (New York: Simon & Schuster, 2007), 22.

9. slow to talk / tantrums / "His slow development" / "patron saint of distracted kids"—Ibid., 8–12.

9. **"I believe in Spinoza's God"**—Ibid., 388–89.

9. **"I believe that a triangle"**—*The Letters,* Letter 56, *Spinoza: Complete Works,* 904.

10. **"God is Nature"**—Steven Nadler, *Think Least of Death: Spinoza on How to Live and How to Die* (Princeton, NJ: Princeton University Press, 2020), 3.

10. **"the trees and the forests"**—Beth Lord, interviewed on broadcast, "Spinoza," *Ideas,* CBC (Canadian Broadcasting Corporation) Radio, June 14, 2013, https://www.cbc.ca/radio/ideas/spinoza-1.2913483.

10. **"we understand Spinoza's God through science"**—Beth Lord, "The Atheist God: Spinoza's Laws of Religion and Politics," recorded at the State Library of New South Wales for The Sydney Seminar for the Arts and Philosophy at the University of Western Sydney, broadcast on *Big Ideas with Paul Barclay,* ABC (Australian Broadcasting Corporation) Radio National, June 12, 2011, https://www.abc.net.au/radionational/programs/bigideas/the-atheist-god-spinozas-laws-of-religion-and/2916064.

10. **Szasz, was adamant that he was neither anti-psychiatry nor anti-medication**—Natasha Mitchell, "Thomas Szasz Speaks (Part 2)," interview of Thomas Szasz, *All in the Mind,* broadcast on ABC (Australian Broadcasting Corporation) Radio National, April 11, 2009, recording and transcript at https://www.abc.net.au/radionational/programs/allinthemind/thomas-szasz-speaks-part-2-of-2/3138880#transcript.

10. **scorned by psychiatry advocates**—Powers, *No One Cares about Crazy People,* 156–74.

11. **"One of the cultural images of Spinoza"**—Susan James, *Spinoza on Philosophy, Religion, and Politics: The Theological-Political Treatise* (Oxford: Oxford University Press, 2012), 1.

11. **"little to improve the lives of the millions"**—Benedict Carey, "Science Plays the Long Game. But People Have Mental Health Issues Now," *New York Times,* April 1, 2021, https://www.nytimes.com/2021/04/01/health/mental-health-treatments.html.

12. **"What is Enlightenment?"**—Immanuel Kant, "An Answer to the Question: What is Enlightenment?" *Berlinische Monatschrift,* November, 1784.

12. **In *Radical Enlightenment***—Jonathan Israel, *Radical Enlightenment: Philosophy and the Making of Modernity 1650–1750* (Oxford: Oxford University Press, 2001).

12. **"in such a way as to preserve"** / **"rejected all compromises with the past"**—Ibid., 11.

12. **"I have taken great care not to deride"**—*Political Treatise,* Chapter 1, *Spinoza: Complete Works,* 681.

13. **"mental illness deniers"** / **"Scientologists"**—Powers, *No One Cares about Crazy People,* 160–74.

13. **"ecstatic rationalism"** / **"the exhilarating sense"**—Goldstein, *Betraying Spinoza,* 186–88.

Chapter 2: Freethinking

15. *Merriam-Webster* defines freethinker—*Merriam-Webster Dictionary*, https://www.merriam-webster.com/dictionary/freethinker.

15. "everyone being allowed to think what he will"—*Theological-Political Treatise*, Chapter 20, *Spinoza: Complete Works*, 572.

15. "the most tyrannical government"—Ibid., 567.

15. "The words 'freethinking'"—John Robertson, *A Short History of Freethought: Ancient and Modern* (London: Watts & Co.1915). 1.

15. "Such a work"—Ibid., 2.

15. "What makes a free thinker is not his beliefs"—Bertrand Russell, *The Value of Free Thought* (Girard, KS: Haldeman-Julius Publication, 1944), 3.

16. "that the masses can no more be freed"—*Theological-Political Treatise*, Preface, *Spinoza: Complete Works*, 393–94.

16. records from 1655 / knife attack on him—Steven Nadler, "Who Tried to Kill Spinoza?" *Jewish Review of Books*, Winter 2019, https://jewishreviewofbooks.com/articles/4991/who-tried-to-kill-spinoza.

16–7. "After experience had taught me"—*Treatise on the Emendation of the Intellect*, *Spinoza: Complete Works*, 3.

17. there were perhaps as many as four hundred of them—Matthew Stewart, *The Courtier and the Heretic: Leibniz, Spinoza, and the Fate of God in the Modern World* (New York: W. W. Norton & Company, 2006), 28.

17. "the bad boy of the early Dutch Enlightenment"—Ibid.

17. Colerus claims that Spinoza was attracted to her "sharp mind"—Johan Colerus, *The Life of Benedict de Spinosa* published in 1706, quoted in Steven Nadler, *Spinoza: A Life* (Cambridge: Cambridge University Press, 1999), 108.

17. showing her to be twenty-seven—Stewart, *The Courtier and the Heretic*, 62.

18. average height and having a "well-formed body"—Ibid., 13.

18. "his choice of a low-income lifestyle"—Ibid., 62.

18. "All the better; they do not force me to do"—Jean-Maximilian Lucas, *The Life of the Late Mr. De Spinoza* (probably completed 1678, published in 1719), in *The Oldest Biography of Spinoza*, ed. A. Wolf (New York: The Dial Press, 1927), 51.

19. he rented a large single room—Nadler, *Spinoza: A Life*, 288–289; Steven Nadler, *Think Least of Death: Spinoza on How to Live and How to Die* (Princeton, NJ: Princeton University Press, 2020), 61.

19. "As a Jew severed from his community"—Stuart Hampshire, *Spinoza: An Introduction to His Philosophical Thought* (New York: Viking Penguin, 1987), 35.

19. "In a sense, Spinoza was"—Clare Carlisle, "Spinoza, Part 1: Philosophy as a Way of Life," *The Guardian*, February 7, 2011, https://www.theguardian.com/commentisfree/belief/2011/feb/07/spinoza-philosophy-god-world.

19. "The freedom that the freethinker seeks"—Russell, *The Value of Free Thought*, 3.

20. **"I take the newer medications"**—*A Beautiful Mind*, directed by Ron Howard (Universal City, CA: Universal Studios, 2001).

20. **"Nash's refusal to take the antipsychotic drugs"**—Sylvia Nasar, *A Beautiful Mind* (New York: Touchstone, 1999), 353.

20. **"The movie is not quite accurate"**—"One on One: Professor John Nash," Nash interviewed by Riz Khan on "Al Jazeera English," 2009, https://www.youtube.com/watch?v=UiWBWwCa1E0.

20–1. **"The change was apparently made"**—Clare Allan, "Don't Use John Nash to Promote the Use of Anti-Psychotic Drugs," *The Guardian*, June 2, 2015, https://www.theguardian.com/society/2015/jun/02/dont-use-john-nash-schizophrenia-a-beautiful-mind-promote-anti-psychotics.

21. **"Ecclesiastic meddling represents a threat"**—Steven Nadler, *A Book Forged in Hell: Spinoza's Scandalous Treatise and the Birth of the Secular Age* (Princeton: Princeton University Press, 2011), 187.

21. ***The Myth of Mental Illness***—Thomas Szasz, *The Myth of Mental Illness* (New York: Harper & Row, 1961).

21. **"Szasz does not deny the existence of suffering"**—Ron Leifer, "The Psychiatric Repression of Thomas Szasz: Its Social and Political Significance," The Thomas S. Szasz Cybercenter for Liberty and Responsibility, 1997, https://www.szasz.com/leifer.html. Also Ron Leifer, "The Concept of Mental Illnesses and Why They Are Not Brain Diseases," *Ethical Human Psychology and Psychiatry* 19, no. 3 (2017): 161–67.

21. **Psychiatrist Paul Hoch**—Jeffrey Oliver, "The Myth of Thomas Szasz, *The New Atlantis*, Summer 2006, https://www.thenewatlantis.com/publications/the-myth-of-thomas-szasz.

21. **"Would you describe yourself as an anti-psychiatrist?"**—Natasha Mitchell, "Thomas Szasz Speaks (Part 2)," interview of Thomas Szasz, *All in the Mind*, broadcast on ABC (Australian Broadcasting Corporation) Radio National, April 11, 2009, recording and transcript at https://www.abc.net.au/radionational/programs/allinthemind/thomas-szasz-speaks-part-2-of-2/3138880#transcript.

22. **"bombastic influence" that created a "post-Szaszian atrocity"**—Ron Powers, *No One Cares about Crazy People: My Family and the Heartbreak of Mental Illness* (New York: Hachette Books, 2017), 158, 170.

22. **profile about Szasz**—Melanie Hirsch, "Home on the Hot Seat," *Post-Standard* (Syracuse), February 19, 1992, republished as "1992 Post-Standard Story Explored Dr. Thomas Szasz's Controversial Views," syracuse.com, September 12, 2012, https://www.syracuse.com/news/2012/09/dr_thomas_szasz_critics_discus.html.

22. **Hartmann was the first openly gay president of the APA**—Jim Beckerman, "How Stonewall Cured Gay People—of Psychiatrists," northjersey.com, June 28, 2019, https://www.northjersey.com/story/entertainment/2019/06/28/how-stonewall-cured-gay-people-psychiatrists/1445470001.

23. **Anatomy of an Epidemic**—Robert Whitaker, *Anatomy of an Epidemic: Magic Bullets, Psychiatric Drugs, and the Astonishing Rise of Mental Illness in America* (New York: Crown Publishers, 2010).

23. **Whitaker was called a "menace to society"**—Rob Wipond, "Lieberman Calls Whitaker 'A Menace to Society,'" *Mad in America*, April 26, 2015, https://www.madinamerica.com/2015/04/lieberman-calls-whitaker-menace-society.

23. **"introduce doubt into weak, unstable minds"**—Nadler, *A Book Forged in Hell*, 230.

23. **"I don't believe in Scientology"**—Mitchell, "Thomas Szasz Speaks."

23. **"Thanks to Scientology"**—Whitaker, *Anatomy of an Epidemic*, 282

24. **"pave the way for publication"**—Nadler, *A Book Forged in Hell*, 237.

24. **"all national institutions of churches"**—Thomas Paine, *The Age of Reason*, 1795 (republished New York: D. M Bennett 1877), 6.

24. **"species of atheism"**—Ibid., 28

24. **"none more derogatory to the Almighty"**—Ibid., 148.

25. **"Paine emerges in most academic accounts"**—Jill Lepore, "The Sharpened Quill: Was Thomas Paine Too Much of a Freethinker for the Country He Helped Free?," *New Yorker*, October 16, 2006, http://www.newyorker.com/magazine/2006/10/16/the-sharpened-quill.

25. **allegory retold by Fred Edwords**—Fred Edwords, "The Saga of Freethought and Its Pioneers: Religious Critique and Social Reform," American Humanist Association, https://americanhumanist.org/what-is-humanism/saga-freethought-pioneers-religious-critique-social-reform.

25. **"more courage than politeness"**—Robert G. Ingersoll, "Thomas Paine," in *The Works of Robert G. Ingersoll*, ed. David Widger (New York: New Dresden Edition, 1900) xi, 321.

25. **"The Fate of Thomas Paine"**—Bertrand Russell, "The Fate of Thomas Paine," in *Why I Am Not a Christian and Other Essays on Religion and Related Subjects*, 1934 (New York: Touchstone, 1957).

26. **"To be worthy of the name"**—Russell, *The Value of Free Thought*, 3.

26. **"For all classes of mental illness"**—Thomas Insel, "Translating Scientific Opportunity into Public Health Impact: A Strategic Plan for Research on Mental Illness," *Archives of General Psychiatry* (now *JAMA Psychiatry*). 66, no. 2 (March 2009): 128–33.

27. **the rate of antidepressant use in the United States increased**—Centers for Disease Control, National Center for Health Statistics Data Brief No. 76, October 2011, https://www.cdc.gov/nchs/products/databriefs/db76.htm.

27. **"the suicide rate increased 35%"**—Centers for Disease Control, National Center for Health Statistics Data Brief no. 362, April 2020, https://www.cdc.gov/nchs/products/databriefs/db362.htm.

27. **U.S. mental illness disability rate**—Whitaker, *Anatomy of an Epidemic*, 6–7.

27. **"10–25 year life expectancy reduction"**—World Health Organization,

"Information Sheet: Premature Death among People with Severe Mental Disorders," 2021, https://www.who.int/mental_health/management/info_sheet.pdf.

Chapter 3: Fear

29. **"thinks of fear as a kind of depressing"**—Susan James, quoted in "Benedict Spinoza: A Philosopher for Our Time," *Heart and Soul*, BBC, broadcast August 7, 2016, https://www.bbc.co.uk/programmes/p043318k.

29. **"To varying degrees, fear"**—Susan James, *Spinoza on Philosophy, Religion, and Politics: The Theological-Political Treatise* (Oxford: Oxford University Press, 2012), 15–17.

29. **"A free man, that is, he who"**—*Ethics*, Part IV, Proposition 67, *Spinoza: Complete Works*, 355.

30. **"On and off, then, from 1661 to 1674"**—Michael L. Morgan ed., Introduction to Spinoza's *Ethics*, *Spinoza: Complete Works*, 213.

30. **barring by some Dutch provinces of the sale**—Jonathan Israel, *Radical Enlightenment: Philosophy and the Making of Modernity 1650–1750* (Oxford: Oxford University Press, 2001), 203.

30. **"implore God's help with prayers"**—*Theological-Political Treatise*, Preface, *Spinoza: Complete Works*, 388–89.

30. **"For if, while possessed by fear"**—Ibid., 388.

30. **"Harmony is also commonly produced"**—*Ethics*, Part IV, Appendix, *Spinoza: Complete Works*, 360

31. **Søren Kierkegaard**—Søren Kierkegaard, *The Concept of Anxiety*, 1844, trans. Alastair Hannay (New York: Liveright. 2015); title translated as *The Concept of Dread* in 1944, Walter Lowrie translation.

34. **"After Decades of Research"**—American Psychological Association, "After Decades of Research, Science Is No Better Able to Predict Suicidal Behaviors," APA website, November 15, 2016, https://www.apa.org/news/press/releases/2016/11/suicidal-behaviors; Joseph C. Franklin et al., "Risk Factors for Suicidal Thoughts and Behaviors: A Meta-Analysis of 50 Years of Research," *Psychological Bulletin* 143, no. 2 (February 2017): 87–232.

35. **"The Clinician's Illusion"**—Patricia Cohen and Jacob Cohen, "The Clinician's Illusion," *Archives of General Psychiatry* (now *JAMA Psychiatry*) 41, no. 2 (1984): 1178–82.

35. **"like one who, having never seen any sheep"**—*Short Treatise on God, Man, and His Well-Being*, Chapter III, *Spinoza: Complete Works*, 64.

35. **"It is fear, then, that engenders"**—*Theological-Political Treatise*, Preface, Ibid., 388–89.

36. **"Man's emotional nature masters"**—Joseph Ratner, *The Philosophy of Spinoza* (New York: Random House, 1927), xlix.

36. **"Paul's idea of Peter tells us more about Paul"**—Ibid., xlv–xlvi.

39. **"Since the very process of correcting erroneous"**—Rebecca Goldstein, *Betraying Spinoza: The Renegade Jew Who Gave Us Modernity* (New York: Schocken, 2006), 183.

Chapter 4: *Ultimi Barbarorum*

42. **harshest writ of herem**—Steven Nadler, *Spinoza: A Life* (Cambridge: Cambridge University Press, 1999), 127.
42. **unspecified "evil opinions and acts"**—Ibid., 120, 129.
42. **tragic story of Uriel da Costa**—Ibid., 66–72.
43. **Spinoza told Leibniz**—Ibid., 306.
43. **Commonly referred to as "Bedlam"**—Steven Casale, Bedlam: The Horrors of London's Most Notorious Insane Asylum" *Huffpost*, December 6, 2017, https://www.huffpost.com/entry/bedlam-the-horrors-of-lon_b_9499118.
43. **"the father of American psychiatry"**—"Benjamin Rush," *Biography*, September 3, 2019, https://www.biography.com/political-figure/benjamin-rush.
44. **proclaimed himself a slave abolitionist**—"Benjamin Rush, Race, Slavery, and Abolitionism," *Dickenson College* (which Rush founded) https://www.dickinson.edu/info/20043/about/3480/benjamin_rush.
44. **Rush also invented treatments**—"Psychiatry: Dr. Benjamin Rush (1745–1813)," *Penn Medicine: History of Pennsylvania Hospital*, http://www.uphs.upenn.edu/paharc/collections/exhibits/psych.
44. **United States led the world in forced sterilizations**—"Nazi Euthanasia Program: Persecution of the Mentally & Physically Disabled," *Jewish Virtual Library*, https://www.jewishvirtuallibrary.org/nazi-persecution-of-the-mentally-and-physically-disabled.
44. **Foster Kennedy**—Foster Kennedy, "The Problem of Social Control of the Congenital Defective: Education, Sterilization, Euthanasia," *American Journal of Psychiatry* 99 (1942): 13–16.
44. **Joseph Dejarnette**—Edwin Black, "Hitler's Debt to America," *The Guardian*, February 5, 2004, https://www.theguardian.com/uk/2004/feb/06/race.usa.
44. **Leon Whitney**—Dusty Sklar, "American Eugenics and German Nazism," *Jewish Currents*, February 20, 2016, https://jewishcurrents.org/american-eugenics-and-german-nazism.
45. **Hitler**—an admirer of U.S. eugenic policies—Black, "Hitler's Debt to America."
45. **estimated 300,000 to 400,000 forced sterilization / T4 program**—"Nazi Euthanasia Program: Persecution of the Mentally & Physically Disabled," *Jewish Virtual Library*.
45. **staff of Hadamer**—Ibid.
45. **public protests led by prominent religious figures**—Ibid.

45. **"How Ethics Failed"**—Jutta Lindert, et al., "How Ethics Failed—The Role of Psychiatrists and Physicians in Nazi Programs from Exclusion to Extermination, 1933–1945," *Public Health Reviews* 34, no. 1 (June 2012): 1–26.

45. **Walter Freeman**—Ron Powers, *No One Cares about Crazy People: My Family and the Heartbreak of Mental Illness* (New York: Hachette Books, 2017), 272–277; also "The Lobotomist," *American Experience* documentary (2008), https://www.youtube.com/watch?v=8izaaZ5dRyU.

46. **Howard Dully**—Howard Dully and Charles Fleming, *My Lobotomy: A Memoir* (New York: Broadway Books, 2007).

46. **electric shock to the genitals**—Brian D. Earp et al., "Brave New Love: The Threat of High-Tech 'Conversion' Therapy and the Bio-Oppression of Sexual Minorities," *AJOB Neuroscience* 5, no. 1 (January 2014): 4–12.

46. **Nuremberg Code**—"Nuremberg Code," *United States Holocaust Museum*, https://www.ushmm.org/information/exhibitions/online-exhibitions/special-focus/doctors-trial/nuremberg-code.

46. **Paul Hoch**—Robert Whitaker, *Mad in America: Bad Science, Bad Medicine, and the Enduring Mistreatment of the Mentally Ill* (Cambridge, MA: Perseus, 2002), 235–38.

47. **David Janowsky**—Robert Whitaker and Dolores Kong, "Doing Harm: Research on the Mentally Ill," *Boston Globe*, November 15, 1998, http://old.narpa.org/doing.harm.htm.

47. ***Boston Globe* series**—Ibid.

47. **"Prediction of Relapse in Schizophrenia"**—Jeffrey Lieberman, et al., "Prediction of Relapse in Schizophrenia," *Archives of General Psychiatry* (now *JAMA Psychiatry*) 44, no. 7 (July 1987): 597–603.

47. **"Behavioral Response to Methylphenidate"**—Darlene Jody, Jeffrey A. Lieberman, et al., "Behavioral Response to Methylphenidate and Treatment Outcome in First Episode Schizophrenia," *Psychopharmacological Bulletin* 26, no. 2 (1990): 224–30.

47. **elected president of the APA**—"Jeffrey Lieberman New APA President-Elect," *Psychiatric Services*, May 2012, https://ps.psychiatryonline.org/doi/full/10.1176/appi.ps.20120p517.

48. ***60 Minutes* reporter Katie Couric**—"What Killed Rebecca Riley?," *60 Minutes*, September 30, 2007, https://www.cbsnews.com/news/what-killed-rebecca-riley.

48. **"Every one of us was very angry"**—Patricia Wen, "Jurors Outraged by Psychiatrist's Conduct," *Boston Globe*, February 11, 2010, http://archive.boston.com/news/local/massachusetts/articles/2010/02/11/jurors_outraged_by_psychiatrists_conduct.

48. **chosen by Kennedy family patriarch Joseph Kennedy**—Powers, *No One Cares about Crazy People*, 188.

48. **"The care we provided was appropriate"**—"What Killed Rebecca Riley?," *60 Minutes*.

49. **A 2019 review of the research on ECT**—John Read, Irving Kirsch, and Laura McGrath, "Electroconvulsive Therapy for Depression: A Review of the Quality of ECT versus Sham ECT Trials and Meta-Analyses," *Ethical Human Psychology and Psychiatry* 21, no. 2 (2019): 64–103.

49. **a signet ring engraved with the word** *caute*—Matthew Stewart, *The Courtier and the Heretic: Leibniz, Spinoza, and the Fate of God in the Modern World* (New York: W. W. Norton, 2006), 106.

50. **"Apparently in a manic mood"**—Jonathan Israel, *Radical Enlightenment: Philosophy and the Making of Modernity 1650–1750* (Oxford: Oxford University Press, 2001), 192.

50. **Koerbagh denied the divinity of Jesus**—Steven Nadler, *A Book Forged in Hell: Spinoza's Scandalous Treatise and the Birth of the Secular Age* (Princeton: Princeton University Press, 2011), 42.

50. **"Spinoza was deeply touched by Koerbagh's death"**—Ibid., 43–44, 51.

Chapter 5: Science

51. **"The depth of his devotion to science"**—Anthony Gottlieb, *The Dream of Enlightenment: The Rise of Modern Philosophy* (New York: Liveright Publishing, 2016), 90.

51. **"Observed data are only"**—Jonathan Israel, *Radical Enlightenment: Philosophy and the Making of Modernity 1650–1750* (Oxford: Oxford University Press, 2001), 252.

52. **including ones on hydrodynamics** —*The Letters,* Letter 41, *Spinoza: Complete Works,* 867–868

52. **"to distinguish 'true ideas'"**—Steven Nadler, *Spinoza: A Life* (Cambridge: Cambridge University Press, 1999), 179.

52. **"This," as Nadler puts it, "is not a project"**—Ibid., 177.

52. **"In studying logic"**—Stuart Hampshire, *Spinoza: An Introduction to His Philosophical Thought* (New York: Viking Penguin, 1987), 92.

52. **he describes four methods**—*Treatise on the Emendation of the Intellect, Spinoza: Complete Works,* 7–9.

53. **In his later** *Ethics,* **Spinoza distinguishes three categories**—*Ethics,* Part II, Proposition 40, *Spinoza: Complete Works,* 267–268.

53. **"Knowledge of the first kind"**—*Ethics,* Part II, Proposition 41, Ibid., 268.

53. **"Knowledge of the second and third kind"**—*Ethics,* Part II, Proposition, 42, Ibid., 268.

53. **connect to three psychological stages**—Alasdair MacIntyre, "Benedict (Baruch) Spinoza," *The Encyclopedia of Philosophy,* Volume 7, ed., Paul Edwards (New York: Macmillan Publishing Co., 1967), 538.

54. *The Analects*—Confucius, *The Analects,* trans. D.C. Lau (New York: Penguin, 1998), 118.

54. **Samuel Cartwright**—Samuel Cartwright, "Report on the Diseases and Physical Peculiarities of the Negro Race, *The New Orleans Medical and Surgical Journal* (1851), https://archive.org/stream/TheNewOrleansMedicalAndSurgical Journal.

55. **Hamilton Rating Scale**—"Hamilton M. A rating scale for depression," *Journal of Neurology, Neurosurgery and Psychiatry* 23 (1960) : 56–62, https://dcf .psychiatry.ufl.edu/files/2011/05/HAMILTON-DEPRESSION.pdf.

58–9. **Bloodletting**—Gerry Greenstone, "The History of Bloodletting," *BC Medical Journal* 52, no. 1 (January/February 2010): 12–14.

59. **Falsifiability**—Karl Popper, *The Logic of Scientific Discovery,* 1935, trans. *Logik der Forschung* (New York: Routledge, 1992).

60. **makes clear are not necessarily false**—*Treatise on the Emendation of the Intellect, Spinoza: Complete Works*, 17.

60. **"Imaginative knowledge"**—Beth Lord, "The Atheist God: Spinoza's Laws of Religion and Politics," recorded at the State Library of New South Wales for The Sydney Seminar for the Arts and Philosophy at the University of Western Sydney, broadcast on *Big Ideas with Paul Barclay*, ABC (Australian Broadcasting Corporation) Radio National, June 12, 2011, https://www.abc .net.au/radionational/programs/bigideas/the-atheist-god-spinozas-laws-of -religion-and/2916064.

61. *The Structure of Scientific Revolutions*—Thomas Kuhn, *The Structure of Scientific Revolutions,* 1962 (Chicago: University of Chicago Press, 2012).

Chapter 6: Unethical

63. **"obsess the minds of the populace"**—*Ethics*, Part IV Appendix, *Spinoza: Complete Works*, 361.

63. **"His wants were few and simple"**—Bertrand Russell, *History of Western Philosophy* (New York: Simon & Schuster, 1945), 569.

63. **"Not only did riches not tempt him"**—Jean-Maximilian Lucas, *The Life of the Late Mr. De Spinoza* (probably completed 1678, published in 1719), in *The Oldest Biography of Spinoza*, ed. A. Wolf (New York: The Dial Press, 1927), 64.

64. **When de Vries tried to make Spinoza his heir**—Steven Nadler, *Spinoza: A Life* (Cambridge: Cambridge University Press, 1999), 261.

64. **"You will not find elsewhere"**—*The Letters*, Letter 47, *Spinoza: Complete Works*, 886.

64. **in his return letter he stated: "I do not know within"**—*The Letters*, Letter 48, Ibid., 887.

64. **"When *The New England Journal of Medicine*"**—Marcia Angell, *The Truth about the Drug Companies: How They Deceive Us and What to Do about It* (New York: Random House, 2004), 143.

65. **ProPublica published "Dollars for Docs"**—Hanna Trudo and Theodoric

Meyer, "Dollars for Docs: The Top Earners," *ProPublica*, March 12, 2013, https://www.propublica.org/article/dollars-for-docs-the-top-earners.

65. **"Psychiatrists Top List in Drug Maker Gifts"**—Gardiner Harris, "Psychiatrists Top List in Drug Maker Gifts," *New York Times*, June 27, 2007, http://www.nytimes.com/2007/06/27/health/psychology/27doctors.html.

65. **A 2007 analysis of Minnesota psychiatrists**—Gardiner Harris et al., "Psychiatrists, Children and Drug Industry's Role," *New York Times*, May 10, 2007, https://www.nytimes.com/2007/05/10/health/10psyche.html.

65. **Biederman / Kifuji said influenced her**—Scott Allen, "MGH Psychiatrist's Work Stirs Debate," *Boston Globe*, June 17, 2007, http://www.psychrights.org/Articles/BostonGlobe6-17-07ChildBipolarBacklash.htm.

65. **increased forty-fold from 1994 to 2003**—Carmen Moreno, et al., "National Trends in the Outpatient Diagnosis and Treatment of Bipolar Disorder in Youth," *Archives of General Psychiatry* (now *JAMA Psychiatry*) 64, no. 9 (September 2007): 1032–39.

65. **Biederman's financial relationships / $1.6 million**—Gardiner Harris, *New York Times*, "Drug Maker Told Studies Would Aid It, Papers Say" March 19, 2009, https://www.nytimes.com/2009/03/20/us/20psych.html.

65. **Biederman had told Johnson & Johnson**—Ibid.

65. **Alan Schatzberg, had $4.8 million stock holdings**—Benedict Carey and Gardiner Harris, "Psychiatric Group Faces Scrutiny Over Drug Industry Ties," *New York Times*, July 12, 2008, http://www.nytimes.com/2008/07/12/washington/12psych.html.

66. **APA: "In 2006, the latest year for which numbers**—Ibid.

66. **"69% of the *DSM* -5 task force members report"**—Lisa Cosgrove and Sheldon Krimsky, "A Comparison of *DSMIV* and *DSM-5* Panel Members' Financial Associations with Industry: A Pernicious Problem Persists," *PLOS Medicine* 9, no. 3 (March 2012), https://www.ncbi.nlm.nih.gov/pmc/articles/PMC3302834.

66. **"By 2010, as much as 75 percent of NAMI's budget"**—Anne Harrington, *Mind Fixers: Psychiatry's Troubled Search for the Biology of Mental Illness* (New York: W. W. Norton, 2019), 251.

66. **Eisenhower warned**—Dwight D. Eisenhower, Farewell Address, January 17, 1961, *Digital History*, https://www.digitalhistory.uh.edu/disp_textbook.cfm?smtID=3&psid=1230.

67. **David Rosenhan**—David Rosenhan, "On Being Sane in Insane Places," *Science* 179, no. 4070 (January 1973): 250–58.

67. **Susannah Cahalan**—Susannah Cahalan, *The Great Pretender: The Undercover Mission That Changed Our Understanding of Madness* (New York: Grand Central Publishing, 2019).

67. **Sabshin / defended the APA's relationship**—Melvin Sabshin, "To Aid Understanding of Mental Disorders," *New York Times*, March 10, 1992, https://www.nytimes.com/1992/03/10/opinion/l-to-aid-understanding-of-mental-disorders-574092.html.

68. *Psychiatry Under the Influence*—Robert Whitaker and Lisa Cosgrove, *Psychiatry Under the Influence: Institutional Corruption, Social Injury, and Prescriptions for Reform* (New York: Palgrave Macmillan, 2015).

68. **Lawrence Lessig**—Ibid., xi.

68. **"financial conflict of interest came to pervade"**—Ibid., 40.

68. **Open Payments database**—Robert Whitaker, "Anatomy of an Industry: Commerce, Payments to Psychiatrists and Betrayal of the Public Good," *Mad in America*, September 18, 2021, https://www.madinamerica.com/2021/09/anatomy-industry-commerce-payments-psychiatrists-betrayal-public-good.

68–9. **"Studies viewed by the FDA as having"**—Erick Turner et al., "Selective Publication of Antidepressant Trials and its Influence on Apparent Efficacy," *New England Journal of Medicine* 358, no. 3 (January 2008): 252–60.

69. **Whitaker and Cosgrove document several studies**—Whitaker and Cosgrove, *Psychiatry Under the Influence*, 177–79.

69. **University of California San Francisco study**—Ibid., 178.

69. **APA guide for psychiatrists, "Commentary on Ethics in Practice"**—American Psychiatric Association, "Commentary on Ethics in Practice," (APA document, 2015), 10–11, downloadable pdf at https://www.psychiatry.org/psychiatrists/practice/ethics.

70. **former FDA Commissioner Scott Gottlieb**—Angelica LaVito, "Former FDA Commissioner Scott Gottlieb Joins Pfizer's Board of Directors," CNBC, June 27, 2019, https://www.cnbc.com/2019/06/27/former-fda-commissioner-scott-gottlieb-joins-pfizers-board.html.

70. **Pfizer's board members were paid**—Angelica LaVito, "Former FDA Commissioner Gottlieb Defends Decision to Join Pfizer Board," CNBC.com, July 2, 2019, https://www.cnbc.com/2019/07/02/former-fda-commissioner-gottlieb-defends-decision-to-join-pfizer-board.html.

Chapter 7: Two Bibles

73–4. **"More than any other work"**—Steven Nadler, *A Book Forged in Hell: Spinoza's Scandalous Treatise and the Birth of the Secular Age* (Princeton: Princeton University Press, 2011), 240.

74. **"a book forged in hell"**—Ibid., xi.

74. **"Spinoza is, without question, one of history's"**—Ibid., 207.

74. **"faulty, mutilated, adulterated, and inconsistent"**—*Theological-Political Treatise*, Chapter 12, *Spinoza: Complete Works*, 503.

75. **"were led by ambitious clergymen"**—Nadler, *A Book Forged in Hell*, 50.

76. **Allen Frances**—Allen Frances, *Saving Normal: An Insider's Revolt against Out-of-Control Psychiatric Diagnosis, DSM-5, Big Pharma, and the Medicalization of Ordinary Life* (New York: William Morrow, 2013).

77. **2010 *Wired* interview**—Gary Greenberg, "Inside the Battle to Define

Mental Illness," *Wired*, December 27, 2010, https://www.wired.com/2010/12/ff_dsmv.

77. *The Book of Woe*—Gary Greenberg, *The Book of Woe: The* DSM *and the Unmaking of Psychiatry* (New York: Penguin Group, 2013).

77. *They Say You're Crazy*—Paula Caplan, *They Say You're Crazy: How the World's Most Powerful Psychiatrists Decide Who's Normal* (Cambridge, MA: Da Capo Lifelong Books, 1995).

77. *Making Us Crazy*—Herb Kutchins and Stuart Kirk, *Making Us Crazy*: DSM: *The Psychiatric Bible and the Creation of Mental Disorders* (New York: The Free Press, 1997).

77. *The Loss of Sadness*—Allan Horwitz and Jerome Wakefield, *The Loss of Sadness: How Psychiatry Transformed Normal Sorrow into Depressive Disorder* (New York: Oxford Press, 2007).

77. *Shyness*—Christopher Lane, *Shyness: How Normal Behavior Became a Sickness* (New Haven: Yale University Press, 2007).

77. *Mad Science*—Stuart Kirk, Tomi Gomory, and David Cohen, *Mad Science: Psychiatric Coercion, Diagnosis, and Drugs* (New Brunswick, NJ: Transaction Publishers, 2013).

77. **bereavement exclusion / upset even Frances**—Allen Frances, "Last Plea to *DSM-5*: Save Grief From the Drug Companies," *HuffPost*, January 7, 2013, https://www.huffpost.com/entry/saving-grief-from-dsm-5-a_b_2325108.

77. **"Schizophrenia is certainly not a disease"**—Allen Frances, "A Clinical Reality Check," *Cato Unbound*, August 8, 2012, https://www.cato-unbound.org/2012/08/08/allen-frances/clinical-reality-check.

78. **"What is Bizarre in Bizarre Delusions?"**—Michel Cermolacce, et al., "What is Bizarre in Bizarre Delusions?" *Schizophrenia Bulletin* 36, no. 4 (July 2010): 667–679.

78. **A 2017 Gallup poll**—*Lydia Saad,* "Record Few Americans Believe Bible Is Literal Word of God," Gallup, May 15, 2017, https://news.gallup.com/poll/210704/record-few-americans-believe-bible-literal-word-god.aspx.

79. **a major 1992 study**—Kutchins and Kirk, *Making Us Crazy*, 52–54.

79. **a kappa of less than .59 considered weak reliability**—Mary L. McHugh, "Interrater Reliability: The Kappa Statistic," *Biochemia Medica* 22, no. 3 (October 2012): 276–82.

79. **Robert Spitzer / kappa of less than .40**—Greenberg, *The Book of Woe*, 226.

79. **DSM-5 field trials, here is a sample of kappa results**—Ibid., 312–13.

79. **"Here he was, announcing a miserable failure"**—Ibid., 314.

79. **fifty senior psychiatrists were asked to distinguish**—Ramin Mojtabai and Robert A. Nicholson; "Interrater Reliability of Ratings of Delusions and Bizarre Delusions," *American Journal of Psychiatry* 152, no. 12 (December 1995): 1804–06.

80. **"Even the sages of the Talmud"**—Nadler, *A Book Forged in Hell*, 108.

80. **Amsterdam rabbinical battle**—Rebecca Goldstein, *Betraying Spinoza: The*

Renegade Jew Who Gave Us Modernity (New York: Schocken, 2006), 149–150.

80. **$10,000 annual royalties from *DSM-IV***—Greenberg, *The Book of Woe*, 139.

80. **Spitzer had publicly criticized**—Ibid., 102–103.

80. **"APA's enemies' list"**—Ibid., 108.

81. **First about *DSM-5*: "The good news about the *DSM-5*"**—Ibid., 362.

81. **"We see that nearly all men parade their own ideas"**—*Theological-Political Treatise*, Chapter 7, *Spinoza: Complete Works*, 456.

81. **"Troubled by the expansion of ecclesiastic power"**—Nadler, *A Book Forged in Hell*, 110–11.

82. **"NIMH will be re-orienting its research away from *DSM* categories"**—Thomas Insel, "Transforming Diagnosis," National Institute of Mental Health, April 29, 2013, https://www.nimh.nih.gov/about/directors/thomas-insel/blog/2013/transforming-diagnosis.shtml.

82. **NIMH would be re-orienting to something called RDoC**—Ibid.

82. **conflict between the *DSM* and RDoC**—Stuart L. Kaplan, "The Most Important Controversy in Current Psychiatry: Dimensional Diagnosis versus Categorical Diagnosis," *Psychology Today*, January 10, 2016, https://www.psychologytoday.com/us/blog/your-child-does-not-have-bipolar-disorder/201601/the-most-important-controversy-in-current.

Chapter 8: Thee Noble Lies

85. **"there is no definition of a mental disorder"**—Gary Greenberg, "Inside the Battle to Define Mental Illness" *Wired*, December 27, 2010, https://www.wired.com/2010/12/ff_dsmv.

85. **"the diagnostic label is just a description"**—Gary Greenberg, *The Book of Woe: The DSM and the Unmaking of Psychiatry* (New York: Penguin Group, 2013), 157.

85. **"If you puncture that noble lie"**—Ibid., 157.

85. **"A lot of false beliefs help people cope"**—Ibid., 281.

86. ***Manufacturing Consent***—Edward Herman and Noam Chomsky, *Manufacturing Consent* (New York: Pantheon, 1988).

86. ***Why Leaders Lie***—John Mearsheimer, *Why Leaders Lie: The Truth about Lying in International Politics* (New York: Oxford University Press, 2011).

86. **"I look at international lying from a strictly"**—Ibid., 11.

86. **He details how the George W. Bush administration**—Ibid., 5.

86. **evaluates positively a major lie of the Kennedy**—Ibid., 66.

87. **"In truth, the 'chemical imbalance'"**—Ronald, Pies, "Psychiatry's New Brain-Mind and the Legend of the 'Chemical Imbalance,'" *Psychiatric Times*, July 11, 2011, https://www.psychiatrictimes.com/view/psychiatrys-new-brain-mind-and-legend-chemical-imbalance.

87. **Alix Spiegel**—Alix Spiegel, "When It Comes To Depression, Serotonin Isn't

The Whole Story," *NPR Morning Edition*, January 23, 2012, https://www.npr.org/sections/health-shots/2012/01/23/145525853/when-it-comes-to-depression-serotonin-isnt-the-whole-story.

88. **In his 1999 review of the research**—Pedro Delgado and Francisco Moreno, "Antidepressants and the Brain," *International Clinical Psychopharmacology* 14, no. 1 (May 1999): 9–16.

88. **"The aim of science, philosophy"**—Beth Lord, interviewed on broadcast, "Spinoza," *Ideas*, CBC (Canadian Broadcasting Corporation) Radio, June 14, 2013, https://www.cbc.ca/radio/ideas/spinoza-1.2913483.

89. **"Furthermore, there is no convincing evidence"**—Elliot Valenstein, *Blaming the Brain: The Truth about Drugs and Mental Health* (New York: The Free Press, 1998), 223.

89. **Pies claims**—Ronald Pies, "Nuances, Narratives, and the 'Chemical Imbalance' Debate," *Psychiatric Times*, April 11, 2014, https://www.psychiatrictimes.com/view/nuances-narratives-and-chemical-imbalance-debate.

89. **A 2006 survey revealed that 80 percent**—Bernice A. Pescosolido, et al., "'A Disease Like Any Other'? A Decade of Change in Public Reactions to Schizophrenia, Depression, and Alcohol Dependence," *American Journal of Psychiatry* 167, no. 11 (November 2010): 1321–30.

89. **A 2015 survey reported that 42 percent**—Kendall Breitman, "Poll: Half of Republicans still believe WMDs found in Iraq," January 7, 2015, https://www.politico.com/story/2015/01/poll-republicans-wmds-iraq-114016.

89. **"One of the saddest lessons of history"**—Carl Sagan, *The Demon-Haunted World: Science as a Candle in the Dark* (New York, Ballantine: 1996), 241.

90. **"My father believed in the God of Spinoza"**—Lynn Margulis and Dorion Sagan, *Dazzle Gradually: Reflections on the Nature of Nature* (White River Junction, VT: Chelsea Green, 2007), 14.

90. **between 1988 and 2008, the rate of antidepressant use**—Laura A. Pratt, et al., "Antidepressant Use in Persons Aged 12 and Over: United States, 2005–2008," National Center for Health Statistics Data Brief no. 76, October 2011, https://www.cdc.gov/nchs/products/databriefs/db76.htm.

90. **A study published in 2020 in the *Journal of Affective Disorders***—Hans, Schroder, et al., "Stressors and Chemical Imbalances: Beliefs about the Causes of Depression in an Acute Psychiatric Treatment Sample," *Journal of Affective Disorders* 276 (November 2020): 537–45.

90. **"Like most medical specialties"**—Greenberg, *The Book of Woe*, 157.

91. **In 2002, Kirsch examined**—Irving Kirsch, et al., "The Emperor's New Drugs: An Analysis of Antidepressant Medication Data Submitted to the U.S. Food and Drug Administration," *Prevention & Treatment* 5, no. 1, Article 23 (2002), https://www.researchgate.net/publication/228550299.

91. **"all antidepressants / no clinically significant benefit over a placebo"**—Irving, Kirsch, "Why Antidepressants are Simply a Confidence Trick: A Leading Psychologist Claims Taking Sugar Pills Would Work Just as

Well," *Daily Mail*, August 3, 2010, https://www.dailymail.co.uk/health/article-1299791/Why-antidepressants-simply-confidence-trick-A-leading-psychologist-claims-taking-sugar-pills-work-just-well.html.

91. **The FDA's "Major Depressive Disorder"**—"Major Depressive Disorder: Developing Drugs for Treatment Guidance for Industry," US Department of Health and Human Services and Food and Drug Administration, 2020, https://www.fda.gov/media/113988/download.

92. **Giovanni Fava**—Giovanni Fava, "Do Antidepressant and Antianxiety Drugs Increase Chronicity in Affective Disorders?" *Psychotherapy and Psychosomatics* 61, no. 3/4 (1994): 125–31.

92. **"Poorer Long-Term Outcomes"**— Jeffrey R. Vittengl, "Poorer Long-Term Outcomes among Persons with Major Depressive Disorder Treated with Medication," *Psychotherapy and Psychosomatics* 86 (September 2017): 302–304.

92. **In 2006, an NIMH-funded study**—Michael Posternak, et al., "The Naturalistic Course of Unipolar Major Depression in the Absence of Somatic Therapy, *Journal of Nervous and Mental Disease* 194, no. 5 (May 2006): 324–29.

93. **"No other element of Spinoza's philosophy"**—Jonathan Israel, *Radical Enlightenment: Philosophy and the Making of Modernity 1650–1750* (Oxford: Oxford University Press, 2001), 218.

Chapter 9: Tolerance and Stigma

95. **Union of Utrecht**—Steven Nadler, *Spinoza: A Life* (Cambridge: Cambridge University Press, 1999), 8.

96. **"the two Enlightenments"**—Jonathan Israel, *Radical Enlightenment: Philosophy and the Making of Modernity 1650–1750* (Oxford: Oxford University Press, 2001), 265–66.

96. **"Those are not at all to be tolerated"**— Ibid., 266.

97. **Erving Goffman**—Erving Goffman, *Asylums: Essays on the Social Situation of Mental Patients and Other Inmates* (New York: Anchor Books, 1961); *Stigma: Notes on the Management of Spoiled Identity* (New York: Simon & Schuster, 1963).

98. **U.S. Joint Commission on Mental Illness**—U.S. Joint Commission on Mental Illness and Health, *Action for Mental Health* (New York: Basic Books, 1961), 59.

98. **"Prejudice and Schizophrenia: A Review"**—John Read et al., "Prejudice and Schizophrenia: A Review of the 'Mental illness is an Illness Like any Other' Approach," *Acta Psychiatrica Scandinavica* 114, no. 5 (November 2006): 303–18.

99. **Mehta's 1997 study**—Shelia Mehta and Amerigo Farina, "Is Being 'Sick' Really Better? Effect of the Disease View of Mental Disorder on Stigma," *Journal of Social and Clinical Psychology* 16, no. 4 (December 1997): 405–19.

100. **"Myth: Reframing Mental Illness"**—"Myth: Reframing Mental Illness as a 'Brain Disease' Reduces Stigma," *Canadian Health Services Research Foundation*, July 17, 2013, https://journals.sagepub.com/doi/abs/10.1177/1355819613485853.

100. **"Biochemical aberrations make them"**—Mehta, "Is Being 'Sick' Really Better?"

101. **"Our findings also suggest that conceptualizing mental disorder"**—Georg Schomerus, et al., "Evolution of Public Attitudes about Mental Illness: A Systematic Review and Meta-Analysis," *Acta Psychiatrica Scandinavica* 125, no. 6 (June 2012): 440–52.

101. **"Childhood Adversities Increase the Risk of Psychosis"**—Filippo Varese et al., "Childhood Adversities Increase the Risk of Psychosis: A Meta-analysis of Patient-Control, Prospective- and Cross-sectional Cohort Studies," *Schizophrenia Bulletin* 38, no. 4 (June 2012): 661–671.

102. **"So when something in Nature appears to us as ridiculous"**—*Theological-Political Treatise*, Chapter 16, *Spinoza: Complete Works*, 528.

102. **Marius Romme**—Marius Romme and Sandra Escher, "Intervoice: Accepting and Making Sense of Hearing Voices," in *Alternatives Beyond Psychiatry*, ed. Peter Stastny and Peter Lehmann (Berlin: Peter Lehman Publishing, 2007), 131–145.

103. **Eleanor Longden**—Eleanor Longden, "The Voices in My Head," *TED*, 2013, https://www.ted.com/talks/eleanor_longden_the_voices_in_my_head.

103. **great deal of research examining just how common voice hearing is**—Saskia de Leede-Smith, et al., "A Comprehensive Review of Auditory Verbal Hallucinations: Lifetime Prevalence, Correlates and Mechanisms in Healthy and Clinical Individuals," *Frontiers in Human Neuroscience* 7, no. 367 (July 2013).

104. **unusual beliefs**—Rufus May, "Reclaiming Mad Experience: Establishing Unusual Belief Groups and Evolving Minds Public Meetings," in *Alternatives Beyond Psychiatry*, 117–27.

104. **Tamasin Knight**—Tamasin Knight, *Beyond Belief: Alternative Ways of Working with Delusions, Obsessions and Unusual Experience* (Berlin: Peter Lehman Publishing, 2013).

105. **Gore Vidal**—Gore Vidal, *The City and the Pillar* (New York: E.P. Dutton, 1948).

105. ***New York Times* refused to accept advertising**—Gore Vidal, *The Essential Gore Vidal*, ed. Fred Kaplan (New York, Random House, 1999), excerpt at https://archive.nytimes.com/www.nytimes.com/books/first/v/vidal-essential.html.

105. **"With a real voice God revealed to Moses"**—*Theological-Political Treatise*, Chapter 1, *Spinoza: Complete Works*, 396.

Chapter 10: Brain Disease

107. **"Schizophrenia is a chronic brain disorder"**—American Psychiatric Association, "What Is Schizophrenia?," APA website, https://www.psychiatry.org/patients-families/schizophrenia/what-is-schizophrenia.

107. **Ron Powers states: "Schizophrenia"**—Ron Powers, *No One Cares about Crazy People: My Family and the Heartbreak of Mental Illness* (New York: Hachette Books, 2017), xv.

108. **(WHO) website**—"What are Neurological Disorders?" World Health Organization, https://www.who.int/news-room/q-a-detail/what-are-neurological-disorders.

108. **WHO's 217 page report "Neurological Disorders**—"Neurological Disorders: Public Health Challenges," World Health Organization, https://www.who.int/mental_health/neurology/neurological_disorders_report_web.pdf.

108. **Brain Foundation's website**—"A–Z of Brain Disorders," The Brain Foundation, https://brainfoundation.org.au/disorders.

108. **National Institute of Neurological Disorders and Stroke**—National Institute of Neurological Disorders and Stroke, "All Disorders," National Institute of Health website, https://www.ninds.nih.gov/Disorders/All-Disorders.

108. **"Push Is On to Reclassify Schizophrenia"**—Batya Swift Yasgur, "Push Is On to Reclassify Schizophrenia as a Neurologic Disease," *Medscape*, July 24, 2019, https://www.medscape.com/viewarticle/908834.

109. **The *DSM* criteria for schizophrenia**—"Schizophrenia," *Medscape*, https://emedicine.medscape.com/article/288259-overview#a2.

109. **"a concept so diffuse as to be unusable"**—Don Bannister, "The Logical Requirements of Research into Schizophrenia," *British Journal of Psychiatry* 114, no. 507 (1968): 181–188, quoted by John Read, "Does 'Schizophrenia' Exist? Reliability and Validity," in John Read, Loren R. Mosher, and Richard P. Bentall, *Models of Madness: Psychological, Social and Biological Approaches to Schizophrenia* (East Sussex, UK: Routledge, 2004), 46.

111. **"The Brain in Schizophrenia" offers colorful**—"The Brain in Schizophrenia," schizophrenia.com, http://schizophrenia.com/schizpictures.html.

111. **"The Myth of Schizophrenia as a Progressive Brain Disease"**—Robert Zipursky et al., "The Myth of Schizophrenia as a Progressive Brain Disease," *Schizophrenia Bulletin* 39, no. 6 (November 2013): 1363–72.

112. **A 2020 *JAMA Psychiatry* study**—Aristotle N. Voineskos et al., "Effects of Antipsychotic Medication on Brain Structure in Patients with Major Depressive Disorder and Psychotic Features: Neuroimaging Findings in the Context of a Randomized Placebo-Controlled Clinical Trial," *JAMA Psychiatry* 77, no. 7 (February 2020): 674–83.

112. **"The infusion of new funds"**—Anne Harrington, *Mind Fixers: Psychiatry's Troubled Search for the Biology of Mental Illness* (New York: W. W. Norton, 2019), 249.

112. **"Above all," Harrington concludes**—Ibid.

112. **brains of the majority of individuals diagnosed with schizophrenia**—Al Siebert, "Brain Disease Hypothesis for Schizophrenia Disconfirmed by All Evidence," *Ethical Human Sciences and Services* 1, no. 2 (1999): 179–89.

113. **dopamine imbalance theory**—John Haracz, "The Dopamine Hypothesis: An Overview of Studies with Schizophrenic Patients," *Schizophrenia Bulletin* 8, no. 3 (January 1982): 438–469.

113. **"supersensitivity" to dopamine**—Guy Chouinard and Barry Jones, "Neuroleptic-Induced Supersensitivity Psychosis: Clinical and Pharmacologic Characteristics," *American Journal of Psychiatry* 137, no. 1 (January 1980): 16–21.

113. **"synaptic pruning"**—Powers, *No One Cares about Crazy People*, 35–36.

114. **"have consistently found that about 40% achieve"**—Zipursky, et al., "The Myth of Schizophrenia as a Progressive Brain Disease."

114. **Courtenay Harding**—Courtenay Harding, "The Vermont Longitudinal Study of Persons with Severe Mental Illness, II: Long-term outcome of subjects who retrospectively met *DSM-III* criteria for schizophrenia," *American Journal of Psychiatry* 144, no. 6 (June 1987): 727–735; Michael DeSisto, Courtenay M Harding, et. al. "The Maine and Vermont Three-Decade Studies of Serious Mental Illness. II. Longitudinal Course Comparisons," *British Journal of Psychiatry*, 167, no. 3 (September 1995): 338–42; Patrick A. McGuire, "A New Hope for People with Schizophrenia," *Monitor on Psychology* 31, no. 2 (February 2000), http://psychrights.org/research/Digest/Effective/APAMonV31No2.htm.

114. **"The most amazing finding"**—Powers, *No One Cares about Crazy People*, 327.

114. **common factor shared by the best-outcome group**—Robert Whitaker, *Mad in America: Bad Science, Bad Medicine, and the Enduring Mistreatment of the Mentally Ill* (Cambridge, MA, Perseus, 2001), 231.

114. **"It is important here to stress"**—Powers, *No One Cares about Crazy People*, 328.

114. **Maimonides's reconciliatory theism**—Rebecca Goldstein, *Betraying Spinoza: The Renegade Jew Who Gave Us Modernity* (New York: Schocken, 2006), 82–83.

115. **"new round of awards for cutting-edge"**—National Institute for Mental Health, "NIH Greatly Expands Investment in BRAIN Initiative," NIMH press release, November 5, 2018, https://www.nimh.nih.gov/news/science-news/2018/nih-greatly-expands-investment-in-brain-initiative.shtml.

Chapter 11: Genetics

118. **"Researchers believe that a number of genetic"**—American Psychiatric Association, "What Is Schizophrenia?," APA website, https://www.psychiatry.org/patients-families/schizophrenia/what-is-schizophrenia.

118. **An estimated 73 percent to 100 percent of individuals**—E. Fuller Torrey

and Robert H. Yolken, "Psychiatric Genocide: Nazi Attempts to Eradicate Schizophrenia," *Schizophrenia Bulletin* 36, no. 1 (January, 2010): 26–32.

119. **As would be expected**—Ibid.

119. **researchers led by Heinz Häfner**—Ibid.; Heinz Häfner et al., "Spatial Distribution of Mental Disorders in Mannheim, 1965," in *Psychiatric Epidemiology: Proceedings of the International Symposium Held at Aberdeen University*, ed. E.H. Hare and J.K. Wing (New York: Oxford University Press, 1970), 341–54; Heinz Häfner et al., "The Contribution of European Case Registers to Research on Schizophrenia," *Schizophrenia Bulletin* 12, no. 1 (January 1986): 26–51.

119. **"based upon a mistaken belief"**—Torrey and Yolken, "Psychiatric Genocide."

120. **The Invisible Plague**—E. Fuller Torrey and Judy Miller, *The Invisible Plague: The Rise of Mental Illness from 1750 to the Present* (Rutgers: Rutgers University Press, 2002).

120. **Anatomy of an Epidemic**—Robert Whitaker, *Anatomy of an Epidemic: Magic Bullets, Psychiatric Drugs, and the Astonishing Rise of Mental Illness in America* (New York: Crown Publishers, 2010).

120. **markedly lower reproductive rate in people diagnosed with schizophrenia**—Matthew C. Keller and Geoffrey Miller, "Resolving the Paradox of Common, Harmful, Heritable Mental Disorders: Which Evolutionary Genetic Models Work Best?," *Behavioral and Brain Sciences* 29, no. 4 (August, 2006): 385–404.

121. **Aaron Rosanoff**—Whitaker, *Mad in America: Bad Science, Bad Medicine, and the Enduring Mistreatment of the Mentally Ill* (Cambridge, MA: Perseus, 2002), 50–51.

121. **Franz Kallmann, a student of Rüdin**—R. C. Lewontin, Steven Rose, Leon Kamin, *Not in Our Genes: Biology, Ideology, and Human Nature* (New York: Pantheon, 1984), 207–209.

121–22. **often treated more similarly / one study, 40 percent**—Ibid., 114–15.

122. **"Most pairs come to the attention of researchers"**—Jay Joseph, *The Gene Illusion: Genetic Research in Psychiatry and Psychology Under the Microscope* (New York: Algora Publishing, 2004), 98.

122. **Jay Joseph details scientific problems with TRA**—Jay Joseph, *The Trouble with Twin Studies: Reassessment of Twin Research in the Social and Behavioral Sciences* (New York: Routledge, 2016), 1–150.

122. **James Shields's 1962 study / "living next door to each other"**—Ibid., 30.

122. **The most well-known TRA study**—Thomas Bouchard, et al., "Sources of Human Psychological Differences: The Minnesota Study of Twins Reared Apart," *Science* 250, no. 4978 (Ocotober 1990): 223–28.

122. **"In direct contrast, the MISTRA researchers"**—Jay Joseph, "Studies of Reared-Apart (Separated) Twins: Facts and Fallacies," *Mad in America*, December 15, 2014, https://www.madinamerica.com/2014/12/studies-reared-apart-separated-twins-facts-fallacies.

122. **described Kendler as a "genius"**—Peter D. Kramer, *Against Depression* (New York: Viking, 2005), 125.

122. **"Although we may wish it to be true"**—Kennith Kendler, "'A Gene for. . .': The Nature of Gene Action in Psychiatric Disorders," *American Journal of Psychiatry* 162, no. 7 (July 2005): 1243–52.

123. **no genetic variants were found to predict schizophrenia**—Thivia Balakrishna and David Curtis, "Assessment of Potential Clinical Role for Exome Sequencing in Schizophrenia," *Schizophrenia Bulletin* 46, no. 2 (March 2020): 328–35.

123. **2021 investigation published in the *Journal of Affective Disorders***—David Curtis, "Analysis of 50,000 Exome-Sequenced UK Biobank Subjects Fails to Identify Genes Influencing the Probability of Developing a Mood Disorder Resulting in Psychiatric Referral," *Journal of Affective Disorders* 281, no. 15 (February 2021): 216–19.

Chapter 12: Coercion

125. **descended from *converso* families**—Steven Nadler, *Think Least of Death: Spinoza on How to Live and How to Die* (Princeton: Princeton University Press, 2020), 7.

125. **"But it is far beyond the bounds of possibility that all men"**—*Theological-Political Treatise*, Chapter 20, *Spinoza: Complete Works*, 569.

126. **"Ecclesiastic authorities"**—Steven Nadler, "Spinoza on Freedom, Toleration & Charlie Hebdo," *The Critique*, January 7, 2016, http://www.thecritique.com/articles/spinoza-on-freedom-toleration-charlie-hebdo.

126. **"Now if men were so constituted by nature"**—*Theological-Political Treatise*, Chapter 5, *Spinoza: Complete Works*, 438.

127. **(APA) guide on "Ethics in Practice"**—American Psychiatric Association, "Commentary on Ethics in Practice," (APA document, 2015), 6, downloadable pdf at https://www.psychiatry.org/psychiatrists/practice/ethics.

127. **Steven Sharfstein**—Steven Sharfstein, "Individual Rights Must Be Balanced with 'Caring Coercion'" and "The Case for Caring Coercion," *Mental Illness Policy Org*, https://mentalillnesspolicy.org/aot/caring-coercion.html.

128. **"Assisted Outpatient Treatment" (AOT)**—for New York State's AOT or "Kendra's Law," see "Understanding AOT," Department of Mental Health, Oneida County, NY, https://www.ocgov.net/oneida/mentalhealth/aot.

128. **D.J. Jaffe**—D.J. Jaffe "Remarks on Assisted Outpatient Treatment," Presented at the Annual Conference of the National Alliance for the Mentally Ill, Chicago, June 30, 1999, quoted in John Monahan, "The Future of Risk Management," in *The Future of Imprisonment*, ed. Michael Tonry (New York: Oxford University Press), 238.

129. **"As Szasz points out, a drunken driver"**—E. Fuller Torrey, *The Death of Psychiatry* (Radnor PA: Chilton Book, Company, 1974), 89.

129. **"have almost unanimously shown a lower arrest rate"**—Ibid., 75.

130. **Torrey reports that research shows that applying AOT**—Robert Whitaker and Michael Simonson, "Twenty Years After Kendra's Law: The Case Against AOT," July 14, 2019, *Mad in America*, https://www.madinamerica.com/2019/07/twenty-years-kendras-law-case-aot.

130. **"4X less likely to perpetuate serious violence"**—"What is AOT?" Treatment Advocacy website, https://www.treatmentadvocacycenter.org/storage/documents/aot-one-pager.pdf.

130. **"these findings should be interpreted in terms"**—Jo C. Phelan, et al., "Effectiveness and Outcomes of Assisted Outpatient Treatment in New York State," *Psychiatry Services* 61, no. 2 (February 2010): 137–43.

130. **"remaining on medication long-term might impede"**—Thomas Insel, "Post by Former NIMH Director Thomas Insel: Antipsychotics: Taking the Long View," National Institute of Mental Health, August 28, 2013, https://www.nimh.nih.gov/about/directors/thomas-insel/blog/2013/antipsychotics-taking-the-long-view.shtml.

130. **In 1969, the World Health Organization**—Robert Whitaker, *Anatomy of an Epidemic: Magic Bullets, Psychiatric Drugs, and the Astonishing Rise of Mental Illness in America* (New York: Crown Publishers, 2010), 110–11.

131. **Ethan Watters**—Ethan Watters, *Crazy Like Us: The Globalization of the American Psyche* (New York: Free Press, 2010).

131. **Martin Harrow / followed the long-term outcomes**—Martin Harrow, et al., "Do All Schizophrenia Patients Need Antipsychotic Treatment Continuously Throughout Their Lifetime? A 20-Year Longitudinal Study," *Psychological Medicine* 42, no. 10 (October 2012): 2145–55.

132. **"I conclude that patients with schizophrenia"**—Harrow at the 2008 annual American Psychiatric Association meeting updating his review, "Factors Involved in Outcome and Recovery in Schizophrenic Patients Not on Antipsychotics: A 15-Year Multifollow-Up Study," *Journal of Nervous and Mental Disease* 195, no. 5 (May 2007), 406–14, quoted in Whitaker, *Anatomy of an Epidemic*, 116.

132. **"While antipsychotics reduce or eliminate flagrant psychosis"**—Martin Harrow, et al., "A 20-Year Multi-Followup Longitudinal Study Assessing Whether Antipsychotic Medications Contribute to Work Functioning in Schizophrenia," *Psychiatry Research* 256 (June 2017): 267–74.

132. **Lex Wunderink**—Lex Wunderink, et al., "Recovery in Remitted First-Episode Psychosis at 7 Years of Follow-Up of an Early Dose Reduction/Discontinuation or Maintenance Treatment Strategy: Long-Term Follow-Up of a 2-year Randomized Clinical Trial, *JAMA Psychiatry* 70, no. 9 (September 2013): 913–20.

133. **"It appears that what we currently call"**—Thomas Insel, "Post by Former NIMH Director Thomas Insel."

132. **"was prescribed oral antipsychotics"**—Ron Powers, *No One Cares about Crazy People: My Family and the Heartbreak of Mental Illness* (New York: Hachette Books, 2017), 58, 170, 28–29.

133. **Elizabeth Rich about her son, Andrew**—Whitaker and Simonson, "Twenty Years After Kendra's Law."

134. **David Cohen**—David Cohen, "It's the Coercion, Stupid!" *Mad in America*, October 21, 2014, https://www.madinamerica.com/2014/10/coercion-stupid.

135. **"Spinoza seems to have had a friendly"**—Steven Nadler, *Spinoza: A Life* (Cambridge: Cambridge University Press, 1999), 289.

135. **Nadler speculates that Van der Spyck**—Ibid., 306.

136. **Noam Chomsky**—Noam Chomsky, *Understanding Power: The Indispensable Chomsky*, ed. Peter Mitchell and John Schoeffel (New York: The New Press, 2002), 201.

136. **"After several weeks of worrisome behavior"**—Joshua Wolf Shenk, *Lincoln's Melancholy: How Depression Challenged a President and Fueled His Greatness* (Boston: Houghton Mifflin, 2005), 21.

136. **Bowling Green's funeral**—Ibid., 95.

Chapter 13: Madness and *Scientia Intuitiva*

137. **"For sometimes we see men so affected by one object"**— *Ethics*, Part IV, Proposition 44, *Spinoza: Complete Works*, 344.

139. **"A foolish faith in authority"**—Walter Isaacson, *Albert Einstein: His Life and the Universe* (New York: Simon & Schuster, 2007), 22.

139. **"His early suspicion of authority"** —Ibid.

139. **"cocky contempt for authority"**—Ibid., 9.

139. **"The ordinary adult never bothers his head"**—Ibid.

140. **"Through the reading of popular scientific books"**—Ibid., 20.

140. **"is grasped in a single act"**—Blake Dutton, "Benedict de Spinoza (1632–1677)," Internet Encyclopedia, https://www.iep.utm.edu/spinoza/#SH4c.

141. **"you come to know the essence"**—"Conversation with Steven Nadler," *The Wright Show*, November 2, 2016, https://www.youtube.com/watch?v=3p8azTXhSrs.

141. **"consists in an immediate, intuitive"**—Steven Nadler, *Spinoza: A Life* (Cambridge: Cambridge University` Press, 1999), 178.

141. **"a deep causal understanding"**—Steven Nadler, *A Book Forged in Hell: Spinoza's Scandalous Treatise and the Birth of the Secular Age* (Princeton: Princeton University Press, 2011), 67.

141. **"This kind of knowledge proceeds"**—*Ethics*, Part II, Proposition 40, *Spinoza: Complete Works*, 267.

141. **Sanem Soyarslan**—Sanem Soyarslan, *Reason and Intuitive Knowledge in Spinoza's Ethics: Two Ways of Knowing, Two Ways of Living*," (PhD diss, Duke University, 2011), 3, 15, https://dukespace.lib.duke.edu/dspace/bitstream/handle/10161/4961/Soyarslan_duke_0066D_11103.pdf.

142. **In his autobiographical essay written for the Nobel Prize**—John F. Nash,

Jr., "Biographical Essay for Nobel Prize," The Nobel Prize website, https://www.nobelprize.org/prizes/economic-sciences/1994/nash/biographical.

142. **"A new idea comes suddenly"**—Isaacson, *Albert Einstein*, 113.

142. **"It's the same for a man of science"**—Ibid., 549.

142. **"No one was more obsessed"**—Sylvia Nasar, *A Beautiful Mind* (New York: Touchstone, 1999), 12.

142. **"Nash always worked backward in his head"**—Ibid., 129.

143. **"Nash knew exactly what he wanted to do"**—Ibid., 224.

143. **"His tolerance for solitude"**—Ibid., 160.

143. **"possibly overreaching and psychologically destabilizing"**—Ibid., 221.

143. **"Madness can be an escape"**—*A Brilliant Madness*, directed by Mark Samels, documentary film (Boston: WGBH Educational Foundation, 2002). Transcript available at http://www.shoppbs.pbs.org/wgbh/amex/nash/filmmore/pt.html.

143. **"beguiled by the idea of alien races"**—Nasar, *A Beautiful Mind*, 12–13.

143. **"How could you," Harvard professor George Mackey**—Ibid., 11.

144. *The Insanity Hoax*—Judith Schlesinger, *The Insanity Hoax: Exposing the Myth of the Mad Genius* (Ardsley-on-Hudson, New York: Shrinktunes Media, 2012).

145. **"Descartes's mind-body dualism involves the claim"**—Clare Carlisle, "Spinoza, Part 5: On Human Nature," *The Guardian*, March 7, 2011, https://www.theguardian.com/commentisfree/belief/2011/mar/07/spinoza-philosophy-ethics-human-nature.

145. **"Thus a thought"**—Matthew Gindin, "An Introduction to Spinoza," *Medium*, August 25, 2019, https://medium.com/@MatthewZGindin/an-introduction-to-spinoza-f0ec03b2c556.

146. **"a nearly constant dance taking place"**—Paris Williams, *Rethinking Madness: Towards a Paradigm Shift in Our Understanding and Treatment of Psychosis* (San Francisco: Sky's Edge, 2012), 146.

146. **"the need to maintain the survival of a dualistic"**—Ibid., 192.

146. **"The *conatus* with which each thing endeavors"**—*Ethics*, Part III, Proposition 7, *Spinoza: Complete Works*, 283.

146. **"dread of non-being"**—Søren Kierkegaard, *The Concept of Anxiety*, 1844, trans. Alastair Hannay (New York: Liveright, 2015); title translated as *The Concept of Dread* in 1944 by Walter Lowrie.

147. **"a mark of spiritual nobility"**—Clare Carlisle, *Philosopher of the Heart: The Restless Life of Søren Kierkegaard* (New York: Farrar, Straus and Giroux, 2019), 175.

147. **Ernest Becker**—Ernest Becker, *The Denial of Death* (New York: The Free Press, 1973).

147. **Louis Sass**—Louis Sass, *Madness and Modernism: Insanity in the Light of Modern Art, Literature, and Thought* (New York: Basic Books, 1992).

147–48. **"Works like abstract expressionism"**—"Art and Schizophrenia: Louis Sass," interviewed by Will Hall, *Madness Radio*, June 30, 2009, https://www.youtube.com/watch?v=lMjDEC5vZmo.

148. "sticking this lump of flesh out into the space"—Ibid.

148. "My basic proposition"—Wouter Kusters, *A Philosophy of Madness: The Experience of Psychotic Thinking* (Cambridge, Massachusetts: MIT Press, 2020), 1.

148. "Being in a condition of madness"—Ibid., xxiii.

148–49. "So a term like 'philochosis'"—Ibid., 15.

Chapter 14: Icarus and Recovery

151. "Now I must arrive at the time"—John F. Nash, Jr., "Biographical Essay for Nobel Prize," The Nobel Prize website, available at https://www.nobelprize.org/prizes/economic-sciences/1994/nash/biographical.

152. insulin coma therapy—Sylvia Nasar, *A Beautiful Mind* (New York: Touchstone, 1999), 291–92, 329.

152. "Alicia drew the line at electroshock"—Ibid., 306.

152. Nash completely stopped psychiatric medications—Ibid., 353.

152. "Much of his past hospitalization"—Ibid., 340.

152. "Princeton functioned as a therapeutic community"—Ibid., 335.

152. "a growing awareness of the sterility"—Ibid., 353.

152. "It is a matter of policing one's thoughts"—Ibid., 351.

152. "I began to intellectually reject some"—Nash, "Biographical Essay for Nobel Prize."

152. "I began to study mathematical problems and to learn the computer"—Nasar, *A Beautiful Mind*, 354.

153. "The self-deprecating humor suggest greater self-awareness"—Ibid., 388.

153. "Personal Story Project"—Oryx Cohen, "Personal Story Project," MindFreedom International, https://mindfreedom.org/personal-stories/stories-index.

154. "A non-Zoroastrian could think of Zarathustra"—Nash, "Biographical Essay for Nobel Prize."

154. Prologue of Nietzsche's Thus Spoke Zarathustra—Friedrich Nietzsche, *Thus Spoke Zarathustra*, 1883–1885, in *The Portable Nietzsche,* ed. Walter Kaufmann (New York: Viking Press, 1954), 121.

154–55. "All superior men who were irresistibly drawn to throw off the yoke"—Friedrich Nietzsche, *Daybreak Thoughts on the Prejudices of Morality*, 1881, trans. R.J. Hollingdale, ed. Maudemarie Clark and Brian Leiter (Cambridge: Cambridge University Press, 1997), 14.

155. the Icarus Project—Maryse Mitchell-Brody, "The Icarus Project: Dangerous Gifts, Iridescent Visions and Mad Community," in *Alternatives Beyond Psychiatry,* ed. Peter Stastny and Peter Lehmann (Berlin: Peter Lehman Publishing, 2007), 137–45.

155. DuBrul began to have "a messianic feeling like"—"Maps to the Other Side: Sascha DuBrul," excerpts from DuBrul interview on *Madness Radio,* quoted in

Outside Mental Health: Voices and Visions of Madness, ed. Will Hall (Madness Radio, 2016), 91.

155. **DuBrul wrote an article in *the San Francisco Bay Guardian***—Mitchell-Brody, "The Icarus Project," 138.

156. **"freaks and kids who feel really alienated and alone"**—Hall, *Outside Mental Health*, 93.

156. **"many of us have found that labels"**—Mitchell-Brody, "The Icarus Project," 141.

156. **Reinhold Niebuhr / "a sublime madness in the soul"**—Chris Hedges, *Wages of Rebellion: The Moral Imperative of Revolt* (New York: Nation Books, 2015), 211.

156. **Kate Clifford Larson concluded that Tubman**—Kate Clifford Larson, *Bound for the Promised Land: Harriet Tubman, Portrait of an American Hero* (New York: Ballantine Books, 2004), xvii, 43, 48, 101, 263; Still quote, 254; Garrett quote, 46.

157–58. **"If we consider psychosis to be essentially"**—Paris Williams, *Rethinking Madness: Towards a Paradigm Shift in Our Understanding and Treatment of Psychosis* (San Francisco: Sky's Edge, 2012), 261.

158. **"Why am I a slave?"**—Frederick Douglass, *Life and Times of Frederick Douglass* (Boston: De Wolfe & Fiske Co., 1892), 56 (e-edition available at https:// docsouth.unc.edu/neh/dougl92/dougl92.html, 56).

158. **"All expressed the importance of maintaining hope"**—Williams, *Rethinking Madness*, 263.

158. **"that someone experiencing long-term psychosis should abandon"**—Ibid., 265.

159. **"fostering a deep connection with their aliveness"**—Ibid., 263, 266.

159. **"the importance of cultivating healthy relationships"**—Ibid., 263.

159. **Daniel Fisher**—"Building Hope in a Culture of Recovery: Interviews with Daniel Fisher, M.D.," National Empowerment Center, 2008, https://www .youtube.com/watch?v=BP_EW9u_TTw.

160. **"engenders, preserves, and fosters superstition"**—*Theological-Political Treatise*, Preface, *Spinoza: Complete Works*, 388.

160. **Voyce Hendrix**—Rachel Levy, "Original Soteria House Members to Speak!" *Mad in America*, October 26, 2020, https://www.madinamerica.com/2020/10/ original-soteria-members-speak.

160. **The Soteria staff was comprised**—Loren R. Mosher, "Non-Hospital, Non-Drug Intervention with First-Episode Psychosis," in *Models of Madness: Psychological, Social and Biological Approaches to Schizophrenia*, ed. John Read, Loren R. Mosher, and Richard P. Bentall (East Sussex, UK: Routledge, 2004), 349–364.

161. **Mosher was fired from his NIMH position**—Fabrice Nye, "The Story of the Soteria House in San Jose," Santa Clara County Psychological Association, February 10, 2015, https://www.sccpa.org/content.aspx?page_id=2507&club_ id=956131&item_id=808&pst=2301&sl=1405529142.

Chapter 15: Pals and Peers

163. **"It is of the first importance to men to establish close relationships"**—*Ethics*, Part IV, Appendix, *Spinoza: Complete Works*, 359.
164. **"Only free men are truly advantageous to one another"**—Ibid., Part IV, Proposition 71, 356.
164. **"He left Amsterdam for good in 1660"**—A. Wolf, *The Oldest Biography of Spinoza* (New York: The Dial Press, 1927), 18.
164. **"For two years he stayed in this retreat"**—Jean-Maximilian Lucas, *The Life of the Late Mr. De Spinoza* (probably completed 1678, published in 1719), in *The Oldest Biography of Spinoza*, ed. A. Wolf (New York: The Dial Press, 1927), 57.
164. **"He had many friends in The Hague"**—Colerus quote in Steven Nadler, *Spinoza: A Life* (Cambridge: Cambridge University Press, 1999), 288.
164. **"all types of curious minds, and even by upper-class girls"**—Ibid., 292.
164. **"sought a less dogmatic and nonhierarchical form of worship"**—Ibid., 139–40.
165. **"more than anyone else was responsible for bringing"**—Ibid., 171.
166. **Historians Paul Avrich and Karen Avrich**—Paul Avrich and Karen Avrich, *Sasha and Emma: The Anarchist Odyssey of Alexander Berkman and Emma Goldman* (Cambridge, MA: Belknap Press of Harvard University Press, 2012).
167. **anti-authoritarian groups that I have studied**—Bruce E. Levine, *Resisting Illegitimate Authority: A Thinking Person's Guide to Being an Anti-Authoritarian—Strategies, Tools, and Models* (Chico, CA: AK Press, 2018).
167. **Judi Chamberlin**—Judi Chamberlin, *On Our Own: Patient-Controlled Alternatives to the Mental Health System* (Lawrence, MA: National Empowerment Center, 1978).
167. **In Chamberlin's chapter**—Judy Chamberlin, "User-Run Services," in *Models of Madness: Psychological, Social and Biological Approaches to Schizophrenia*, ed. John Read, Loren R. Mosher, and Richard P. Bentall (East Sussex, UK: Routledge, 2004), 283–90.
167–68. **"A person who has been seen"** / **"more practical help"**—Ibid., 286.
168. **Sera Davidow**—Tracy Frisch, "An Open Mind: Sera Davidow Questions What We Think We Know about Mental Illness," *The Sun*, April 2017, https://www.thesunmagazine.org/issues/496/an-open-mind.
170. **Joanna Moncrieff**—Joanna Moncrieff, *The Myth of the Chemical Cure: A Critique of Psychiatric Drug Treatment* (New York: Palgrave Macmillan, 2008).
170. **"What psychiatric drugs essentially do is like using alcohol"**—"Myth of the Chemical Cure," 2010 interview with Joanna Moncrieff, in *Outside Mental Health: Voices and Visions of Madness*, ed. Will Hall (Madness Radio, 2016), 157.
170. **elsewhere acknowledges**—Joanna Moncrieff, "Psychedelics—The New Psychiatric Craze," September 2, 2021, *Mad in America*, https://www.madinamerica.com/2021/09/psychedelics-new-psychiatric-craze.
171. **John McKnight**—John McKnight, *The Careless Society: Community and Its Counterfeits* (New York: Basic Books, 1995).

171. *"I, the professional servicer, am the answer"*—Ibid., 46.
171. "While institutions and professionals war against human fallibility"—Ibid., 170.
171. "Human service professionals with special"—Ibid., 105–106.
171. "Modern heretics are those professional practitioners"—Ibid., 49.
171. Open Dialogue—Jaakko Seikkula and Birgitta Alakare, "Open Dialogues," in *Alternatives Beyond Psychiatry*, ed. Peter Stastny and Peter Lehmann (Berlin: Peter Lehman Publishing, 2007), 223–39.
172. Ronald Bassman—Ronald Bassman, *A Fight to Be: A Psychologist's Experience from Both Sides of the Locked Door* (New York: Tantamount Press, 2011).
172. Michel Foucault—Michel Foucault, *Madness and Civilization: A History of Insanity in the Age of Reason*, 1961, trans. Richard Howard (New York: Vintage Books Edition, 1988); *Discipline and Punish: The Birth of the Prison*, 1975, trans. Alan Sherridan (New York: Vintage Books Edition, 1995).
173. "The idea of 'heresy'"—Jonathan Israel, *Radical Enlightenment: Philosophy and the Making of Modernity 1650–1750* (Oxford: Oxford University Press, 2001), 191.
173. "to enlighten the people by showing how lawyers dupe"—Ibid., 187.
173. "Fired with zeal"—Ibid., 191.

Chapter 16: Freedom from Bondage

175. "whether, in fact, there was something whose discovery"—*Treatise on the Emendation of the Intellect*, *Spinoza: Complete Works*, 3.
176. *mental health* is "a state of well-being—Silvana Galderisi et al., "Toward a New Definition of Mental Health," *World Psychiatry* 14, no. 2 (June 2015): 231–233.
176. "people would gradually retrain"—Clare Carlisle, "Spinoza, Part 8: Reading the Ethics," *The Guardian*, March 28, 2011, https://www.theguardian.com/commentisfree/2011/mar/28/spinoza-reading-ethics.
177. "*Conatus* is simply"—Rebecca Goldstein, *Betraying Spinoza: The Renegade Jew Who Gave Us Modernity* (New York: Schocken, 2006), 160.
177. "nothing is more advantageous to man"—*Ethics*, Part IV Proposition 18, *Spinoza: Complete Works*, 331.
177–78. "I shall, then, treat of the nature and strength of the emotions"—*Ethics*, Part III, Preface, *Spinoza: Complete Works*, 278.
178. "We are in bondage in proportion"—Bertrand Russell, *History of Western Philosophy* (New York: Simon & Schuster, 1945), 573.
179. "if we are conscious that we have done our duty"—*Ethics*, Part IV, Appendix, *Spinoza: Complete Works*, 362.
180. Matthew Stewart points out—Matthew Stewart, *The Courtier and the*

Heretic: Leibniz, Spinoza, and the Fate of God in the Modern World (New York: W. W. Norton & Company, 2006), 176.

180. **"For a man at the mercy of his emotions is not"**—*Ethics*, Part IV, Preface, *Spinoza: Complete Works*, 320.

180. **"Spinoza's ethical theory"**—Steven Nadler, "Baruch Spinoza," *Stanford Encyclopedia of Philosophy*, June 29, 2001, https://plato.stanford.edu/entries/spinoza.

180. **"He thinks that as you"**—Susan James, interviewed on broadcast, "Spinoza," *Ideas*, CBC (Canadian Broadcasting Corporation) Radio, June 14, 2013, https://www.cbc.ca/radio/ideas/spinoza-1.2913483.

181. **"Spinoza does not, like the Stoics"**—Russell, *History of Western Philosophy*, 575.

181. **a meta-analysis of eleven randomized controlled trials**—Halle R Amick et al., "Comparative Benefits and Harms of Second Generation Antidepressants and Cognitive Behavioral Therapies in Initial Treatment of Major Depressive Disorder: Systematic Review and Meta-Analysis," *BMJ* (formerly *British Medical Journal*) 351 (December 2015).

182. **"What matters, according to Spinoza"**—Steven Nadler, *Think Least of Death: Spinoza on How to Live and How to Die* (Princeton: Princeton University Press, 2020), 39.

182. **Donald J. Robertson**—Donald J. Robertson, "Spinoza's Philosophical Psychotherapy: Rational Techniques of Emotional Therapy in Spinoza and the Stoics," *Medium*, September 22, 2019, https://medium.com/stoicism-philosophy-as-a-way-of-life/spinozas-philosophical-psychotherapy-94ff758f6f15.

183. **"Spinoza argues," notes Nadler**—Nadler, "Baruch Spinoza," *Stanford Encyclopedia of Philosophy*.

183. **"the mind passes to the highest state"**—Blake Dutton, "Benedict de Spinoza (1632–1677)," Internet Encyclopedia, https://www.iep.utm.edu/spinoza/#SH4c.

183. **"Blessedness is not the reward of virtue, but virtue itself"**—*Ethics*, Part V, Proposition 42, *Spinoza: Complete Works*, 382.

183. **"one love may be extinguished by another which is greater"**—*Short Treatise on God, Man, and His Well-Being*, Chapter XXI, ibid., 93.

183. **"Reason has no power to lead us to the attainment of our well-being"**—*Short Treatise on God, Man, and His Well-Being*, Chapter XXII, ibid., 93.

183. **"So that when we get to know God after this manner"**—Ibid., 93–94.

185. **"For I do not presume to have found the best philosophy"**—*The Letters*, Letter 76, ibid., 949.

185. **"mystical insight"**—Neal Grossman, *The Spirit of Spinoza: Healing the Mind* (Princeton NJ: ICRL Press, 2014), 105.

186. **"If the road I have pointed out as leading"**—*Ethics*, Part V, Proposition 42, *Spinoza: Complete Works*, 382.

186. **"All things excellent are as difficult"**—Ibid.

Chapter 17: *Tractatus Psychiatrico-Politicus*

188. **interviewed by Mike Wallace on network television**—"The Mike Wallace Interview: Erich Fromm," ABC, May 5, 1958, https://www.youtube.com/watch?v=OTuoqJGoNfU.

188. *The Art of Loving*—Erich Fromm, *The Art of Loving* (New York: Harper & Row, 1956).

188. **"though giving the individual a new feeling of independence"**—Erich Fromm, *Escape from Freedom*, 1941 (New York, Avon Books, 1965), 123.

188. **"Acting against the command of authority"**—Ibid., 50.

189. **"Today the function of psychiatry"**—Erich Fromm, *The Sane Society*, 1955 (New York: Fawcett Publications, 1968), 151.

189. **"Yet, many psychiatrists and psychologists refuse"**—Ibid., 15.

189. **"the person who is normal"**—Fromm, *Escaper from Freedom*, 160.

189. **Walter Reich**—Walter Reich, "The World of Soviet Psychiatry," *New York Times*, January 30, 1983, https://www.nytimes.com/1983/01/30/magazine/the-world-of-soviet-psychiatry.html.

190. **Benjamin Rush / "the father of American psychiatry" / on the seal**—Seal can be viewed at https://web.archive.org/web/20171020182607/https:/www.ucsf.edu/sites/default/files/fields/field_insert_file/blog_posts/American-Psychiatric-Association-Logo.jpeg.

190. **"excess of the passion for liberty" / "anarchia"**—*The Selected Writings of Benjamin Rush*, ed. Dagobert D. Runes (New York: Philosophical Library, 1947), 333, https://archive.org/stream/selectedwritings030242mbp/selectedwritings030242mbp_djvu.txt.

190. *The Protest Psychosis*—Jonathan Metzl, *The Protest Psychosis: How Schizophrenia Became a Black Disease* (Boston: Beacon Press, 2010).

190. **"The main story"**—"Black Politics and Schizophrenia: Jonathan Metzl," in *Outside Mental Health: Voices and Visions of Madness*, ed. Will Hall (Madness Radio, 2016), 249.

190. **Project MK-Ultra**—John Marks, *The Search for the "Manchurian Candidate": The CIA and Mind Control: The Secret History of the Behavioral Sciences* (New York: W. W. Norton, 1979).

191. **enabling interrogations that employed torture**—James Risen, "American Psychological Association Bolstered C.I.A. Torture Program, Report Says," *New York Times*, April 30, 2015, https://www.nytimes.com/2015/05/01/us/report-says-american-psychological-association-collaborated-on-torture-justification.html; Rupert Stone, "Leading Psychologists Secretly Aided U.S. Torture Program," *Newsweek*, July 10, 2015, https://www.newsweek.com/torture-cia-american-psychological-association-defense-department-352728.

191. **Martin Seligman / U.S. Army's Comprehensive Soldier Fitness**—Benedict Carey. "Mental Stress Training Is Planned for U.S. Soldiers," *New York Times*, August 18, 2009, http://www.nytimes.com/2009/08/18/health/18psych.html.

191. **one in six U.S. armed service members**—"Medicating the Mili-

tary—Use of Psychiatric Drugs Has Spiked; Concerns Surface about Suicide, Other Dangers," *Military Times*, March 29, 2013, https://www.militarytimes.com/2013/03/29/medicating-the-military-use-of-psychiatric-drugs-has-spiked-concerns-surface-about-suicide-other-dangers.

192. **antipsychotic drugs grossed over $18 billion**—Richard Friedman, "A Call for Caution in the Use of Antipsychotic Drugs," *New York Times*, September, 25, 2012, https://www.nytimes.com/2012/09/25/health/a-call-for-caution-in-the-use-of-antipsychotic-drugs.html.

192. **2021 *New York Times* investigation**—Katie Thomas, et al., "Phony Diagnoses Hide High Rates of Drugging at Nursing Homes," *New York Times*, September 11, 2021, https://www.nytimes.com/2021/09/11/health/nursing-homes-schizophrenia-antipsychotics.html.

192. **foster children**—Lucette Lagnado, "Drugged as Children, Foster-Care Alumni Speak Out," *Wall Street Journal*, Feb. 23, 2014, http://www.wsj.com/articles/SB10001424052702303442704579361333470749104.

192. **inmates in prisons and jails**—Matt Davis, "Overmedicating Young Inmates Called Chemical Restraint," *The Lens*, July 27, 2011, http://thelensnola.org/2011/07/27/jailedjuvenilesanddrugs.

192. **Among U.S. veterans**—Ilse R. Wiechers et al., "Increased Risk Among Older Veterans of Prescribing Psychotropic Medication in the Absence of Psychiatric Diagnoses," *American Journal of Geriatric Psychiatry* 22, no. 6 (June 2014): 531–39.

192. **"Mother's Little Helper"**—"History of Valium," valiumaddiction.com, http://www.valiumaddiction.com/history-of-v.htm.

192. **CDC reported that 23 percent of women**—Craig M. Hales et al., "Prescription Use Among Adults Aged 40–79 in the United States and Canada," National Center for Health Statistics, Data Brief no. 347, August 2019, Centers for Disease Control, https://www.cdc.gov/nchs/products/databriefs/db347.htm.

193. **"Biological determinism (biologism)"**—R.C. Lewontin, Steven Rose, and Leon Kamin, *Not in Our Genes: Biology, Ideology, and Human Nature* (New York: Pantheon Books, 1984), 7, 23.

193. **Stephen Jay Gould**—Stephen Jay Gould, *The Mismeasure of Man* (New York: W. W. Norton, 1981).

193. **Results from a 2013 national survey**—"Results from the 2013 National Survey on Drug Use and Health: Mental Health Findings," Substance Abuse and Mental Health Services Administration, https://www.samhsa.gov/data/sites/default/files/NSDUHmhfr2013/NSDUHmhfr2013.pdf.

194. **Adverse Childhood Experiences (ACE)**—Vincent J Felitti, et al., "Relationship of Childhood Abuse and Household Dysfunction to Many of the Leading Causes of Death in Adults: The Adverse Childhood Experiences (ACE) Study," *American Journal of Preventive Medicine* 14, no. 4 (May 1998): 245–58.

194. **"Adverse experiences, particularly in childhood"**—Noël Hunter, *Trauma*

and Madness in Mental Health Services (New York: Palgrave Macmillan, 2018), 4.

195. *Schizophrenia and Civilization*—E. Fuller Torrey, *Schizophrenia and Civilization* (New York: Jason Aronson1980), 12–13, 40, 43–76, 187.

196. **"This alienation and automatization"**—Fromm, *The Sane Society*, 312.

196. **"They both are thoroughly materialistic in their outlook"**—Ibid., 311.

196. **70 percent of Americans were disengaged**—Richard Ellison, "How to Increase the Number of Engaged Employees in Your Organization," *Forbes*, October 3, '2019, https://www.forbes.com/sites/forbescoachescouncil/2019/10/03/how-to-increase-the-number-of-engaged-employees-in-your-organization/#306cb961c8df.

196. **2018 Wisconsin Medical Society survey**—Anne Hauer et al., "Physician Burnout in Wisconsin: An Alarming Trend Affecting Physician Wellness," *Wisconsin Medical Journal* (December 2018): 194–200.

196. **Amazon, which by 2020 had approximately 900,000 employees**—Monica Nickelsburg, "Amazon Tops 935k Employees as of This Week, as Pandemic-Driven Hiring Spree Continues," *Geek Wire*, April 30, 2020, https://www.geekwire.com/2020/amazon-tops-935k-employees-week-pandemic-driven-hiring-spree-continues.

196. **"Confidence in Institutions"**—"Confidence in Institutions," Gallup Poll, 2020, https://news.gallup.com/poll/1597/confidence-institutions.aspx.

Chapter 18: Bento's Conclusions

199. **"a focus of general indignation"**—Jonathan Israel, *Radical Enlightenment: Philosophy and the Making of Modernity 1650–1750* (Oxford: Oxford University Press, 2001), 285–286.

200. **"Intending to put into print the book"**—*The Letters*, Letter 68, *Spinoza: Complete Works*, 935.

200. **plotting to establish a free republic in Normandy**—Israel, *Radical Enlightenment*, 183.

201. **sketched with charcoal and ink**—Steven Nadler, *Spinoza: A Life* (Cambridge: Cambridge University Press, 1999), 204.

201. **"the complex business of saving and deploying"**—Israel, *Radical Enlightenment*, 287.

201. **"good that follows from mutual friendship"**—*Ethics*, Part V, Proposition 10, *Spinoza: Complete Works*, 369.

201. **"A sizeable group, including copiers"**—Israel, *Radical Enlightenment*, 288.

201. **"purity of our Holy Catholic Faith"**—Ibid., 289.

202. **"scarcely any other fruit"**—Ibid., 293.

202. **"The illegal sale of Spinoza's texts could not be stopped"**—Ibid.

202. **"laying down legally the separation between"**—Ibid., 294.

202. "So when they something occurring"—*Ethics*, Part IV, Preface, *Spinoza: Complete Works*, 321.

203-04. "that insane and evil man"—Matthew Stewart, *The Courtier and the Heretic: Leibniz, Spinoza, and the Fate of God in the Modern World* (New York: W. W. Norton, 2006), 11, 313.

207. "in the broad river of anarchy"—Peter Marshall, *Demanding the Impossible: A History of Anarchism* (Oakland: PM Press, 2010), 11.

207. "the first to give a clear statement of anarchist principles"—Ibid., 191.

207. "Godwin's position resembles Spinoza's description"—Ibid., 37.

207. "Spinoza is often presented"—Daniel Garber, "Hobbes vs. Spinoza on Human Nature: Political Ramifications," lecture, March 26, 2014, https://www.youtube.com/watch?v=tn9NpyHtnMw.

208. suicide is now the second leading cause of death—Centers for Disease Control, "Increase in Suicide Mortality in the United States, 1999–2018," National Center for Health Statistics Data Brief no. 362, April 2020, https://www.cdc.gov/nchs/products/databriefs/db362.htm.

208. "Therefore nobody, unless he is overcome by external causes"—*Ethics*. Part IV, Proposition 20, *Spinoza: Complete Works*, 332.

210. "A sad example of this truth"—*Theological-Political Treatise*, Chapter 18, Ibid., 556.

211. On the last pages of that unfinished chapter on democracy—*Political Treatise*, Chapter 11, *Spinoza: Complete Works*, 752–54.

212. George Eliot—*Spinoza's Ethics*, trans. George Eliot, ed. Clare Carlisle (Princeton, NJ: Princeton University Press, 2020).

212. "some readers have found in her novels"—Clare Carlisle, "George Eliot Meets Spinoza," *Lapham's Quarterly*, January 14, 2020, https://www.laphamsquarterly.org/roundtable/george-eliot-meets-spinoza.

213. "Indeed, I would prefer that they disregard this book"—*Theological-Political Treatise*, Preface, *Spinoza: Complete Works*, 394.

INDEX

ABC paradigm, 181, 184
active placebos, 91. *See also* placebos
addiction, 11–12
adequate ideas, 203
Adverse Childhood Experiences (ACE), 194–5
advocacy, 23
Afiya House, 169–70
African Americans, 190
"After Decades of Research, Science Is No Better Able to Predict Suicidal Behaviors" (report), 34
The Age of Reason (Paine), 24, 64
Alakare, Birgitta, 172
alcohol, 170
Alcott, Bronson, 166
alienation, 196
aliveness, 159
altruism, 4–5
American Crisis (Paine), 25
American Eugenics Society, 44
American Psychiatric Association (APA): and CIA, 191; "Commentary on Ethics in Practice," 69; conflicts of interest, 65, 66, 67, 69; on depression, 89; "Ethics in Practice," 127; and homosexuality, 3; and Lieberman, 23, 47; and ODD, 5;

power of, 198; and reliability, 78–79; and Rush, 43–44; and Schatzberg, 65; and schizophrenia, 55, 107, 118; and Spitzer and Frances, 80; and Szasz, 22. See also *Diagnostic and Statistical Manual of Mental Disorders*
American Revolution, 25
amusement, 7
The Analects (Confucius), 54
anarchia, 190
anarchy, 135, 155–56, 166, 207–208
Anatomy of an Epidemic (Whitaker), 23
Anda, Robert, 194
Andreasen, Nancy, 137–8
anecdotal evidence, 57–9
Angell, Marcia, 64
anger, 29, 31–2, 55. *See also* fear; tension
anosognosia, 127
"An Answer to the Question: What is Enlightenment?" (Kant), 12
anthropomorphism, 9
antidepressants. *See* medication
anti-psychiatry, 21–22
anti-stigma strategy, 97–101
anxiety, 30–1, 146–47
aristocracy, 210–11
arrogance, 39, 69, 102, 142, 152
art, 137–38, 147–48, 156

assimilation, 4–5
"Assisted Outpatient Treatment" (AOT), 128, 129–30, 132–33
Asylums (Goffman), 97
atheists, 96
attention deficit hyperactivity disorder, 9, 48, 57
auditory verbal hallucinations (AVH), 102–103, 105, 156–57. *See also* allusions
authoritarianism, 1
authority: evaluating, 38; and ODD diagnosis, 5–6, 31–32, 139; resisting, 5, 139–40; and tension of uncertainty, 16
autism spectrum disorder (ASD), 9
aversion therapies, 46
Avrich, Paul and Karen, 166
axioms, 31, 37–39, 61

Balling, Pieter, 164, 200
banned books, 41
Bannister, Don, 109
barbarism, 41, 43–50
Barberini, Francesco, 201
Bassman, Ronald, 172
A Beautiful Mind (film), 20–21, 140, 151, 153. *See also* Nash, John
Becker, Ernest, 147
"Behavioral Response to Methylphenidate [Ritalin]... " (Lieberman), 47
"On Being Sane in Insane Places" (Rosenhan), 67
bereavement exclusion, 77
Bethlem Royal Hospital ("Bedlam"), 43
Betraying Spinoza (Goldstein), 7
Beyond Belief (Knight), 104
bias, 13, 34–35
Bible: as coercive, 1; and DSM, 73, 75–76, 78, 80, 81–82; and Einstein, 139–40; and God, 74–75, 78, 81–82, 87; inconsistencies, 74; Spinoza's views,

1, 73–75, 204; and voice hearing, 105. *See also Theological-Political Treatise*
Biederman, Joseph, 65
biochemical mental illness, 37, 87–89, 93, 99–100, 112–13, 195
biochemical/genetic determinism, 193
biogenetic causal beliefs, 37, 98, 99
biological theories, 59
bipolar disorder, 8, 65, 108
bizarre delusions, 78, 79–80. *See also* delusions
Blaming the Brain (Valenstein), 89
blasphemy, 173
blessedness, 53, 175, 183, 185
bloodletting, 35, 36, 44, 58–59
bondage, 29–30, 53, 177–79, 181, 182, 185–86
A Book Forged in Hell (Nadler), 74. *See also* Nadler, Steven
The Book of Woe: The DSM and the Unmaking of Psychiatry, 77, 80
borderline personality disorder, 36
Bouchard, Thomas, 122
Bouwmeester, Johannes, 201
brain disease, 59, 107–109, 111–16, 158, 205-2-7. *See also* chemical imbalances
Brooks, George, 114
Brown University Medical School, 64
Bruno, Giordano, 20
burnout, 196
Bush, George W., 86, 191

Cahalan, Susannah, 67
Campbell, Joseph, 147
capitalism, 188, 196
careers/employment, 193, 196
The Careless Society: Community and Its Counterfeits (McKnight), 171
Carey, Benedict, 11–12
caring, 136, 152. *See also* supportive relationships
Carlisle, Clare, 18–19, 145, 147, 176

Cartwright, Samuel, 54
Catholicism, 125, 201–202, 210
causality, 58–9. *See also* biogenetic
  causal beliefs; societal causes
cause/cure, 3
Center for Schizophrenia Research,
  160–61
Central Intelligence Agency (CIA),
  190–91
Chamberlin, Judi, 167–88
Channing, Ellery, 166
charity, 75
chemical imbalances, 37, 87–89, 93,
  99–100, 112–13, 195. *See also* brain
  disease
"Childhood Adversities Increase the
  Risk of Psychosis" (report), 101–102
childhood trauma, 101–102, 103, 194–105,
  197
children, 4–5, 48, 65, 90, 192
Chomsky, Noam, 86, 135
Chouinard, Guy, 113
Christianity, 24, 25, 125, 164. *See also*
  Catholicism; religion
Church of Scientology, 23
Citizens Commission on Human Rights
  (CCHR), 23
The City and the Pillar (Vidal), 105
classifications, 3
clergy, 21, 74, 75, 187, 192, 206
Clinician's Illusion, 35, 110–11, 167
clonidine, 48
coercion: overview, 127–28; debate on,
  135; defined, 125; and fear, 32–33,
  129; fear of, 129; and freethinkers,
  167; laws, 130; and Nash, 151–52;
  of religion, 125–26; and resentment, 208; and Szasz, 22. *See also*
  "Assisted Outpatient Treatment";
  hospitalization
cognitive constructs, 158
Cognitive-behavioral therapy (CBT),
  180–82, 184
Cohen, David, 134
Cohen, Jacob, 35

Cohen, Oryx, 154
Cohen, Patricia, 35
Colerus, Johan, 17, 164
Collegiants, 164
comas, induced, 46, 152
"Commentary on Ethics in Practice"
  (APA guide), 69
Common Sense (Paine), 25
communism, 189–90, 196
Comprehensive Soldier Fitness, 191–2
conatus, 146, 163–64, 176, 177–78
conceptualizations, 203, 205
confidence, 178
conflicts of interest, 63, 64–66, 67–71
Confucius, 54
consensus reality: vs. reality, 7, 8, 54–55,
  203; and recovery, 158; rejection
  of, 7–8; and remission as term, 153;
  on schizophrenia, 8, 117, 119–20;
  Spinoza challenging, 9; and superstitions, 58; and Tubman, 157
control, 81, 157, 192
conventional wisdom: about mental
  illness, 8; and recovery, 158–59; and
  slavery, 8, 157; and Tubman, 157; vs.
  wisdom, 7
coronavirus epidemic, 42
corruption, 63, 64–66, 67–71
Cosgrove, Lisa, 68, 69
counterfeit communities, 171
Couric, Katie, 48
The Courtier and the Heretic (Stewart), 7,
  203–204
Crazy Like Us (Watters), 131
creativity, 137–38, 144, 147–48, 156
criminal justice system, 193–94. *See also*
  prison
Critical Psychiatry Network, 170
Cromwell, Oliver, 210
Cuban Missile Crisis, 86
cures, 3, 114–15

da Costa, Uriel, 42

Damasio, Antonio, 6
Davidow, Sera, 168–70
de Vries, Simon, 63–64, 165, 200
de Witt, Johan, 43, 200
death, 27, 29–30, 146–47
The Death of Psychiatry (Torrey), 129
de-escalating, 38
DeJarnette, Joseph, 44
Delgado, Pedro, 88
delusions, 78, 79–80, 109, 110, 151, 152, 154. *See also* auditory verbal hallucinations
democracy, 1, 12, 24, 126, 135, 171–72, 187, 197–98
The Denial of Death (Becker), 147
Depakote, 48
depression, 55–56, 77, 87–9, 90–94, 181
derailments, 149
Descartes, René, 145
despair, 178
diagnosis: and behavior, 57; increasing, 76; reliability, 67, 78–80; resisting, 206; schizophrenia, 77–78, 112, 153; as telling of professionals, 36
Diagnostic and Statistical Manual of Mental Disorders (DSM): about, 73, 76; and Bible, 73, 75–76, 78, 80, 81–82; as bible, 7; criticisms of, 76–77, 82, 85; expansion of, 76; Insel rejecting, 26; as invalid, 61; and RDoC, 82–83; revising from criticisms, 82; schizophrenia criteria, 109; and Torah Commandments (Mitzvot), 80. *See also* American Psychiatric Association
DSM-II, 76
DSM-III, 5, 56, 76, 79
DSM-IV, 76
DSM-5, 56, 66, 76–77, 79, 81
dialogue, 38
disability, 27
Discipline and Punish (Foucault), 172
dismissing criticism, 23–24
dogma, 6, 165, 178–79
"Doing Harm: Research on the Mentally

Ill" (Whitaker and Kong), 47
"Dollars for Docs: The Top Earners" (*ProPublica*), 65
dopamine imbalance theory, 46–47, 113
Douglass, Frederick, 158
drapetomania, 54, 57
The Dream of Enlightenment (Gottlieb), 51
drug companies. *See* medication
dualism, 145–46
Duality Unity Integrative Model, 146
DuBrul, Sascha, 155–56, 161
Dully, Howard, 45–46
Dutch Golden Age, 95
Dutton, Blake, 140, 183

ecstatic rationalism, 13
Edmond J. Safra Center for Ethics, 68
Edwords, Fred, 25
Einstein, Albert, 6, 9, 55, 139–40, 142, 145
Einstein: His Life and the Universe (Isaacson), 9
Eisenhower, Dwight, 66
electroconvulsant therapy (ECT), 49
electroshock, 49
Eliot, George, 212
elites, 86–7
Emerson, Ralfph Waldo, 166
emotions, 43, 57, 134–35, 175, 177–78, 179–81. *See also* anger; fear; tension
Enlightenment, 12, 17, 26, 198, 202
enslaved people, 54, 156–57, 158
Escape from Freedom (Fromm), 188, 189
Escher, Sandra, 102–103
essence, 52–53
ethics, 63, 93, 127
Ethics (Spinoza), 3, 30, 41, 53, 137, 165, 175, 176–80, 183, 186, 199–200, 201, 204, 208
"Ethics in Practice" (APA guide), 127
eugenics, 44–5, 117, 118–19
Evans, Marian, 212
"Evolution of Public Attitudes about

Mental Illness" (report), 101
experimental method, 51–52
experiments on patients, 46–47
extreme states, 168
Ezra the Scribe, 74, 80

Fabricus, J. Ludwig, 64
faith, 10
false notions, 39. *See also* chemical
    imbalances; *Diagnostic and Statistical
    Manual of Mental Disorders*; noble
    lies
falsifiability, 59
fanaticism, 156
"The Fate of Thomas Paine" (Russell),
    25–26
Fava, Giovanni, 92
fear: vs. anxiety, 30–31, 146–47; axioms
    of, 31, 37–39; and barbarism, 43–45;
    of blame, 36–37; causing coercion,
    133; of coercion, 129; of death, 29–30,
    146–47; defined by Spinoza, 178, 179;
    and dialogue, 38; and disconnecting
    from consensus reality, 160; as dis-
    empowering, 29; and freedom, 149;
    harmony in, 30; of homosexuality,
    3–4; and inadequate ideas, 2; and
    irrational thinking, 35–36, 160, 161,
    205; of mental health professionals,
    32, 33, 34, 36; of Native Americans,
    4–5; patients and others, 35; and
    peer-to-peer support, 38–39; and
    recovery, 158; relief of, 35–36; and
    stigmatization, 104–105; and super-
    stitions, 29, 30; and tension of un-
    certainty, 29; and Tubman, 156–57;
    of violence, 127, 128–29, 133–34. *See
    also* tension
Felitti, Vincent, 194
fictions, 52
A Fight to Be (Bassman), 172
First, Michael, 81
Fisher, Daniel, 159

flight-or-flight state, 38
*A Flower Garden of All Kinds of Loveliness
    without Sorrow* (Koerbah, A. and
    Kowerbah, J.), 173
Food and Drug Administration (FDA),
    68–9, 70, 91–2
forced sterilizations, 44–45
foster children, 192
Foucault, Michel, 172
Frances, Allen, 76–77, 80, 85, 90
Franklin, Joseph, 33–34
Frazer, Alan, 88
free speech, 12
free thought: overview, 13–14; and
    animosity, 26; defined, 15–16, 26; and
    ecclesiastic authorities, 74, 187; and
    freedom, 19; and guillotine allegory,
    25; history of freethinkers, 15; and
    majority of seventeenth century,
    26; and moderately enlightened
    thinkers, 26; and oppression, 19;
    and radical thinkers, 12, 26; Spinoza
    meeting others, 17–18; and Spinoza's
    therapy, 209; as torturous, 16
freedom: from bondage, 175, 177–78;
    defined, 180; in democracy, 187; and
    Foucault, 172; and freethinkers, 19;
    and greater insecurity, 188; and life,
    29–30
Freeman, Walter, 45
French Revolution, 25
Freud, Sigmund, 176
Fromm, Erich, 188–89, 196
funding, 115

Garber, Daniel, 207–208
Garrett, Thomas, 156–57
The Gene Illusion, 122
genetics, 117–22, 123
genuine community, 208
Gindin, Matthew, 145
Glazemaker, Jan, 201
God: and the Bible, 74–75, 78, 81–82, 87;

and knowledge, 53; manipulation of, 177; and mankind, 9–10; and the masses, 87; and miracles, 75; and reality, 210–11; and Spinoza, 96 (*see also* God/Nature); and Tubman, 156–57; validity of prayer, 60, 92–93, 177; and voice hearing, 105

God/Nature: and love, 209; and natural law, 203; reality as aspects of God, 9–10; and reason, 141, 177; Spinoza as naturalist, 116; Spinoza's views, 178–79; as therapy, 182–84

Godwin, William, 207

Goffman, Erving, 97

Goldman, Emma, 166

Goldsman, Akiva, 20

Goldstein, Rebecca, 7, 13, 39, 114–15, 177

Gottlieb, Anthony, 51

Gottlieb, Scott, 70

Gould, Stephen Jay, 193

government, 70, 210

Great Depression, 44

The Great Pretender (Cahalan), 67

Green, Bowling and Nancy, 136

Greenberg, Gary, 77, 79, 80, 85

Grossman, Neal, 185

gyrators, 44

Hadamer Psychiatric Institution, 45

Häfner, Heinz, 119

Hage, Patsy, 102–103

Hall, Will, 156

Hamilton, Max, 55

Hamilton Rating Scale for Depression (HAM-D), 55

Hampshire, Stuart, 18–19, 52

happiness, 17

Harding, Courtenay, 114, 131

harmony, 30

Harrington, Anne, 66, 112

Harrow, Martin, 131–32

Hartmann, Lawrence, 22

hatred, 178

Healing Voices Network, 102–103

hearsay, 52-3, 56. *See also* opinion

Hendrix, Voyce, 160–61

herem, 42

heresy, 19, 173

Herman, Edward, 86

hierarchy, 86, 173-4, 197–98, 212

History of Western Philosophy (Russell), 6

Hitler, Adolph, 45

Hobbes, Thomas, 163–64

Hoch, Paul, 21

Hoffmann, Banesh, 139

homelessness, 130

homosexuality, 3–4, 46, 102, 105, 110–11

hope, 158–59, 178, 179

hospitalization, 127–28, 130, 133, 151, 167

"How Ethics Failed..." (article), 45

humiliation, 42

Hunter, Noël, 194

Hussein, Saddam, 86

Icarus (myth), 155–56

Icarus Project, 155–56

"The Icarus Project" (Mitchell-Brody), 156

idiot savants, 25

imaginative knowledge, 60–61. *See also* opinion

immaturity, 12

inadequate ideas, 2, 53–54, 56, 60, 203

incompetence, 32

inconsistent behavior, 57

industrial complexes, 66

Ingersoll, Robert, 25

The Insanity Hoax: Exposing the Myth of the Mad Genius (Schlesinger), 144

Insel, Thomas, 2, 11–12, 26–27, 82, 96–97, 115, 132

insomnia, 55–56

institutional confidence, 196–97

institutionalization, 97

insulin coma therapy, 46, 152

interconnectedness, 145–46

interventions, 8
intolerance, 41, 49
intuitive knowledge, 53, 137, 140–44, 157, 183, 185
invalidity, 54, 57, 61
"involuntary euthanasia," 45
involuntary psychiatric treatment. *See* coercion
Iraq war, 86
"Is Being 'Sick' Really Better?" (Mehta), 99–100
Isaacson, Walter, 9, 139
Israel, Jonathan, 12, 50, 51, 93, 96, 173, 198, 199, 201, 202
"It's the Coercion, Stupid!" (Cohen), 134

Jaffe, D.J., 128–29
James, Susan, 11, 29, 180
Jamison, Kay Redfield, 137–38
Janowsky, David, 46–47
jargon, 172–73
Jelles, Jarig, 201
Jesus, 185
Jewish community: banishing Spinoza, 6, 18, 20, 42–43; converso families, 125; and guillotine allegory, 25; stigmatization, 95; victims of barbarism, 41
Johnson & Johnson Center for Pediatric Psychopathology Research, 65
Jones, Barry, 113
Joseph, Jay, 122
journals and corruption, 68
justice, 75
Justice Department, 191

Kallmann, Franz, 121
Kamin, Leon, 121, 193
Kant, Immanuel, 12
Kaplan, Stuart L., 82–83

Kendler, Kenneth, 122
Kendra's Law, 130
Kennedy, Foster, 44
Kennedy, John F., 86
KGB, 190
Kierkegaard, Søren, 31, 146–47
Kifuji, Kayoko, 48, 65
Kirk, Stuart, 79
Kirsch, Irving, 90–91
Knight, Tamasin, 104
knowledge, 52–53, 60–61, 140–44, 172, 176. *See also various knowledge*
Koerbagh, Adriaan, 30, 49–50, 172–73, 200
Koerbagh, Johannes, 200
Kong, Dolores, 47
Kramer, Peter, 122
Kuhn, Thomas, 61
Kupfer, David, 80
Kusters, Wouter, 148–49
Kutchins, Herb, 79

Larson, Kate Clifford, 156
laws, 126, 127–29, 130, 135, 155, 203
Leibniz, Gottfried, 6
Leifer, Ron, 21
Lepore, Jill, 25
Lessig, Lawrence, 68, 70
Letter Concerning Toleration (Locke), 96
Lewontin, R.C., 121, 193
LGBTQ+, 3–4, 46, 102, 105, 110–11
liability concerns, 169
liberalism, 156
Lieberman, Jeffrey, 23, 47
The Light upon the Candlestick (Balling), 164
Lincoln, Abraham, 136
Lincoln's Melancholy (Shenk), 136
Lippman, Walter, 86
Listening to Prozac (Kramer), 122
lobotomies, 45–46
Locke, John, 96
Longden, Eleanor, 103

Looking for Spinoza (Damasio), 6
Lord, Beth, 10, 60, 88
love, 159–60, 178, 182–85, 209
love of fate, 180
LSD, 46
Lucas, Jean-Maximilian, 5–6, 7, 17
Ludwig, Arnold K., 137–38
Ludwig, Karl, 64
lying, 86, 93. *See also* noble lies

MacIntyre, Alasdair, 53
Mad Pride, 156, 166–67
madness, as term, 148–49
Madness and Civilization (Foucault), 172
Madness and Modernism (Sass), 147–48
Maimonides, 114–15
Making Us Crazy (Kutchins and Kirk), 79
Manufacturing Consent (Herman and
    Chomsky), 86
marginalization, 19–20
Marks, John, 191
Marshall, Peter, 207
Massachusetts General Hospital, 65
May, Rufus, 104
McKnight, John, 171
McNamara, Ashley, 156
Mearsheimer, John, 86
medication: and aliveness, 159; as
    causing brain effects, 112, 113; and
    CBT, 181; and coercion, 127–28, 130
    (*see also* coercion); as contributing
    to depression, 92; controlling
    populations, 192; and conventional
    wisdom, 8; corruption of drug com-
    panies, 64–66, 67–71; increasing use
    of, 27; and informed choices, 161;
    and military, 191–92; Nash's refusal
    of, 20–21, 151; and noble lies, 88,
    90–91, 93; placebos, 58–59, 90–91;
    psychedelics, 170–71; psychotropics,
    182, 192, 209; and RCL, 170; and
    schizophrenia, 26, 114, 130–33; side
    effects, 133; as tranquilizing, 170. *See*

also various medications
Mehta, Shelia, 99–100
memory loss, 49
men and suicide, 33–34
mental health, 176
mental illness: and chemical imbalance,
    87–89, 99–100; vs. creativity, 144;
    as escape, 143; as human condition,
    138–39; and opinion/imaginative
    knowledge, 176; vs. physical illness,
    97–99; psychotic breakdown, 35; and
    reduced morbidity, 27; as socially
    useful fiction, 21; Spinoza's possi-
    ble views in conclusion, 204–10;
    sublime madness, 156–57; as term,
    172–73; as undefinable, 77. *See also*
    brain disease
"mental illness deniers," 13
Mental Patients Liberation Front, 167
mescaline, 46
metaphysics, 148
Metzl, Jonathan, 190
Meyer, Lodewijk, 165, 201
microscopes, 3
military, 66, 191–92, 197
military-industrial complex, 66
Mind Fixers (Harrington), 112
mind/body, 145–46
MindFreedom International, 153–54,
    166–67
miracles, 74, 75
Mitchell-Brody, Maryse, 156
MK-Ultra, 190–91
moderate enlightenment, 26
Moncrieff, Joanna, 170
money, 63–64, 204
monism, 144–45
Montagu, Ashley, 193
morals, 4, 73, 75
Morgan, Michael, 30
mortality, 27
Moses, 105
Mosher, Loren, 160–61
"The Most Important Controversy in
    Current Psychiatry" (Kaplan), 82–83

fMRI, 112
murder, 45, 48, 118
Murray, Henry, 191
mutual aid, 166, 169, 197
My Lobotomy (Dully), 46
mysticism, 185
The Myth of Mental Illness (Szasz), 21
"The Myth of Schizophrenia as
    a Progressive Brain Disease"
    (Zipursky), 111–12
The Myth of the Chemical Cure
    (Moncrieff), 170–71
"Myth: Reframing Mental Illness…"
    (CHSRF report), 100

Nadler, Steven, 9–10, 21, 24, 50, 52,
    73–74, 75, 80, 81, 126, 135, 140–41, 164,
    180, 182, 183
Nasar, Sylvia, 20, 142–43, 151–53
Nash, Alicia, 151–52
Nash, John, 20, 140, 142, 151–53, 154, 155
Nash, Marsha, 152
National Alliance on Mental Illness
    (NAMI): and *A Beautiful Mind*
    (film), 21; and brain disease theory,
    20; conflicts of interest, 66; and
    destigmatization, 49; and *DSM*, 82;
    and laws, 129; RDoC, 82–83; and
    schizophrenia, 55
National Empowerment Center (NEC),
    154, 159, 167
National Institute of Mental Health
    (NIMH), 2, 115, 130, 131, 160–61
National Institute of Neurological
    Disorders and Stroke, 108
Native Americans, 4–5
natural law, 155, 203
"The Naturalistic Course of Major
    Depression…" (study), 92
nature, 177, 179, 184, 203. *See also* God/
    Nature
Nazi Germany, 44–45, 118–20, 155
Neercassel, Johannes van, 201–202

Nero, 180
neuroimaging, 112
neurology, 107–109
New York State Psychiatric Institute, 46
Newton, Isaac, 55
Niebuhr, Reinhold, 156
Nietzsche, Friedrich, 154–55
No One Cares about Crazy People
    (Powers), 22, 107, 113–14, 132–33
noble lies, 86, 87, 89, 107, 117. *See also*
    chemical imbalances; *Diagnostic and
    Statistical Manual of Mental Disorders*
Not in Our Genes (Lewontin, Rose and
    Kamin), 121, 192–93
Nuremberg Code, 46
nursing homes, 192

Oaks, David, 166–67
Oldenburg, Henry, 200
One Flew Over the Cuckoo's Nest (film),
    66
Open Dialogue, 135, 171–72
Open Payments database, 68
Opera Posthuma (Spinoza), 202
opinion, 53, 56, 60, 116, 176, 204–205, 211
oppositional defiant disorder (ODD):
    overview, 5–6; causing fear and ten-
    sion, 31–32, 139; and Einstein, 9; po-
    litical dissidents, 188–89; Spinoza's
    possible views, 7, 204
ostracism, 36–37
On Our Own (Chamberlin), 167
overdoses, 11–12

Paine, Thomas, 24
paradigms, 60–61
patriarchy, 211
peer-to-peer support, 38–9, 166–71,
    173–74, 197–198, 206–207. *See also*
    supportive relationships
"Personal Story Project," 153–54

Pfizer, 70
pharmaceutical companies. *See*
medication
Philosopher of the Heart (Carlisle), 147
Philosophia S. Scripturae Interpres
(Meyer), 30
philosophy, 10, 15, 19
A Philosophy of Madness (Kusters),
148–49
The Philosophy of Spinoza (Ratner), 36
"Phony Diagnoses Hide High Rates of
Drugging at Nursing Homes" (investigation), 192
physician, 196
"Physician Burnout in Wisconsin"
(report), 196
Pies, Ronald, 87, 89
placebos, 58–59, 90–91, 92–93
political judgement, 23–24
Political Treatise (Spinoza), 12, 201, 211
politics, 23–24, 188–89, 190–95
Pollock, Jackson, 147
"Poorer Long-Term Outcomes..."
(Vittengl), 92
Popper, Karl, 59
poverty, 193–94
power: of APA, 198; and causes of suffering, 58–59, 101; and community, 171;
of ecclesiastic authorities, 21, 187,
192, 206; and fear, 74; and knowledge, 172, 173; and pleasure, 177–78
Powers, Ron, 22, 107, 113–14, 132–33
prayers, 60, 92–93, 177
"Prediction of Relapse in
Schizophrenia" (Lieberman), 47
"Prejudice and Schizophrenia" (Read),
98–99
preservation, 19–20
prison, 128, 192, 193–94. *See also* criminal
justice system
"The Problem of Social Control of the
Congenital Defective" (Kennedy),
44
productivity, 36–37, 117
professionalism, 197

Project MK-Ultra, 190–91
*The Protest Psychosis: How Schizophrenia
Became a Black Disease* (Metzl), 190
pseudoscience, 4, 59
psychedelics, 170–71
"Psychedelics—The New Psychiatric
Craze" (Moncrieff), 170–71
"Psychiatric Genocide: Nazi Attempts
to Eradicate Schizophrenia" (report), 118–19
psychiatric survivors, 153–54, 166–67
Psychiatry Under the Influence (Whitaker
and Cosgrove)), 68, 69
psychiatry/psychiatrists: overview, 189;
acknowledging lack of success, 2,
11–12, 26–27, 61; and brain disease
theory, 107, 108–109; crisis of, 66–68,
76–77, 82–83; deciding mental
illness, 3, 80; defined, 108; diagnosis
and professionals, 36 (*see also* diagnosis); dissent professionals, 172;
duel roles of, 129; empirical studies
for opposite positions, 10; and fear,
32, 33, 34, 36, 160 (*see also* fear); as
inherently coercive, 134; jargon,
172–73; liability concerns, 169; as
object of derision, 66–68; and politics, 187–89, 190–95; in Soviet Union,
189–90; as unethical, 63
psychosocial stressors, 100, 101–102
psychotic breakdown, 35
psychotropics, 182, 192, 209
punishment, 128
punk rock, 155–56
"Push Is On to Reclassify Schizophrenia
as a Neurologic Disease" (report),
108
psychosis, as term, 148–49

Quakers, 25

racism, 44, 54, 190
radical, defined, 26
radical Enlightenment, 12, 26, 198
Radical Enlightenment (Israel), 12. *See also* Israel, Jonathan
random experience, 52–53
randomized control trials (RCT), 59, 132
rationality, 10, 11, 13, 39
Ratner, Joseph, 36
Read, John, 98–99
"Reason and Intuitive Knowledge in Spinoza's *Ethics*" (Soyarslan), 141
reasoning: and adequate idea of God, 179; and disobedience, 188; and God/Nature, 141; and knowledge, 53, 140, 141; preventing suffering, 177–78; and Spinoza's works, 213; and well-being, 183
reconciliatory theism, 114–15, 119, 121
recovery: Cohen's methods, 154; connecting to aliveness, 159; and consensus reality, 158; and conventional wisdom, 158–59; culture of, 159; vs. cure, 114; and fear, 158; hope for, 158–59; and love, 159–60; and medication, 130, 131–32; Nash, 151–53; and natural law, 155; and negativity, 99; "Personal Story Project," 153–54; as reorganizing cognitive constructs, 158; and schizophrenia, 99, 114–15, 130, 131–32. *See also* caring; therapeutic communities
Recovery Learning Community (RLC), 168–70, 171
reform, 26
Regier, Darrel, 79
Reich, Walter, 189–90
Reign of Terror, 25
reliability, 56, 67, 78–80
religion: and dogma, 165; *Ethics* causing harm to, 201–202; and free thought, 74; Koerbagh and blasphemy, 173; Paine's ideas, 24; power of ecclesiastic authorities, 21, 187, 192, 206; and superstitions, 16, 58; true religion, 75. *See also* Bible; clergy; God; *various religions*
"Remarks on Assisted Outpatient Treatment (AOT)" (Jaffe), 128–29
remission, 153
Research Domain Criteria (RDoC), 82–83
resentment, 135, 136
residential schools, 4–5
Rethinking Madness (Williams), 145–46, 157–59
revolution, 210
revolutionary science, 61
Rich, Andrew and Elizabeth, 133
Rieuwertsz, Jan, 165, 201, 202
Riley, Rebecca, 48, 65
Ritalin, 47
Robertson, Donald J., 182
Robertson, John, 15
Romme, Marius, 102–103
Rosanoff, Aaron, 121
Rose, Steven, 121, 193
Rosenhan, David, 67
Rüdin, Ernst, 121
Rush, Benjamin, 43–4, 190
Russell, Bertrand, 6, 15–16, 19, 25–26, 63, 178, 181

Sabshin, Melvin, 67
Sagan, Carl, 89
The Sane Society (Fromm), 188–89, 196
Sasha and Emma (Avrich P. and Avrich K.), 166
Sass, Louis, 147–8
Saving Normal (Frances), 76
Schatzberg, Alan, 65
schizophrenia: and anosognosia, 127; and APA, 55, 107, 118; and brain tissue, 111–12; and childhood trauma, 101–102, 103; and coercion, 127; consensus reality, 8, 119–20; as construct, 77–78; and death, 12; defined, 107, 118; diagnosing, 77–78, 112, 153;

as disease of civilization, 195; and
dopamine, 113; dopamine hypothesis
of, 46–47; and *DSM*, 109; and fear,
104; and genetics, 117–21, 123; in
Germany, 118–19; and hyper-focus,
148; and medication long-term, 26,
130–33; and misdiagnosis, 153; and
mortality, 27; NAMI and APA, 55; as
neurological disorder, 108; as not
valid construct, 110, 123; and racism,
190; recovery, 99, 114–15, 130, 131–32;
reproductive rate, 120; Soteria
House, 160–61; and stigmatization,
97, 99, 102–103, 104, 111; synaptic
pruning, 113–14; WHO reports,
130–31

Schizophrenia and Civilization (Torrey),
195

Schizophrenia and Related Disorders
Alliance of America, 108

Schlesinger, Judith, 137–38

Schuller, Georg, 201

science: and anger, 55; and consensus
reality/conventional wisdom, 8;
medical advances and technology,
51; vs. pseudoscience, 59; and reason, 11; reliability, 56; revolutionary,
61; and superstitions, 57–58; true
ideas vs. fictions, 52–54; and understanding God, 10; validity, 54–55, 57,
60–61

scientia intuitiva, 53, 137, 140–44, 157, 183,
185

*The Search for the "Manchurian
Candidate"* (Marks), 191

Seikkula, Jaakko, 172

self-love, 184

self-preservation, 20

Seligman, Martin, 191

Seneca the Younger, 180

Seroquel, 48

serotonin deficiency theory, 88–90, 91

Sharfstein, Steven, 127

Shenk, Joshua Wolf, 136

Shield, James, 122

Shive, Bonfire Madigan, 156

A Short History of Freethought
(Robertson), 15

*Short Treatise on God, Man, and His Well-
Being* (Spinoza), 35, 175, 183

Simonson, Michael, 133

sin, 188

societal causes, 192–97, 208, 210

Soteria House, 160–61

"Sources of Human Psychological
Differences" (Bouchard), 122

Soviet Union, 189–90

Soyarslan, Sanem, 141

Spiegel, Alix, 87–88

Spinoza, Baruch de (Bento): about,
1–2, 5–7, 11, 16–19, 95, 125, 163–66,
199; acquiring knowledge, 52–53;
on aims of science and religion,
88–89; animosity towards, 26; and
atheism, 96; attacked, 13, 16; banishment from Jewish community,
6, 18, 20, 42–43; and Burgh, 185;
challenging convention, 9; and Clara
Maria, 17–18; cursed, 42; declining
professorship, 64; and elitism, 87;
and experimental method, 51–52;
and free thought, 16–18 (*see also* free
thought); and freedom, 175 (*see also*
freedom); and friendship, 163–66;
interest in science, 51; and Koerbagh,
50; on madness, 137; and money,
63–64; and own emotions, 43, 134–55;
political judgement, 24; and radical
Enlightenment, 12; and reconciliatory theism, 114–15; romantic and
family life, 17–19; shunned, 42; and
surveillance, 199; and Van der Spyck,
43, 135, 136, 201; views on women,
211–12

Spinoza, Hanna (mother), 18

Spinoza, Miguel (father), 16

Spinoza: A Life (Nadler), 3. *See also*
Nadler, Steven

Spinoza: Complete Works (Morgan), 30

Spinoza on Philosophy, Religion, and

Politics (James), 11
"Spinoza's Philosophical Psychotherapy" (Robertson), 182
The Spirit of Spinoza (Grossman), 185
Spitzer, Robert, 79, 80
Stahl, Stephen, 68
Stein, Eli, 143
sterilization, 117, 118, 121. *See also* eugenics
Stewart, Matthew, 7, 17, 180, 203–204
Stigma (Goffman), 97
stigmatization: and advocates, 98; anti-stigma strategy, 97–101; of atheists, 96; and authority of professionals, 101; defined, 97; and dysfunction, 97; and fear, 104–105; fear of, 36–37; and hospitalization, 128; of Jews, 95; and violence, 129, 134. *See also* homosexuality; tolerance
Still, William, 157
Stoicism, 179–80
Stone, Allan, 22
"Stressors and Chemical Imbalances" (report), 90
The Structure of Scientific Revolutions (Kuhn), 61
sublime madness, 156–57
submissive compliance, 31
Substance Abuse and Mental Health Services Administration (SAMHSA), 193
suffering, 7, 13–14, 46–47, 54–55, 177
suicide: and ACE, 194; and criminal justice system, 193–94; of da Costa, 42; in *Ethics*, 208; evaluations, 33–34, 56; fear of, 37; increasing, 11; and Lincoln, 136; and love, 159–60; and poverty, 193–94; predicting, 33–34; rate increase, 27; and RCL, 169; reporting thoughts, 56; and schizophrenia, 132; and treatment coercion, 133; and unemployment, 193; in United States, 208
supernatural occurrences, 75
superstitions, 16, 29, 30, 57–59

supportive relationships: overview, 163; anarchists, 166; genuine community, 171; peer-to-peer support, 38–39, 166–71, 173–74, 197–98, 206–207; and Spinoza, 163–66. *See also* caring; mutual aid; therapeutic communities
synaptic pruning, 113–14
Szasz, Thomas, 10, 21–22, 23, 77, 209–10

T4 program, 45
taboo: overview, 13; brain disease critiques as, 60; challenging labels, 109; sexuality in *The City and the Pillar*, 105; Spinoza and Paine as, 25; validity of brain-disease paradigm, 61; without threats, 169
telescopes, 3
tension: and axioms of fear, 37–38; and blame, 36–37; dualism and unity, 146; and homosexuality, 3–4; and insecurity, 188; and Native Americans, 4–5; and ODD, 31–32; and "passions," 29; relief of, 38; and schizophrenia, 118; tolerating, 39; of uncertainty, 16. *See also* fear
terror, 31, 35. *See also* fear
Theological-Political Treatise (Spinoza), 1, 15, 16, 23, 24, 30, 41, 73–74, 175, 185, 187, 199, 206
therapeutic communities, 152, 155–56. *See also* caring; supportive relationships
therapists. *See* psychiatry/psychiatrists
Thoreau, Henry David, 18–19, 166
threats, 33
Thus Spoke Zarathustra (Nietzsche), 154
tolerance, 95–96, 102–103, 104–105, 152, 197, 205. *See also* stigmatization
Torah Commandments (Mitzvot), 80
Torrey, E. Fuller, 119, 129–30, 195
tranquilizing chairs, 44
transnational corporations, 64–66, 67–71. *See also* medication

transorbital lobotomies, 45–46
trauma, 101–102, 103, 168, 194–95, 197
Trauma and Madness in Mental Health Services (Hunter), 194
Treatise on the Emendation of the Intellect (Spinoza), 16–17, 52, 175
Treatment Advocacy Center, 130
The Trouble with Twin Studies (Joseph), 122
true ideas, 52, 59, 60–61
true religion, 75
The Truth about the Drug Companies (Angell), 64
Tubman, Harriet, 156–57
Tufts-New England Medical Center, 48
Turner, Erick, 68–69
twin studies, 121–22
twins reared apart (TRA), 122

Underground Railroad, 156–57
unemployment, 193
unity, 145–46
U.S. Joint Commission on Mental Illness and Health, 98

validity, 54–55, 57, 60–61, 109–10, 123
"The Value of Free Thought" (Russell), 15–16
Van den Enden, Clara Maria, 17–18
Van den Enden, Franciscus, 17, 200
Van der Spyck, Hendrik, 43, 135, 136, 201
Van Gent, Petrus, 201
veterans, 192
Vidal, Gore, 105
violence, 127, 128–29, 133–34
Vittengl, Jeffrey, 92
voice hearing, 102–103, 105, 156–157
"The Voices in My Head" (TED talk), 103
Voltaire, 211

Walden (Thoreau), 166
Watters, Ethan, 131
West, Louis Jolyon "Jolly," 191
Western Mass Recovery Learning Community (RLC), 168–70, 171
Western State Hospital (Virginia), 44
"What is Bizarre in Bizarre Delusions? A Critical Review" (article), 78
"What Killed Rebecca Riley?" (TV program), 48
Whitaker, Robert, 22–23, 47, 68, 69, 120, 133
Whitney, Leon, 44
Why Leaders Lie (Mearsheimer), 86
Williams, Paris, 145–46, 157–59
Wolf, A., 164
women, 33–34, 164, 192, 211–12
World Health Organization (WHO), 108, 130–31, 176
"The World of Soviet Psychiatry" (Reich), 189
Wunderink, Lex, 132

Yalom, Irvin, 147

Zipursky, Robert, 111–12, 114

AK PRESS is small, in terms of staff and resources, but we also manage to be one of the world's most productive anarchist publishing houses. We publish close to twenty books every year, and distribute thousands of other titles published by like-minded independent presses and projects from around the globe. We're entirely worker run and democratically managed. We operate without a corporate structure—no boss, no managers, no bullshit.

The **FRIENDS OF AK PRESS** program is a way you can directly contribute to the continued existence of AK Press, and ensure that we're able to keep publishing books like this one! Friends pay $25 a month directly into our publishing account ($30 for Canada, $35 for international), and receive a copy of every book AK Press publishes for the duration of their membership! Friends also receive a discount on anything they order from our website or buy at a table: 50% on AK titles, and 30% on everything else. We have a Friends of AK ebook program as well: $15 a month gets you an electronic copy of every book we publish for the duration of your membership. *You can even sponsor a very discounted membership for someone in prison.*

Email **friendsofak@akpress.org** for more info, or visit the website: **https://www.akpress.org/friends.html**.

There are always great book projects in the works—so sign up now to become a Friend of AK Press, and let the presses roll!